On Actors and Acting

EXETER PERFORMANCE STUDIES

Exeter Performance Studies aims to publish the best new scholarship from a variety of sources, presenting established authors alongside innovative work from new scholars. The list explores critically the relationship between theatre and history, relating performance studies to broader political, social and cultural contexts. It also includes titles which offer access to previously unavailable material.

Series editors: **Peter Thomson,** Professor of Drama at the University of Exeter; **Graham Ley,** Lecturer in Drama at the University of Exeter; **Steve Nicholson,** Head of Theatre Studies and Principal Lecturer at the University of Huddersfield.

On Actors and Acting

Peter Thomson

UNIVERSITY
of
EXETER
PRESS

First published in 2000 by
University of Exeter Press
Reed Hall, Streatham Drive
Exeter, Devon EX4 4QR
UK
www.ex.ac.uk/uep/

Reprinted 2002

British Library Cataloguing in Publication Data
A catalogue record of this book is available
from the British Library

ISBN 0 85989 671 4

Typeset in Plantin Light 10/12pt by Exe Valley Dataset Ltd, Exeter

Printed in Great Britain
by TJI Digital, Padstow

*This book is dedicated to the Drama Department at the
University of Exeter: to colleagues and students present and past.
It hasn't always been easy, but it's always been serious.*

Contents

Illustrations

Acknowledgements

Chapter One is reprinted, with the permission of the editors, from *Studies in Theatre and Performance*, vol. 20 no. 1.

Chapter Two is a revised version of a paper published in *European Medieval Drama I*, edited by Sydney Higgins (Turnhout: Brepols, 1997).

Chapter Twelve consists largely of extracts from *Shakespeare Survey*, vol. 24, 26, 27, 28 and 29, which are reproduced here with permission from Cambridge University Press.

Illustration 1 is reproduced with permission from the Tate Gallery, London 2000.

Illustration 2 is reproduced with permission from the Board of Trustees of the National Museums and Galleries on Merseyside (Walker Art Gallery, Liverpool).

Illustration 6 is reproduced with permission from the University of Bristol Theatre Collection.

Illustrations 7, 10 and the cover illustration are reproduced with permission from the Board of Trustees of the Victoria and Albert Museum (V & A Picture Library).

Illustration 8 is reproduced with the permission of the Society for Theatre Research.

Illustration 12 is reproduced with the permission of A.&C. Black (Publishers) Limited.

Assistance, direct and more commonly indirect, from various sources has been acknowledged in footnotes, but the Dedication of this book acknowledges a wider debt to the hundreds of people who have made the Exeter University Drama Department the extraordinary thing that it is.

Introduction

If all our theatres were closed by Act of Parliament, all our directors wiped out by plague, and artificial light abolished, there would still be performances. All you need is actors and audiences. I hadn't realized, until I set about shaping this book, how much I have been preoccupied with actors in particular and with audiences in general. When I have written about Shakespeare or Brecht, almost anything really, it has been with performance in mind. For someone who started his adult life as a student of literature, that represents a journey; and I know when and where it began: 27 September 1964 in Manchester. I was eleven months married, two days a father, and attending a staff meeting four days before my appointment as an assistant lecturer in drama was due to take effect. Hugh Hunt, very much a director, chaired the meeting: he was the professor in the three-year-old Drama Department. John Prudhoe, lymphatic and improbably blond, was the senior lecturer—a Germanist with a passion for Noel Coward. Graham Woodruff, fairly recently a graduate from the Bristol Drama Department and fierily focused on theatre, was a lecturer, very silent and palpably impatient in meetings. Clare Venables, who had just graduated at Manchester (those were the days!), had been appointed an assistant lecturer along with me. Neither of us said much. And then there was Stephen Joseph; a dark man as big as the room he seemed to me then. I knew that he was something to do with theatre-in-the-round and that he was Hermione Gingold's son, but that was about all I knew.

The subject of the meeting was 'the syllabus'. Wasn't it time we had one? Shakespeare and his contemporaries were taught by the English Department: Prudhoe did Goethe, Schiller, Restoration comedy and Coward (plus anything European on the strength of his fluency in *hoch Deutsch*—Corneille, Racine, Molière, Ibsen, Strindberg, you name it); Hunt, having directed at the Abbey, was happy to take on the Irish drama; I can't remember what Woodruff did—the Greeks and Romans I think; I volunteered Chekhov (Prudhoe already did him) and Gorky. Shouldn't there be some structural principle? That was the question. Suddenly—in my memory, at least, it was suddenly—Stephen Joseph's voice came down from the ceiling: 'I don't think we should do plays at all. Anyone can read a play.'

I loved my time (most of it anyway) in the Manchester Drama Department. There was a visceral engagement in the students that I had not been prepared for by my experience as a supervisor of English at Cambridge. These were people who wanted to be up and doing— thorns in the flesh of a syllabus designed for those who only sit and read and think. It was Stephen Joseph who taught me the distinction between drama and literature. He was curious about so much more than I was: anthropology, electronics, popular culture, social history, architecture. The pity is that he was too troubled by scholarly traditions to devise a syllabus that would have satisfied *him*. There would have been plenty of reading in it, but reading that interrogated rather than deterred activity. Under Stephen's casual influence, the ways in which I encountered play-texts changed. I began, I suppose, to read like an actor. Not that I ever became a good actor, though I worked hard at it. I took quite a major role in Graham Woodruff's imaginative production of *Ironhand*, which was a rousing success in the University Theatre. Mr Shields, who ran the staff bar, told me it was the best student show he'd ever seen and that I was 'the worst thing in it'. (It gave me some comfort that he thought Mr Prudhoe 'the next worst'.) I haven't acted much since then, but I have never lost my respect for actors nor my delight in good acting.

The essays in this book are about actors and audiences of the British theatre. They are independent of each other, but that is not to say that they are unconnected. I am interested in the historical conditions of past performances and aware that, though much changes, some things remain the same. It pleased me to learn that John McEnery recognized the need for 'purposefulness' when acting at the New Globe, for example, because it was a quality I had already proposed as a constituent of effective performance in the early modern theatre in the opening chapters of this book. The final essay has implicit links with those in Part One. I would like to be the advocate of a popular theatre. The actors who excite me most now, and those past actors who have best held my attention, are in discernible ways outrageous. I remember the stage whisper with which Donald Wolfit opened his production of *The Master of Santiago*. It was the only time I saw Wolfit on stage. When the curtain rose, he was standing upstage with his back to us, dimly silhouetted against a large window (this is my true memory—Michael Kilgarriff tells me that Wolfit entered slowly ten minutes in). He held his pose for a meaningful while before turning to walk down. What he actually said in his formidably audible stage whisper was quite trivial:

'Still not here', 'Late, always late'—something like that. But it was given such weight by the mode of delivery that I felt the need to hold my breath. Wolfit and Olivier are among the most outrageous actors I have seen, but Olivier in the 1960s was more confidently in tune with my time. Wolfit, like Quin after Garrick's arrival or Kemble after Kean's, seemed frozen in *his* time. The splendour he undoubtedly had was a lonely splendour. Irving, too, lived long enough to be isolated, but his special relationship with his audience makes him a necessary subject in a book concerned with actors and the spirit of their times.

The theatres of the eighteenth and nineteenth centuries are almost as remote from us as those of the medieval and early modern periods. The significant difference is in the quantity and quality of surviving critical comment. The (mostly) silent heroes of Part Two of this book are the writers whose powers of graphic description allow posterity to support intuition with something like hard evidence: Cibber, Lichtenberg, Churchill, Hazlitt, Leigh Hunt, G.H. Lewes, Clement Scott, Joseph Knight and many others. I have included in Part Three some excerpts from my own attempts at emulation. It is not easy to record accurately, and as objectively as possible, the experience of watching a play in performance. I had Hazlitt as my model, certainly not the primarily judgemental style of modern theatre criticism. The first duty, I thought and think, of a critic is to provide some impression of what it was like to be *there* to readers who were not. It is in the actor's voice and body that the present-tenseness of the theatrical experience resides. There should be some attempt on the reviewer's part to hold the tense: it will be read in the past but should be written in the present. Directorial domination is, of course, an impediment to this. The theatres of which I write in this book belonged primarily to the actors. It is a matter for continuing debate whether the return to an actors' theatre will bring back audiences. I argue in the final chapter that it may.

I regret the paucity of female presence in this book; there are two reasons for it. The first is that the critical treatment of actresses through history has been blighted by prejudice and over-affected by mere appearance. The second, and more significant, is that actresses have been better covered in recent scholarly studies than actors. I admit ingloriously that I have little to add to such studies that does not ring of the commonplace. I would have liked, in particular, to write about Susannah Cibber, Peg Woffington and Kitty Clive in the eighteenth century, and about Charlotte Cushman, Marie Wilton/Bancroft and Ellen Terry in the nineteenth. Sarah Siddons does not tempt me. Her acting wasn't outrageous enough.

Part One

ACTORS AND ACTING IN THE EARLY MODERN THEATRE

1

The Elizabethan Actor
A Matter of Temperament

Debates about Elizabethan acting styles have tended to polarize rhetorical formalism and 'true-to-lifeness'. The argument of this essay, though necessarily contingent on such debates, is not primarily designed to privilege either camp. My interest is in the relationship between actor and character during the decades that witnessed the emergence of a professional theatre in London. It is a matter of some weight, morally as well as aesthetically. The social status of actors, those who best observed communal protocols and who best exploited economic opportunities, rose during the reigns of Elizabeth I and James I, but the moral status of actors remained controversial. 'This above all' was Polonius' advice to an audience that would have been predisposed to agree, 'to thine own self be true'; but these words from the mouth of a player must have resounded with rank hypocrisy when they were first spoken—unless it was Polonius, rather than the player, whom the audience heard. That is the razor-edge of the question, and it cut more deeply at the beginning of the seventeenth century than we can readily understand today. The issues confronted in, and the passions aroused by, Diderot's *Paradoxe sur le comédien* (not published until 1830) are of the same kind, but not of the same intensity. Between William Prynne's *Histriomastix* (1632) and Diderot's *Paradoxe*, actors had come to be granted some aesthetic distance from the sin of deceit; but such allowances were not made overnight. If Prynne was unwilling, and Diderot willing, to admit the possibility that the actor might vanish into the character, when and how did the responses of John Citizen and his wife change? The suspension of disbelief that constitutes theatrical docility in the twentieth century should not lead us to assume that Shakespeare's company could rely on that same docility at the Globe.

My supposition—and it seems to me the only plausible one—is that the evolution of audience expectations occurred alongside an evolution of acting styles. It is the early stages of that evolution that I wish to explore here, but historical enquiries about audiences are always impeded by the current resonances of the word 'audience', and I must begin there.

We now take it for granted that the relationship of actor to character is at the heart of the theatrical enterprise. At the 'Towards the Millennium' Conference in Cambridge in December 1995, a successful young director (Jude Kelly) asked John Barton to define his attitude to character in Shakespeare's plays. Barton's scholarly response was understandably hesitant. Shakespeare, he explained, would have associated the word 'character' with the formation of letters in writing or printing, not with invented creatures, not with people at all. Kelly, who had recently directed a well-received *King Lear* in Leeds and London, rather brushed the point aside. Her concern was with the cultural context of twentieth-century practice, in which Shakespeare is commonly perceived as a subtle-souled psychologist. An enquiry into the childhood circumstance that had produced Goneril and Regan had seemed to her pertinent in the rehearsal of *Lear*. Barton might, of course, have asked, 'and how many children had Lady Macbeth?', but, to his credit, he said nothing to deride Kelly's priorities. She had, after all, a point. Psychology may have been in its awkward adolescence when Shakespeare wrote his plays, but those plays exist now in a world inhabited by armchair psychologists. Actors' dressing rooms are part of that world. In a theatre in which Stanislavsky is still dominant and A.C. Bradley's ghost an immanence, the mind of the fictional character is the actor's playground.

Whilst approaches to sixteenth-century drama are increasingly, though not consistently, assimilating current shifts in cultural and performance theory, for most actors *and* for the unreconstructed spectator, character occupies the foreground. Rehearsal time will be spent on debates about the sort of person Cordelia *is*, on the unvoiced assumption that what she *does* is Shakespeare's cryptic clue to her essential being. Whilst we can be quite sure that the King's Men made no such assumption, we have also to recognize that a theatre's responsibility towards its own history is not a straightforward one. The approach to Shakespearean production through character is self-evidently *a* way. It is the twentieth-century tendency to view it as the *only* way that gives legitimate offence; above all, perhaps, because its consequence is a taming of the wildness of Elizabethan drama. The ultimately inexplicable malice of Goneril and Regan is given a local habitation if we can link it to abused childhood. It is axiomatic, in any performance based on character, that everything can be explained, that motiveless malignity is an impossibility. Moreover, the explanations lie within the experience of our world *now*. Such a performance is inherently conservative of the dominant ideology of its time. It is even arguable that it is yet another instrument of political hegemony. Viewing his century's shift in sensibility from the enlightened vantage point of the 1760s, Richard Hurd observed, 'What we have gotten by this revolution is a great deal of good sense. What we have lost is a world of fine fabling'.[1] The same could certainly be said of much post-Stanislavskian Shakespeare.

It scarcely needs saying that if Marlowe or Ben Jonson—anyone but Shakespeare—were our chosen model, the idea of character in Elizabethan drama would be apprehended quite differently. Lunatic, lover and poet would, in Jonson, have been three people rather than Hamlet.

However reluctantly, I am forced to admit that Shakespeare created dramatic characters before there was a reliable word to describe his creations. But it is simply nonsense to suppose that his dramatis personae sprang into independent life the moment he took up his quill. It is only through imposition that we perceive dramatic characters in most of the plays of the 1590s, endowing Juliet with a psyche and the Jaques of *As You Like It* with a biography. Indeed, it seems to me that the effective staging of the great majority, if not all, of Shakespeare's plays is impeded by an actorly approach through character. For a period of about five years, as the old century was ending and the new one beginning, Shakespeare invented a number of roles which tested the players of those roles in an unfamiliar way. The influence of Plutarch is discernible here. For Plutarch, the nature of great men is curiously linked with the great historical events they are known to have precipitated. Writing *Julius Caesar* with North's translation of Plutarch propped open beside him, Shakespeare assimilated what he plagiarized. The culmination was the creation of Hamlet, a dramatic character *avant la lettre*. But it is not at all clear to me that Shakespeare knew what he had done. If *Measure for Measure* came immediately after *Hamlet* in the historical line, what are we to make of the Duke? As indirect as Hamlet, and similarly manipulative and introspective, the Duke resolutely refuses the plot's invitation to him to become a character. It is a refusal that places him in theatrical confrontation with Hamlet; and that confrontation would have been particularly striking if, in the re-opened, post-plague playhouse of 1604, both parts were being played by Richard Burbage. The 'representational' style allowed to the actor of Hamlet is distinct from the 'presentational' style demanded of the actor of the Duke.

The distinction is one to which I will return. For the moment, I wish only to stress that a fruitful interaction between house-playwright and leading actor must have contributed to Shakespeare's extraordinary

---

1. Hurd, *Letters on Chivalry and Romance* (London: 1762), p. 120.

dramatic variety. Having written *Hamlet*, he went on to write plays that were very different from *Hamlet*, in many ways more archaic, certainly less 'modernist'. Trouper that he was, Burbage could perform his part in all of them. But, whether or not he knowingly turned his back on it, Shakespeare had laid claim to new histrionic territory in the writing of *Hamlet*. Had he apprehended, without an articulated mental process, a contradiction in Burbage's self-presentation on stage, a jolting dislocation between speech and act that adumbrated an inner life?

For the Elizabethans, speech and act were distinct branches of the player's craft. 'Others speak', wrote Ben Jonson in his enigmatic homage to Edward Alleyn, 'but only thou dost act'.[2] From a twentieth-century perspective, it is tempting to read this as the description of a man, unique among mere mouthers of lines, who inhabited his part. Such a reading would distinguish between the run-of-the-mill members of the Admiral's Men and the one towering actor whose gift it was to translate words into character, to personalize language. But this interpretation of Jonson's epigram collapses under historical scrutiny. The distinction is not between outward expression and inner feeling, but between word and deed. Jonson's chosen verbs, 'speak' and 'act', have surrendered to linguistic evolution their original import, but we might wish to note that it was Hamlet's defect to speak when he should have acted. It is not Hamlet but the First Player, weeping for Hecuba, who suits the word to the action, the action to the word. The hiatus between speech and action is a Leitmotiv of Shakespearean drama, but it is Jonson who here sites it explicitly on the platform, among the actors. The discrepancy Jonson has observed between players who speak and a player who acts challenges our preconceptions about Elizabethan performance. This address to Alleyn might be seen as the single most significant piece of theatrical criticism to have come down to us from the golden age of English drama, if only we could comprehend it fully.

But can we? I confess my own uncertainty. Even granting the hyperbole of encomium, and leaving open the possibility that, with the Chamberlain's Men in mind, he might have said the same thing about Burbage, Jonson is clearly trying to mean something specific. My best guess is that he was distinguishing between players whose speeches simply foreshadowed the subsequent action of the play and Alleyn, who seemed by the sheer force of his on-stage presence to make it happen. It is, after all, only the behaviour of the actors that can persuade us in the

---

2. C.H. Herford and P. and E. Simpson (eds), *The Works of Ben Jonson* (Oxford: Clarendon Press, 11 vols, 1925–52), vol. 8, p. 56. The quotation is from Epigram LXXXIX.

audience that what is about to occur on the stage has not already occurred on the page; and, given the quantity of roles an Elizabethan player had to hold in his head on any given day, it would not be astonishing if the habitual presentation of any one of them was perfunctory. It is equally possible that Alleyn, like the greatest actors throughout history, overwhelmed audiences by the carnal delight he took in what Brecht has called the fundamental *Gestus*—the *Gestus* of showing.

Alleyn was self-consciously a star in the Elizabethan firmament. We have his part in Robert Greene's *Orlando Furioso*, a 17ft scroll lacking scene divisions and marked up with the briefest of cues. Greene's text has, in several places, been emended by Alleyn himself—and who and how was Greene to object? The part belonged to the player, not to the playwright. The amended text is with Alleyn's papers at the college he founded in Dulwich. There is an intensity of ambition in this manuscript. It expresses an actor's necessary greed: not this is my *part*, but this is *my* part. There is something of the prowling possessiveness of an Edmund Kean here, the possessiveness that led Keats to hope that Kean would promote a production of *Otho the Great* 'if he smokes the hotblooded character of Ludolph'.[3] How much, I wonder, do Marlowe's overreachers owe to Alleyn's overreaching? But if Marlowe was writing with Alleyn in mind, as much in *The Jew of Malta* as in *Tamburlaine*, it was certainly not a one-toned performer that he was envisaging. Alleyn may have been, presumably was, a master of the mighty line, but more than that mastery is required from the player of Barabas. It was Alleyn's versatility that Thomas Heywood featured in his prologue to the 1633 edition of *The Jew of Malta*. He celebrates there

> a man
> Whom we may rank with (doing no one wrong)
> Proteus for shapes, and Roscius for a tongue,
> So could he speak, so vary . . . .

Heywood's emphasis is on vocal variety, on speech. Thomas Nashe, writing about Alleyn in 1592, anticipates Jonson's emphasis on the act: 'Not Roscius nor Aesop, those admyred tragedians that haue lived euer since before Christ was borne, could euer performe more in action than famous Ned Allen'.[4] There may be an unvoiced distinction here between

3. H.E. Rollins (ed.), *The Letters of John Keats* (Cambridge: Cambridge University Press, 2 vols. 1958), vol. 2, p. 217.
4. R.B. McKerrow (ed.), *The Works of Thomas Nashe* (Oxford: Oxford University Press, 2 vols. 1958), vol. 1, p. 215.

performance in speech and performance in action, and once again we are set a puzzle by linguistic evolution. What, in conversational debate, might Nashe have been meaning by the assertion that Alleyn performed more in action than, say, Thomas Pope? Something beyond graceful movement is certainly implied, but gesture accurately synchronized with speech ('the action to the word') cannot be ruled out. The greater likelihood, though, is that Nashe was recording something that struck Jonson, too—the egregious purposefulness of Alleyn's on-stage behaviour. Nearly fifty years later, in Richard Brome's *The Antipodes* (1638), Lord Letoy generously excuses the faulty memory of one of his household players:

> . . . one, that never will be perfect in a thing
> He studies: yet he makes such shifts extempore,
> (Knowing the purpose what he is to speak to),
> That he moves mirth in me 'bove all the rest.   (II.ii.16–19)

This is an actor who, though he may not know his lines, knows his function in the narrative. At the Berliner Ensemble, Brecht would form his stage groupings according to the principle that the story should be clear, even if a soundproof glass wall were erected between the audience and the actors. It may be that Nashe and Jonson recognized in Alleyn a performer whose embodiment of purpose told the story of the play.

Purpose, I suggest, is a much more useful word than character to define the enactment of conflict on the Elizabethan stage. At least until Shakespeare created Brutus and Hamlet, it was the crossing of purposes rather than the clashing of subjectivities that audiences heard and spectators observed. The modern theatre's concern for character has obscured this primary feature of Elizabethan dramaturgy, and the responsibility for that lies equally with actors and audiences. It would be possible, I think, to construct an argument that, as Shakespeare's heroes from Brutus onwards faltered in their purposes, the actor Richard Burbage was set apart from the actor Edward Alleyn. Or, to put it another way, the infiltration of the idea of dramatic character into the art of the actor was significantly accelerated when Shakespeare created tragic heroes (Brutus and Hamlet above all) who were vividly at cross-purposes with *themselves*. There seems to me little doubt that the plays Shakespeare wrote at the turn of the century placed the players' craft under new scrutiny. They enforced the notion that the physical body of the performer might be, in some mysterious way, assimilated in the fictional body of the role. Beyond the immediate ken of audiences, and in ways imperfectly understood by the players themselves, a predominantly presentational style of acting was being shifted towards the representational.

The performative application of the verb 'represent' dates, probably, from the post-Restoration period, but the word had accumulated many of its contemporary meanings before the end of the sixteenth century. For example, persuasive statement was 'representation', as was the ascription of a specific quality to a thing or to a person. To perform a play was to 'represent' it, and a person might 'represent' an abstract concept by symbolizing or embodying it. To act on behalf of another, in a court of law for example, was to 'represent' him or her. The aesthetic application of the term, though, was normally confined to the visual arts. Hermione, in the concluding scene of *The Winter's Tale*, might have been seen to 'represent' a statue by Julio Romano, but it is most unlikely that anyone referred to the boy-actor's 'representing' of Hermione. That said, Elizabethan playgoers must sometimes have felt the need, in discussion, to distinguish between the straightforward 'presentation' of a wall by Snout in *A Midsummer Night's Dream* and the kind of activity undertaken by Burbage in *Hamlet*. The rather lumpen 'personate' was first in the field, when 'imitation', as in 'imitate the action of a tiger', was still more commonly applied to attempts to reproduce the behaviour of animals. But personation, if we mean to propose by it that one whole human being (Burbage, say) can substitute for another whole human being (Hamlet), was at best embryonic on the early modern stage. Personation did not abolish the performer's self from the playing space. He had access to the audience, and so could slip easily from dialogue to aside to dialogue to direct address or soliloquy. The idea of acting as if the audience is not there (a highly improbable one at the Globe or at the regal court) is a post-Stanislavskian phenomenon, and it is vital that we recognize the longevity of presentational performance; a style sturdy enough to survive the separation of actors and audience into two rooms and the darkening of one of those rooms.

Nevertheless, an evolution towards a representational style of acting can conveniently be adduced from a chronological study of Shakespeare's plays, with *Hamlet* in the seminal position. I take, by way of illustration, a metatheatrically fraught exchange in that play. It was Muriel Bradbrook's proposal that, for the Globe audience at least, the Elsinore players embodied (presented? personated?) the Chamberlain's/King's Men on a provincial tour, and that Hamlet's admiration for the First Player contains Shakespeare's homage to Richard Burbage.[5] Decked in a Burbage beard, and perhaps in a costume Burbage was currently

5. Bradbrook, *Shakespeare the Craftsman* (London: Chatto and Windus, 1969), p. 129.

wearing in another part, the First Player as Burbage recites for Burbage as Hamlet his set piece of grief. It is a recitation without warm-up, the casual cadenza of an accomplished platform performer. There is no suggestion that he must first take time to recover Aeneas' emotional context, to 'get into character'. But the response the recitation elicits from Hamlet is, in effect, a critical commentary on acting:

> Is it not monstrous that this player here,
> But in a fiction, in a dream of passion,
> Could force his soul so to his own conceit
> That from her working all his visage wan'd;
> Tears in his eyes, distraction in's aspect.
> A broken voice, and his whole function suiting
> With forms to his conceit? And all for nothing!
> For Hecuba?
> What's Hecuba to him or he to Hecuba,
> That he should weep for her?   (II.ii.585–94)

It is the presentation of grief, not the personation of Aeneas, that excites Hamlet's comment. A genuinely grieving Aeneas (or Hamlet) would look and sound quite different:

> What would he do
> Had he the motive and the cue for passion
> That I have? He would drown the stage with tears,
> And cleave the general ear with horrid speech;
> Make mad the guilty, and appal the free;
> Confound the ignorant, and amaze, indeed,
> The very faculties of eyes and ears.   (II.ii.594–600)

I put it to you, Hamlet seems to be saying, is that what you critics who complain of the rhetorical formality of presentational acting really want? It would be unbearable! And anyway, is it possible to perform *true* grief on someone else's behalf? Who is leading the debate here—Hamlet, Burbage or Shakespeare? It scarcely matters, beyond the added poignancy, whether the original First Player was knowingly personating Burbage. What is here under scrutiny is the craft of the presentational actor. In another play, he may present 'wall' or 'moonshine'; to Hamlet, and to us, he is presenting grief. And where is Burbage meanwhile? Where is the company's leading presentational actor? It seems to me that he is getting very close to concealing himself in the personation of Hamlet, representing at high intensity a subjectivity that is decidedly not

10

his own. Shakespeare is setting off an established acting style against another that is not yet current, and almost inviting the audience to vote.

It would be a serious mistake to conclude that Shakespeare was temperamentally disposed to favour representational acting. As I have said, none of the plays written after *Hamlet* was quite so hospitable to it, and the tendency of the late romances is even towards the broadly presentational, the folkloric. Elizabethan audiences were not much concerned with aesthetic purity, and neither were the players. Most dramatists went with the flow, too. A cursory reading of Dekker's wonderfully anomalous reworking of *Old Fortunatus* speaks much more to the dramatic taste of his time than Jonson's purist frustrations over the stage version of *Sejanus*, and we should not too readily take Jonson's side in the war of the theatres. There is no evidence, in the new century, of a felt need to reform acting styles, to stabilize dramaturgy, or to pursue new methodologies in the training of apprentice players. I doubt very much whether even Burbage ever consciously did more than speak Shakespeare's lines (those he could remember) according to the impulses he sensed in them. I have heard John Barton offering, as the most practical hints to would-be speakers of Shakespeare, firstly, that they should play the question marks, and secondly, that they should recognize his habit of thinking antithetically, and train their voices to accommodate antithesis. It is the tonal variety of the best Elizabethan drama that distinguishes it. A single player in a major role in a Shakespeare play (and many, sometimes most, had more than one role) will find the claims of the part changing from scene to scene. The definitive dramatic unit is not the 'Act', certainly not the 'Play', but the 'Scene', and versatility was a performer's craft. If there were thoroughbreds on the Elizabethan stage, I cannot name them. The Elizabethan actor was a mongrel. Whatever new characteristics he accrued were added to the old stock.

This mixed-breeding, mongrel style was wittily explored by Francis Beaumont in *The Knight of the Burning Pestle* (*c*.1607). Beaumont's surprising play is a layered disquisition on acting. At least, it is more fruitfully viewed in that way than as a satire of vulgar taste in drama: a satire which may expose Beaumont as an intellectual snob ill-acquainted with the current dramatic repertoire. Having recently directed the play, I am more than ever convinced that he was more engaged in testing the nature of actor/audience relationships than in making a monkey of the citizenry. It is not so much the Pirandellian confrontation between purported fact and impeded fiction that interests me (though Beaumont should be credited with that) as the play's implicit challenge to an early Jacobean audience's prejudices about acting. *The Knight of the Burning*

Pestle is set in a playhouse. I hope, though I cannot know, that the audience had been informed by the playbills that they were about to see a new comedy called '*The London Merchant*', and that they were taken aback to find the performance hijacked by a grocer, his wife, and their apprentice. '*The London Merchant*' has a trite plot, one which calls for shamelessly presentational acting from the professional troupe that has bought the manuscript. The two families—the prosperous Venturewells and the increasingly penurious Merrythoughts—on which the intrigue depends are made up of types. There is nothing to indicate an inner life. Cast according to physique, the parts play themselves. To know them is to know their purposes, and nothing more is required than to follow those purposes. Nothing, that is, if it were not for the disconcerting interventions of the self-righteous grocer and his outstandingly insensitive wife. These interventions expose the people inside the stage costumes. The 'real' actors' right to act is under supposedly un-predictable threat from the 'real' citizens. But the citizens are, in fact, actors too: actors presented with the extremely difficult task of convincing the audience that they are *not* acting—or, rather, that they are acting 'not-acting' well enough to license the continuation of the performance of a planned fiasco. Ralph, the apprentice, and his two friends have the complementary task of persuading the audience that they *can't* act, which returns to the 'real' actors—those performing '*The London Merchant*'—the responsibility of demonstrating that they *can*. And they have to carry out that demonstration whilst sharing the stage, at regular intervals, with three actors who are pretending that they can't act and two actors who are pretending that they're not acting.

There is, of course, no significant distinction in the level of skill required of the three groups if a production is to be effective. We know, from the publisher's dedication in the first quarto of 1613, that the play failed when first presented a few years earlier. We do not know why it failed, though it was surely inauspicious to entrust the premiere of this metatheatrical stab-in-the-dark to a boys' company. Beaumont was intervening, from inside the theatre, in a debate about the relationship of acting and truth. It is not, I admit, a profound intervention, but it was evidently sufficient to expose significant inadequacies in the original performers—or a limited tolerance in the original audience. In *The Knight of the Burning Pestle*, the stage is fictionally peopled by three groups with distinct attitudes towards the profession of acting: the first lives by it; the second would relish the opportunity of living by it; and the third is hostile to actors and questions the propriety of acting. However jokily, this offers a paradigm of the playhouse, its patrons and its inquisitors. It also raises, with some benevolence, pertinent points about the boundary between performance and the reality which performance might claim to 'represent'. Beaumont's own limitations restrict the scope of the enquiry. The questions he asks are asked from the periphery of the profession. *The Knight of the Burning Pestle* is quizzical, but ultimately disengaged. Its interest in the nature of acting is journalistic. It offers no insight into how actors act, as *Hamlet* supremely does. It is, in effect, simultaneously a critique of presentational acting and an advertisement for representational acting—though with two provisos. As a critique, it must salvage as much as it destroys, for fear of devaluing its subject. As an advertisement, it is not itself the product.

I am uneasily aware that I may seem to be proposing a 'progress' from presentation, through personation, to representation. That is not my intention. We need to take account of the material circumstances that conditioned performance on the Elizabethan and Jacobean stage. The player, whose prologue to '*The London Merchant*' is interrupted by the grocer, protests that it is far too late for the company to contemplate the performance of an alternative play, more to the grocer's taste. They bought this one a month ago. That does not mean, of course, that they have been rehearsing it for a month. If final copy was delivered four weeks before opening, that copy has had to be copied at least twice (once to furnish a promptbook, once to be cut up into its separate parts for distribution among the actors—and probably once more for despatch to the Master of the Revels with a view to obtaining a licence to perform) during the intervening period. It was probably only two weeks ago that the actors received their parts. The actor's peremptory task, on receipt of the part, is to take it to a private place and set about learning it. In appearance, an actor's part was an untidy monodrama, with two-word cues interpolated, and nothing to indicate the progress of the plot. We can reasonably assume, though we do not *know*, that, once the parts had been distributed, the actors assembled for a reading of the play; but any actor absent from that reading would have to memorize his part in a narrative vacuum. This is not a routine that encourages subtleties of characterization. The lonely memorizer needs to know his part's place in the pecking order of power, but he should be able to deduce its moral flavouring and appropriate temperament from the lines. It is generally possible, in reading or watching Elizabethan plays, to substitute the word 'temperament' where the twentieth-century actor would use 'character'. From Timothy Bright's *Treatise of Melancholy* (1582) to Burton's extraordinary *Anatomy of Melancholy* (1621), renaissance descriptions of the perturbation of the human psyche posited, with varying ingenuity, significant correspondences between physiology and behaviour. Outward signs of temperament (sometimes a synonym for 'humour'), whether in costume or in gesture, would be confirmed by appropriate conduct in the world of the play. The player's task was to suit gesture, movement and vocal inflection to the appropriate temperament. This is the style of performance invited by the twentieth-century parlour game sometimes called 'Adverbs'. Having chosen an adverb ('fiercely, 'independently', 'erotically'), the player's job is to carry out a set of tasks, proposed by people in the room ('play tennis in the manner of the word', 'bath a baby in the manner of the word' etc.), in such a way as to enable the onlookers to guess the adverb. Success in the charade will depend on precision, on the elimination of superfluous or misleading gestures. By the late sixteenth century, this unadorned, adverbial presentation of moral symbols—'characters' in an almost scribal sense, clearly written and therefore clearly legible—had evolved to a more complex presentation of temperaments at war on the human stage; but the bedrock of Elizabethan performance remained the unambiguous, adverbial delivery of a part that could forward the purpose of the plot even if the individual player was hard-pressed to distinguish it from the plot of the play he had performed yesterday or the one scheduled for tomorrow.

The move towards representation did not necessitate an abandonment of the principles of presentation. Although the historical Richard Burbage may not have taken the part of the First Player in *Hamlet*, he *could* have wept for Hecuba. Nor would he have felt demeaned by being asked to play the manifestly presentational role of Leontes in *The Winter's Tale*. The evolution of acting styles has proceeded through accretion, and *Hamlet* was less a revolution than a negotiation. Lesley Soule has recently drawn attention to a feature of Elizabethan dramatic writing; a delight in the creation of composites. For example, she reads in the language allotted to Rosalind in *As You Like It* 'a composite of fictional female and theatrical adolescent male',[6] dubbing the outcome an *anti-character*. As a free theatrical agent, the anti-character resists the confinement of representation, refuses to dwindle or be squeezed into a defined 'character', prefers to range boldly between styles and even genders. Soule's argument is quite complex, and I cannot here do justice to her analysis of theatricality in the boisterous relationship between boy, woman and audience.[7] But my view is that Elizabethan and Jacobean actors had a freedom which we have either lost or, intermittently and against protest, rediscovered: the freedom to range between styles. There

6. Soule, *Character, Actor and Anti-Character*, unpublished thesis at the University of Exeter, 1994, p. 363.
7. Lesley Soule summarizes this aspect of her argument in 'Subverting Rosalind: Cocky Ros in the Forest of Arden', *New Theatre Quarterly* 26 (1991), pp. 126–36.

was a lively dialectic of actor and character that has been buried in neo-Stanislavskian protocol. Because they could combine the presentational and the representational, virtually all late Elizabethan and Jacobean actors had access to the sheer theatricality of the anti-character; a tertium quid who may serve, at any moment, as a disconcerting mediator between the player and the part, or between the player, the part and the audience.

2

Making an Entrance

From Chaucer to Tarlton

There are people who engage our interest as soon as they come through the door. There are other people who come in almost invisibly. My concern here is with the way in which an actor enters the playing space. This is something not much commented on in the modern theatre, perhaps because entrances are generally less important than they used to be. Irene Vanbrugh would cite as particularly unhelpful the stage direction, 'Enter Madame X having just drunk a cup of tea'. She belonged to a generation that took its cue from Henry Irving. Irving would not have forgiven a Lyceum audience that allowed his first entrance to pass unremarked. 'The *manner of coming on* made it extraordinary with great actors', wrote Edward Gordon Craig at the outset of his famous description of Irving's technique and impact as Mathias in *The Bells*. 'It was this manner of timing the appearance, measuring its speed and direction, which created a rhythm that was irresistible.'[1] Confident in the knowledge that the Lyceum faithful had come to see *him*, Irving did everything he could to make the first encounter memorable. The preceding dialogue was calculated to prepare for it; there was atmospheric music to announce and enhance it; a kettledrummer hidden from view in the orchestra pit would augment the applause; the limelight men (there were twenty-five of them for the production of *Faust*) picked out his face and hands.

The historical return journey from Mathias' scenically calculated entry to the unadorned 'In comes I' of the Mummer is a long one, and it is with the unaided entrance, a characteristic of medieval performance, that I am principally concerned here. The Mummer who 'came in' as the Turkish Knight, say, told his audience all they needed to know about the 'character' by his mode of entry—and then repeated the information in a spoken self-description. The medieval actor was not in the business of fooling the audience. If he entered disguised, he told them so. In all other respects, appearance was to be trusted.

1. Craig, *Henry Irving* (London: J.M. Dent, 1930), p. 55.

We are given a wonderful glimpse of the difference between the actor out of role and the actor in role in Chaucer's *Nun's Priest's Tale*. There is an implicit reference, throughout this boisterous narrative, to medieval modes of theatrical performance. To begin with, the resplendent Chanticlere is an actor on display in full costume: jet-black bill, lily-white nails, azure legs and a body-suit of burnished gold. He is not, however, on stage yet. On the contrary, he is exhibiting tell-tale signs of dressing-room nerves. He has had a nightmare that threatens his ability to play his part in the customary way, and he confesses as much to his leading lady, Pertelote. On the strength of his wide reading, Chanticlere is convinced that dreams and nightmares are portents. Pertelote, a common-sense housewife off stage, recommends laxatives as an antidote, and their dressing-room debate develops into a parody of the classic agon, with Chanticlere on the side of dreams and Pertelote speaking up for aperients. It ends when Chanticlere deploys a mistranslation of his own Latin tag, thus winning the argument whilst appearing to concede victory to the monoglot Pertelote. Now he can make his entrance, now he can leave the tiring house and swoop into the yard. 'In comes I, Chanticlere', king of the farmyard, summoning my harem of hens. Like many an actor, Chanticlere is more alive on stage than off it. The entry to the yard is a power surge. He bears himself regally, Chaucer tells us, is no longer afraid—and has been restored to his sexual athleticism: 'He fethered Pertelote twenty tyme, / And trad hire eke as ofte, er it was pryme'.

The entrance of Chanticlere's antagonist is of a very different kind. Chaucer prefaces it with allusions to the Fall, a scene often played out in biblical pageants. A comparison between the serpent in the Garden of Eden and the wily fox in the widow's yard is enforced. The stage serpent's entrance was presumably a sidling one. I am reminded of a stage direction in the Elizabethan play *Patient Grissil*: 'Enter Grissil stealingly' (IV.i.90). But the fox insinuates himself into the *Nun's Priest's Tale* even more unobtrusively; almost invisibly in fact. Like an actor concealed until then among the audience, he is suddenly *there*. The scene is carefully set. Pertelote, *prima inter pares*, is flouncing in her sandbath, Chanticlere singing more merrily than a mermaid. It is a post-coital idyll, observed by a butterfly. But a fall is imminent in this Eden. Looking at the butterfly, Chanticlere sees the fox, an insidious actor who has hovered out of the light for as long as possible. What follows is a composite double act which pits two fast talkers against each other. In the first *lazzo*, the fox follows a preconceived plan to trick Chanticlere through flattery; in the second, Chanticlere turns the tables through inspired improvization. As in the wonderful farce of the chase, there is a clear reference to popular performance. The fox, who entered the yard

17

like a mystery-play serpent, leaves it like the tricked trickster of a jig. And Chanticlere, like many comic protagonists, establishes his supremacy by thinking his way out of a hole of his own digging. This, as we shall see, was a characteristic device of Richard Tarlton.

In the *Nun's Priest's Tale*, both the leading actors know their purposes from the moment they enter the playing space—one to *be* and the other to *eat* the cock of the walk. To know and to embody purpose remained the actor's primary skills, at least until the innovative comedy of the post-Restoration stage set new challenges to deportment and vocal patterning. Provided he knew his function in the story, a performer could get away with forgetting his lines, but his purpose must enter with him. Elizabethan play texts are punctuated with phrases like 'Lo where he comes', 'Here comes the lady', 'Here comes one in haste', but such lead-ins are uncommon in medieval drama. The unheralded actor had generally to announce himself in role. Among interesting exceptions, 'The Slaying of Abel' in the Towneley Cycle may be taken as representative. The design on the audience is palpable here. Cain's boy is sent first into the playing space with the specific purpose of preparing the audience to dislike his foul-mouthed and foul-tempered master. A modern show-business parallel can be found in the mock combats of professional wrestling, in which the ring announcer forewarns the waiting spectators of the wickedness of one of the combatants. The invited jeers of the crowd are vital to the spectacle. To a critical observer, these hyped-up bouts between the dirty fighter and the clean one may seem crudely manipulative, but they energize the fans of wrestling. They rephrase the archetypal combat between Cain and Abel, and this is a combat that can still set the popular pulse racing. We may rediscover something of the way in which a medieval actor entered the playing space by observing a professional wrestler's climb into the ring.

It is not as easy as it sounds for an actor to recognize and stick to his purpose, though the naming of parts made things easier in the moral interludes. Given the role of Cloaked Collusion (in Skelton's *Magnificence*), it should not have been difficult for the actor to dress the part and to determine a mode of entry. But it is not always so straightforward, as I discovered when cast as Felicity in what I believe to have been the first revival of *Magnificence* in its country of origin. Felicity opens the play with a distinctly dispirited homily. If he is 'Happiness', it is a morning-after kind of happiness. My own losing struggle with the speech began with Felicity's entrance. Paula Neuss' edition was not then published, but neither of the alternatives she proposes would have been of much help. Having in mind a first performance at the Merchant Tailors' Hall in Threadneedle Street, London, she suggests that he either entered through a door in the screen or was already in place before the play started, 'beginning his speech when the audience becomes silent'.[2] We were performing in the chapel of Jesus College, Cambridge, on a raised platform with central access from the inner chapel and with an additional entrance through a small door behind that section of the audience seated in the north transept (the main body of the audience was end-on in the nave). For Felicity to enter through the screen (i.e. from the inner chapel) would have accorded him an inappropriate Godwardness. To have him standing on the platform (in yellow tights and in front of half the College rugby team) until all the audience was seated would have been plain daft. I am less confident than Neuss that Skelton's audience, or any audience before the twentieth century, was of the kind that simply 'becomes silent'. Interludes more typically begin with filler lines that enable the actor, more or less *in propria persona*, to ask for a hearing. Felicity has no such help from the text. He has to plunge straight in—something which, having made an untidy entrance through the small door at the foot of the tower staircase, I found very difficult. At the original performance, surely, there was a musical introduction to prepare the audience for Felicity's speech. I would have loved the cover of music for my entrance.

Most of the first appearances in *Magnificence* are of the 'In comes I' kind, but the title character (perhaps wearing a costume borrowed from Henry VIII himself) has the favour of an announcement. Even so, he is allotted two lines to declare himself: 'To assure you of my noble port and fame, / Who list to know, Magnificence I hight' (163–4). Name, appearance, bearing and nature must all coincide for the play to function, and the same is true of all the Vices and Virtues that surround and tug at him. There are eighteen parts in *Magnificence*, but the episodes are so arranged as to bring the play within the compass of a small household company like Cardinal Wolsey's Men. Four men and a boy *could* have performed it. But we should remember that the playing of multiple roles draws particular attention, in a performance, to every new entrance. Not only is the variation in costume to be noted, but also the variation in physical and vocal style of the same actor in a different suit. If, as Neuss suggests, the player of Felicity also appeared as Cloaked Collusion (a much better part), Poverty, Good Hope, and Folly (a gift to a good comedian), he would have been expected to make each 'quality' distinct from the moment of entry. It seems to me unlikely that medieval or Elizabethan actors made any attempt to deceive the

2. John Skelton, *Magnificence*, ed. P.Neuss (Manchester: Manchester University Press, 1980), p. 67.

audience over doubling; on the contrary, they were at pains to display it as evidence of their skill and to gratify the audience's delight in virtuosity.

The player of Felicity would certainly have looked forward to his entrance as Folly. Neuss has plausibly emended the Latin stage direction to read, in translation, 'Here let Folly enter, shaking a bauble and making a commotion, beating on tables and suchlike' (1041). His passage through the Hall to the playing space would necessarily have entailed some improvised by-play with the socially distinguished assembly, splendidly unpredictable if Folly's dog was a real one. For the original audience, the visual reference was to a household Fool, probably a 'natural' (i.e. mentally impaired), whose uncontrollable behaviour provoked both laughter and alarm. Robert Armin would later recall one such in *Foole upon Foole* (1600). Jack Oates belonged to the household of Sir William Hollis, along with an unnamed 'artificial' fool (i.e. a man employed to play the fool, though not naturally foolish). Oates was moody, and sometimes violent, as on the night when he had to be calmed by the diners after laying in to a piper:

> By and by enters my artificiall foole in his olde cloathes making wry mouthes, dauncing, looking asquint, who when Jacke beheld, sodainly he flew at him, and so violently beate him that all the Table rose, but could scarce get him off.[3]

This is the kind of threat which Folly imports to the play; and Skelton has timed his entrance carefully. We are at the midway point, Magnificence's household is in disarray, and we are presented with a pageant of mayhem. Folly is a role which looks tailor-made for the yet-to-be-born Richard Tarlton, and one which demonstrates the fact that even so innovative a Clown as Tarlton had his antecedents.

Before coming to Tarlton, though, it will be helpful to look at an Elizabethan reminiscence of the days of the small household companies. I am referring to Act Four Scene Two of the play of *Sir Thomas More* (c.1603), in which Anthony Munday (if it was he) looks back nostalgically at a performance by Cardinal Wolsey's Men. Two points of interest must be briefly noted. Firstly, given Skelton's out-and-in relationship with Wolsey, it may have been the Cardinal's Men who performed *Magnificence*, and secondly, Munday (and the same would be true of any of his collaborators) never saw them act. They arrive at More's house

---

3. *The Collected Works of Robert Armin* (New York and London: Johnson Reprint Company, 2 vols, 1972), vol.1, B1.

unannounced, when he is entertaining to dinner the Lord Mayor and his associates, and it is an extraordinary courtesy on More's part to receive them: four men and a boy, under the leadership of the actor who will play the coveted role of the Vice. We know the name of only one of the company, and he (Luggins) is indubitably the lowest in the pecking order. From the list of seven plays in their repertoire, More selects *The Marriage of Wit and Wisdom*, and the actors make ready. They are very much in earnest, so serious, in fact, that they request a brief postponement when they discover that a beard has gone missing from the property basket. With so much doubling in the job, there must be a store of beards—ideal for quick changes—and it might reasonably be supposed that any of them would suffice in an emergency like this. But no, the Cardinal's Men are perfectionists. The missing beard is the long one, perhaps destined to signify the transformation of the rash young Wit after his marriage to Wisdom. And who has gone to fetch it? Luggins, of course. He is the company gofer. Unless the performance is delayed he will not be there for his first entrance as Good Counsel. It is for the host, however, not for the actors, to determine how to proceed. In jocular good humour, More offers to substitute himself for the absent Luggins. No one is better equipped to improvise his way through Good Counsel. By the time Luggins returns with the beard, the interlude has been running for five minutes—and what have we seen so far? The first entrances of every member of the company bar Luggins.

They are all distinct. First comes the Prologue, heralded by a trumpet. His is a straightforward task—to introduce Wit. This is a role for a handsome juvenile, no longer a boy. He enters 'ruffling' (i.e. swaggering) in such a way as to advertise his pride of manhood. If there are women in the audience, he has licence to catch their eyes, and he has a song of sex to present to them. But he is accompanied, and possibly pushed into the shade for a while, by Inclination, the Vice. Apart from the boy's three female roles, the doubling in this play falls mostly to the Prologue and Luggins. Inclination has his set mode of entry, one which is designed to engage the audience. Almost at once he is playfully threatening them with his dagger of lath, just in case they are tempted to give the game away when he tries to deceive the gullible Wit into believing that the lady he is about to meet is Wisdom. Thomas More, in the audience, is neither deceived nor deterred for a moment. The boy's seductive entry and two lines of song do not signal Wisdom to him: 'This is Lady Vanity, I'll hold my life. / Beware, good Wit, you take not her to wife'. Such instant recognition signals the impact of an entrance on the Elizabethan, as well as the medieval, stage. David Mann has interestingly proposed the use of the ornithological term 'jiz' to describe the combination of outline, bearing and voice that immediately identifies the performer.[4] The jiz of the boy-actor in *The Marriage of Wit and Wisdom* signifies Vanity to More. As for Luggins, he gets the beard and the sort of reproof to which assistant stage managers are liable. Not that it was his fault that he took so long. He went straight to Oagles' house, but Oagles was out and Mrs Oagles wouldn't let him have the beard. Poor Luggins. The proposal to start the performance again after supper is rescinded when More is called to a meeting of the Privy Council. Luggins never even makes his first entrance.

Minor performers such as Luggins are quickly swallowed by history. He is not to be found in Edwin Nungezer's *Dictionary of Actors*,[5] and must, then, be an invention of the playwright's. But why 'Luggins'? To a modern ear, he is obviously first cousin to Buggins (whose turn it is) and Muggins (always the fall guy), but centuries would pass before their birth.[6] Is there something essentially exploitable about 'uggins'? To judge from some of the extant anecdotes about Tarlton, people sometimes made the mistake of taking him for a Luggins and lived to regret it. Tarlton can usefully be seen as the last of the medieval *and* the first of the Elizabethan actors. He was certainly formidable, 'the first plebeian artist to achieve national recognition in England',[7] and equally certainly bent on making an impact. There is a famous story of his disconcerting first appearance with the touring Queen's Men in a small (unnamed) town. We have to picture an unsophisticated audience, agog in, perhaps, a Moot Hall in Gloucestershire. In the privileged seats are the local dignitaries, proud hosts on this great occasion. One of them in particular catches the eye:

> Amongst other cholericke wise justices he was one that, having a play presented before him and his touneship by Tarlton and the rest of his fellowes, her Majesties servants, and they were now entring into their first merriment (as they call it), the people began exceedingly to laugh, when Tarlton first peept out his head. Whereat the justice, not a little moued, and seeing with his becks and nods hee could not make them cease, he went with

---

4. Mann, *The Elizabethan Player* (London: Routledge, 1991), p. 27.
5. Nungezer, *A Dictionary of Actors and of Other Persons Associated with the Public Representation of Plays in England before 1642* (New Haven: Yale University Press, 1929).
6. My shorter *OED* (1977 edn) dates Muggins, in this sense, from 1872 and omits Buggins altogether.
7. R. Weimann, *Shakespeare and the Popular Tradition in the Theater* (Baltimore: Johns Hopkins University Press, 1978), p. 186.

his staffe, and beat them round about vnmercifully on the bare pates, in that they, being but fermers and poore countrey hyndes, would presume to laugh at the Queenes men, and make no more account of her cloath in his presence.[8]

This is Thomas Nashe's version of a comic actor's device that had been copied by others long before Tarlton was dead. We cannot be sure that it originated with Tarlton, but we can be fairly confident that he employed it. I am reminded of Eric Morecambe's trick of poking his head through the upstage curtain to the consternation of Ernie Wise. Morecambe, like Tarlton, was a master of the insouciant entrance. Was this the actor in role or the man caught unawares on the stage? The area of interaction between the fictional circumstance and the non-fictional self is comic territory for a gifted clown; and, at the liminal moment of entrance—before, that is, the entering actor can be expected to have fully engaged in the fiction—performers like Tarlton are focused on the audience, not the play.

It was impossible, unless by absolute intention, to enter (or exit) unobtrusively on the open stages of the Elizabethan playhouses, and unobtrusive entrances were not part of the Clown's repertoire. The passage from the stage door to the area of action was Tarlton's playground. It is visible in the crude dramaturgy of *The Famous Victories of Henry V*, in which we can read the only surviving role that can be certainly identified with him. The playwrights have contrived for Derick a sequence of *lazzi*, framed by entrances and exits. They knew their man, and they fed him. The audience first encountered Tarlton/Derick in a context of high farce. The scene has opened with a meeting of the neighbourhood watch; a cobbler and a costermonger whose ineptitude anticipates Dogberry and Verges in *Much Ado About Nothing*. Tarlton is then given one of those fatuous 'Now you see him, now you don't' appearances that delight pantomime audiences. He enters precipitately, shouts 'Whoa! Whoa, there! Whoa, there!', and exits. The stage direction stipulates that he is 'roving' (i.e. looking around), and his shout implies that the object of his search is a horse. Even on a flat stage with side access, this kind of eye-blink presence is an invitation to the actor to improvise comic business. On the stage of the Rose, where Derick would presumably have come on through one stage door, circled the platform, and gone out through the other stage door, there was a workable distance to cover. The *joke*, though, is that Tarlton as 'roving' Derick has had his horse stolen and is looking for help from the watch. He sees the

8. Nashe quoted in Nungezer, pp. 356–57.

audience, registers it in his own inimitable way, but fails to see the very people he has come to find. Not much of the art of the Clown is readily discernible in the printed text.

The book of *Tarltons Jests*, however slight its authenticity, records a reputation that cannot simply be dismissed as a fabrication. Tarlton was too recently dead when it was published to be totally misrepresented. We have to take account, then, of an actor whose bodily presence was not without a hint of danger. My own impressions are tinged with a memory of the young Alexi Sayle performing in front of a student audience. The way he came onto the stage was already a provocation. Tarlton seems to have been able to provoke antagonism simply by entering a room:

> There was one Banks, in the time of Tarlton, who served the Earl of Essex, and had a horse of strange qualities, and being at the crosse-keyes in gracious streete, getting mony with him, as he was mightily resorted to. Tarlton then, with his fellowes, playing at the Bel by, came into the Crosse-keyes, amongst many people, to see fashions, which Banks perceiving, to make the people laugh, saies: signior, (to his horse), go fetch me the veryest foole in the company. The jade comes immediately, and with his mouth drawes Tarlton forth. Tarlton, with merry words, said nothing, but 'God a mercy horse'. In the end, Tarlton, seeing the people laugh so, was angry inwardly, and said: sir, had I power of your horse, as you have, I would doe more than that. What ere it be, said Banks, to please him, I will charge him to do it. Then saies Tarlton: charge him to bring me the veriest whore-master in the company. The horse leades his master to him. Then 'God a mercy horse, indeed,' saies Tarlton.[9]

The jest is typical of many in the collection. It takes place in a drinking establishment; it begins with Tarlton as *provocateur*; it presents a Tarlton who is initially outfaced; it reveals his smouldering anger and resultant antagonism; and it shows Tarlton turning the tables with a judicious and economical use of language. His recorded victories were rarely easy. Many of them involve a recovery from humiliation comparable with Chanticlere's, though not so life-threatening. Like Chanticlere, Tarlton seemed to invite trouble simply by the way he came in. There is a

9. The quotation is from *Tarltons Jests*, but the edition in which I read it (ed. W. Carew Hazlitt, 1866) is a regrettably bowdlerized one. There is an account of William Banks and his horse Marocco in Arthur Freeman, *Elizabeth's Misfits* (1978).

reference in Wilson's *Commendation of Cockes and Cock-fighting* (1607) to a Norwich cock which was given the name Tarlton 'because he always came to the fight like a drummer, making a thundering noyse with his winges'.[10] Tarlton's jiz—his combination of outline, bearing and voice—was the jiz of a cockerel. It links him with Chanticlere.

Modern theatre technology has greatly reduced the opportunities for actors to make unaided entrances. Our reception of the performer is conditioned, whether or not we are aware of it, by lighting and scenic design. No longer an 'In comes I' necessity, the unsupported entrance has become an occasional effect, as it memorably was in *The Taming of the Shrew* at Stratford in 1978. Like Folly in *Magnificence*, Jonathan Price trespassed menacingly into *our* space on his way to the stage. How were *we* to know he was an actor, not a drunken hooligan? And when he started tearing down the painted scenery, he was spoiling *our* play. It was a very different theatre, and a very different kind of audience, when Beaumont's grocer first heckled the actors (as if he were one of *us*, not *them*) in *The Knight of the Burning Pestle*. The Stratford audience recovered its equanimity and watched Michael Bogdanov's production respectfully enough. Beaumont's first audience evidently rejected his play. It would be very intriguing to know what went wrong. There is no question, I think, that 'great' actors have still a way with entrances, but it is a different way. It may, of course, turn out that the New Globe will re-introduce us to the old excitement. Perhaps it already has. 'Enter Juliet somewhat fast' has a ring about it on the open, unlit stage.

10. Quoted in Nungezer, p. 356.

3

The Missing Jig

The best known reference to the post-play Elizabethan jig is that of the Swiss traveller, Thomas Platter:

> After dinner on the 21st of September [1599], at about two o'clock, I went with my companions over the water, and in the strewn roof-house saw the tragedy of the first Emperor Julius with at least fifteen characters very well acted. At the end of the comedy they danced according to their custom, with extreme elegance. Two in men's clothes and two in women's gave this performance, in wonderful combination with each other.

Platter says nothing about the content of the jig. Perhaps he didn't understand it. It was the elegance of the presentation that struck him. The probability is that he had just witnessed an obscene playlet featuring failed seduction or triumphant adultery, and that he found the sung dialogue in colloquial English largely incomprehensible. What he *saw* was very different from what he failed to *hear*. There is nothing surprising about that. Not knowing the language of birds, we may find the courtship of the great crested grebe spectacularly elegant whatever is being vocally communicated ('not you again! I know a *coot* with a bigger crest than that'), and however basic the sex drive.

In fact, though, Platter has provided us with a wonderfully terse account of a visit to the newly opened Globe. The day's main meal comes first, and then the crossing of the Thames (someone has to pay the waterman). I suppose the Globe had its own dock or pier and its own traffic jams, and that not all the spectators were in place when the play began (Platter's sense of time is decidedly approximate). Access to the playhouse seems to have been easy enough to require no comment, and the story of Julius Caesar was sufficiently familiar to allow foreign visitors to follow the events of the play without much difficulty. It is a pity that Platter gives no detail of his vantage point. The number of actors surprised and their quality gratified him. And when the comedy (i.e. the play) was over, the jig began. It seems likely that, if there was a significant interval, Platter would have mentioned it. But I am a little troubled here. Evidence from elsewhere suggests that the audience for the jig increased rather than diminished. I doubt whether the clown would have been prepared to make his entrance until the house was ready for it. But I am equally tempted by the idea that Brutus' body had scarcely been borne from the stage before the carnival broke out of the tiring house. The theatrical experience did not end with the death of Brutus but with four clowns, two of them cross-dressed, and all bent on jollity.

It is a fair assumption that Platter is describing a visit to the Globe to see the Chamberlain's Men in Shakespeare's *Julius Caesar*, though it is only an assumption. The competitive Admiral's Men were not above staging a rival Roman play a short distance upstream in the Rose. They had lost their monopoly of a catchment area and were keeping a close watch on the newcomers. But the timing fits well with *Julius Caesar*, and the new Globe was a greater tourist attraction than the Rose. It is just possible that Platter witnessed a reformist jig. Kemp, the supreme jig-maker of the 1590s, had just left the Chamberlain's Men. We don't know whether he jumped or was pushed, and his abrupt departure has invited conjecture. The move to a new playhouse forces on any company a reassessment of priorities, and there have been several supporters of the view that Kemp's style was too 'low' to meet the aspirations of his colleagues. Jigs were directed towards the least sophisticated section of the audience, or to that part in the make-up of every member of the audience that is most resistant to sophistication. David Wiles, on the way to a suggestion that we might regard them as 'a form of soft commercial pornography', explains that '[w]e have to understand the function of the stage jig in relation to the sexual needs of a population which included innumerable men severed from family and parish life'.[1] He has his eye on the proximity of playhouses and brothels along the south bank between the Globe and the Rose. What Platter's evidence confirms is that the Chamberlain's Men did not dispense with jigs the moment they had dispensed with Kemp. It just *may* be, though, that they were trying to sanitize them a little.

There is very little doubt that Shakespeare and Kemp had different views on the relative merits of plays and jigs, but in 1599 it would have been an act of suicidal boldness to dispense with jigs altogether. Only the previous year, another foreign visitor to London, the disapproving

1. Wiles, *Shakespeare's Clown* (Cambridge: Cambridge University Press, 1987), pp. 45–46.

German Paul Hentzner, had noted the excessive applause that greeted them. They were, after all, the parade ground of the company clowns, and intrinsic to the afternoon's entertainment. Wiles has noticed how rarely the clown is provided with any closure within the narrative of the play.[2] He had no need of dramatic finality because the theatrical finality of the jig lay ahead of him. It was not the playing of Peter in *Romeo and Juliet* that capped the day for Will Kemp, but the freedom of the stage when the play was over. If Peter was not on stage for the sad conclusion, it was because Kemp was in the tiring house getting ready for his big entrance.

To come to terms with the jig, we need to know about the clown. The word 'clown' is an Elizabethan coinage (probably derived from Low German) which came into currency because it usefully distinguished those who used it from those they used it about. That is to say that it was the linguistic product of a new class-consciousness that accompanied the decline of feudalism. A clown was a rustic and a boor, boorish because of his rusticity. Courtly aspirants to gentility found his behaviour amusing but were contemptuous of his values. Just how and when the clown got in among the dramatis personae is a matter for dispute, but the decisive contribution was Richard Tarlton's. Tarlton was the first great star of the Elizabethan theatre, and he was a clown. That is to say that he carried onto the stage his developed off-stage persona of the rustic boor. It was not entirely an invented persona. To the city sophisticates, people who, like Tarlton, had immigrated to London *were* rustics. There were thousands of them, and Tarlton spoke to and for them. He was funny and he was formidable.

Any attempt to reconstruct Tarlton's life is doomed to failure since the life can no longer be detached from the legend. No other Elizabethan actor was so much spoken and written about during his life and after his death. In the minds of many Elizabethans, he represented more than the theatre. In the mind of the unknown compiler of the posthumously published book of *Tarlton's Jests*, he represented sturdy individualism opposed to petty authority, charlatanism and any kind of prissiness. Jest books were a literary sub-genre, hovering on the borders of fiction, but *Tarlton's Jests* confirmed rather than created his reputation as a spokesman for the underprivileged. Rightly or wrongly, he is present in history as a prodigious plebeian with an insatiable appetite for confrontation. We do not know his exact route to the stage, though he seems to have gained a reputation as a solo performer before he became, formally, an actor. There are references to his keeping an inn in Colchester, the Saba Tavern in Gracechurch Street, and an ordinary in Paternoster Row. It

2. Wiles, p. 53.

was probably in such places, before his entry into the theatrical profession, that he inaugurated his 'themes', those extemporized (often rhymed) responses to subjects suggested by drinkers to challenge his ingenuity that first brought him to public attention. His transportation of this tavern-based tableside style to the public theatres was his peculiar contribution to acting in general and to jigs in particular. Tarlton delighted in word play and double entendre. To the exasperated lady-in-waiting who threatened to cuff him he readily assented, provided that they reversed the consonants. This is a characteristically masculine nod and a wink and a gesture, transferable almost without adaptation to the world of the jig.

In the latter half of the 1570s, Tarlton joined the acting company of Thomas Radcliffe, Earl of Sussex and the Queen's Lord Chamberlain. The Earl had a ribald sense of humour, appreciated his new clown, and promoted his adoption as unofficial jester to Elizabeth I. There is, then, some legitimacy in the association of Yorick's skull with Tarlton, whose death in 1588 would have been remembered by the greater part of *Hamlet*'s first audience. But it was above all as a founder-member of the revived Queen's Men, from 1583 until his death, that Tarlton established his theatrical supremacy in the jig. None that he wrote has survived, but we can be sure that they exploited his talents as a singer and wordsmith. However he varied his costume, it was as the archetypal rustic clown, dressed in a russet suit and buttoned cap, that he stamped his enduring image on the city. It was in this guise that he appeared on alehouse signs and, presumably, in many of his jigs. What Tarlton made of the jig is what his successors inherited. Shaped as short farces, Tarlton's jigs featured sexual misdemeanour and cross-dressing, drew attention to the functions and appurtenances of the human body's lower half, and served above all as the vehicle for clownish antics. Tarlton could even get away with the defamatory mockery that is a characteristic of Elizabethan libels in a way that other clowns could not. His impact on audiences of the new drama forced playwrights to involve a clown in the action, however incongruous his contribution.

The clown of Will Kemp, Tarlton's best remembered successor, tended to flounder among words. He lacked Tarlton's clown's native shrewdness and durability, but was protected from shame by his own ignorance. In the jig, his medium was dance. The attribution to Kemp of four surviving texts (two of them in German) is not reliable, but Wiles has found them worthy of analysis and I cannot better his conclusion.

[The clown] starts the jig in a predicament, and the audience's pleasure consists in seeing how he extricates himself. The clown

29

is an anti-hero in the misrule tradition, for he is the lowest of the low in all respects—wealth, status, fighting ability, even intelligence (for his ploys are never his own idea)—in everything, in short, except dancing ability.[3]

One of the texts Wiles has used, the richest we have in English, is *Singing Simpkin*. We can be fairly sure it is the one listed in the Stationers' Register for 1595 as 'a ballad called Kemp's new jig betwixt a soldier and a miser and Sim the clown'. There are various printed versions, and I refer to the one reproduced by C.R. Baskervill only because it is accessible.[4] In this form, it is Kemp's jig as emended for seventeenth-century audiences by Robert Cox, but the probability that Cox was still performing it (illicitly) at the Red Bull in the 1650s confirms its appeal. *Singing Simpkin* is a fifteen-minute sung farce, which seems to make use of only two tunes. It begins with the double entry of a pensive wife and Simpkin the clown, who converse to a tripping melody with refrain. The wife, as we will eventually discover, is much younger than her husband, and much lustier. The opening dialogue foreshadows the whole action:

WIFE: Blind Cupid hath made my heart for to bleed,
        Fa la, la, la, la, la, la, la, la.
SIMP: But I know a man can help you at need,
        With a fa la, la, la, la, fa, la, la, la, la, la.

Cupid, in the jig, aims his arrows at the loins, not the heart. The wife flirts with Simpkin because he is there, not because he is special. The first song concludes when they are interrupted by a knock at the door:

WIFE: You know my affection, & no one knows more,
        With a fa la, la, &c.   *Knock within.*
SIMP: 'Uds niggers noggers who knocks at the door?
        With a fa la, la &c.

With the servant's entry to report the arrival of a roaring lout (he is given the name of Bluster in the dramatis personae), the tune changes to accommodate the rapid interchanges that are required for the rest of the narrative. Simply to hear of the arrival of a swearing, tearing roisterer is

3. Wiles, p. 52.
4. Baskervill, *The Elizabethan Jig and Related Song Drama* (Chicago, University of Chicago Press, 1929), pp. 444–49.

enough to throw Simpkin into a panic, and he is quick to follow the wife's suggestion that he hide in a chest. '*A chest set out*', says a stage direction in Cox's text. By whom? Two dancing servants? The simpler thing would be to pre-set it, of course—but there would have been no time for that if the jig burst onto the empty stage at the end of a tragedy, and why bother, anyway, when the introduction of a piece of furniture can be enlivened by a dance routine? The chest is a vital property in the jig. Simpkin/Kemp spends almost all the remaining time in it, out of contact with the on-stage actors but in constant touch with the audience. Frequently he has the punch line at the end of the sung stanza, and his interventions are commentaries on the action or on his own dilemma. Bluster, as his name implies, talks bigger than he acts:

BLUST: Where is the foole thy husband?
          Say, whither is he gone?
WIFE: The Wittall is a hunting.
BLUST: Then we two are alone:
          But should he come and find me here,
          What might the Cuckold think?
          Perhaps hee'd call the neighbours in,
SIMP: And beat you till you stink.

The essence of the comedy is that the wife is available to Simpkin or Bluster, but neither of them has the confidence to cuckold her elderly husband. Is he so formidable? We are obviously intended to suppose that he is. Meanwhile, Simpkin can share jokes (obscene ones preferably) with the audience:

BLUST: Within this chest Ile hide my self,
          If it chance he should come.
WIFE: O no my love, that cannot be,
SIMP: I have bespoke the room.
WIFE: I have a place behind here,
          Which yet is known to no man.
SIMP: She has a place before too,
          But that is all to[o] common.

This is the point of the piece at which we hear, but not yet see, the husband for the first time. He ought to have a huge voice to explain Bluster's panic (Bluster is, after all, built like Tarzan), but once again the resourceful wife comes up with a ruse. Bluster must pretend that he has chased a thief into the house: 'Draw quickly out your furious blade, [and don't miss the opportunity of a double-take on the double entendre] And seem to make a strife.' It is a fine show for the dangerous off-stage husband, who is about to make his first appearance. Bluster's bluster falters. Enter the husband—a classic stage wimp—who begins the strangest stanza in the jig:

> OLD MAN: She's big with child, therefore take heed
> You do not fright my wife.
> BLUST: But know you who the Father is?
> SIMP: The Roarer on my life.
> OLD MAN: She knows not of your enemy,
> Then get you gone you were best.
> WIFE: Peace husband, peace, I tell you true,
> I have hid him in the chest.

The dramaturgy is simple, but wonderfully effective. A bold wife receives three men. The first is stout (since Kemp was stout) and cowardly, the second is big and cowardly, the third is wizened and cowardly. Which is the father of this surprise foetus? None of them seems capable, so that we are permitted to anticipate the arrival of a fourth man, as bold as the wife herself. In fact, no such person arrives, but the focus has anyway shifted in the dramatically crucial last two lines, sung by the wife *aside* to her husband. A sung aside is a great context for stage business. How does Kemp respond? The cat is out of the bag, but the clown is still in the chest, with only the audience for company.

The plot from now to the conclusion is forced. We have to accept that the husband takes pity on the thief in the chest, persuades Bluster to leave, and goes off to buy a restorative quart of wine for Simpkin. Kemp's version probably ended here, with the clown and the wife performing a dance of cuckoldry. The three stanzas that bring the husband back to beat Simpkin off the stage are Cox's moralizing addition. In Kemp's time, the jig paid no heed to conventional morality. It opposed the carnival spirit of misrule to the orderly conclusion of the preceding play. Kemp's nine-day dance away from the Globe to Norwich belongs to the same tradition. The civic authorities would have been pleased if the Chamberlain's Men turned their back on jigs after Kemp's departure. The decision taken at the General Session of the Peace in Westminster on 1 October 1612, to confirm 'An order for the suppressinge of Jigges at the ende of Playes', was not an isolated instance of official disapproval. A fear of riotous assembly was endemic in Tudor legislators, and the continuing popularity of jigs at the north-bank playhouses was a regular cause for anxiety. It might have been a good cause, too. There was surely an element of mob mentality in the section of the population that waited until the play was over to push their way into theatres, just for the jig. For them, it made no difference whether the unseen play had been a tragedy or a comedy. For the majority, though, who were present throughout the afternoon's entertainment, there would have been a qualitative distinction. Comedy, whether romantic or hard-edged or both, generally ended in marriage. The jig offered a low-life picture of bedroom reality after the romance of true love gratified. Tragedy dealt generally with kings and princes. The jig caricatured state quarrels as domestic brawls between artisans. Either way, the last word was with the clown and his carnival collaborators.

It took them a long time, but the legislators seem to have won. *Hamlet* without the Prince is an anomaly, but *Hamlet* without the jig is the norm. In fact, if we accept David Wiles' ingenious commentary on the text, *Hamlet* never had one:[5]

> In *Hamlet*, symbolically, we see the jig being swallowed up and dissolved within the play. The jig became a residual form . . . once the juxtaposition of rule and misrule ceased to be the organizing principle for drama. In Shakespeare's 'dark' comedies and tragedies, the possibility of perfect order disintegrates; the celebration of anarchy ceases, necessarily, to be an admissible complement to the play.

It is an argument that takes no account of the continuing trade in jigs at London's other theatres and assumes their abandonment at the Globe. In the end, I think, it is *too* ingenious. There is some literary sleight of hand in the claim that Hamlet, by declaring himself Ophelia's 'only jig-maker', has already subsumed within himself the role of the clown. There is nothing in the play that precludes the subsequent performance of a jig. Kemp's clowning successor had, presumably, the role of the loquacious Gravedigger. Unless he was uncommonly compliant, he would have demanded a second bite at the audience. The problem here has been our ready acceptance of the claim that Robert Armin replaced Kemp, man for man, in the composition of the Chamberlain's Men. But the company had other clowns. They danced with Kemp. I am entirely persuaded that Armin's post-Kemp promotion shifted Shakespeare's comic focus from clown to fool, but there were many other writers who served the Chamberlain's Men. Where, in their texts, are the philo-

5. Wiles, pp. 57–60.

sophical farewells to the jig? Armin was an actor, not a clown, and certainly not a natural successor to Kemp. He advertised himself by writing whereas Kemp advertised himself by putting on funny clothes and dancing in the open air. Theatre companies are pragmatic entities. Their decisions are not based on the anticipated evaluations of posterity. Because Kemp had left, we do not have to assume that Armin was selected as the next star, certainly not that he must have been one of the dancers praised by Thomas Platter in September 1599. What about the man who had played Bluster opposite Kemp's Simpkin? And what about Richard Cowley who shared with Kemp the double act of Dogberry and Verges and who seems never to have advertised himself at all?

The idea that the Chamberlain's Men abandoned jigs because Armin wasn't a clown seems to me as preposterous as the idea that they came to some sort of consensus that the jig was 'a residual form' now that 'the juxtaposition of rule and misrule [had] ceased to be the organizing principle for drama'. Come up with that at a company meeting, and you're liable to be met with stony silence. The performance of plays was effectively curtailed during the Civil Wars and the Commonwealth Interregnum, but Robert Cox and others ensured that jigs survived in the new guise of 'drolls', and not always surreptitiously. It would measurably increase the public enjoyment of early modern drama if we were to revive them in the twenty-first century, above all in their natural home at the New Globe.

The first problem, of course, is the shortage of texts. Baskervill has published, in whole or in fragments, thirty-five (by no means all in English), but *Singing Simpkin* is the only one I would confidently risk in the modern theatre. We need to write our own, in the sort of spirit in which Henry Livings offered his Pongo Plays as modern English responses to the Japanese *kyogen*. The task is not a difficult one, since jig-writers did not, need not and should not set themselves high literary standards. The greatest risk of offence is to political correctness, something of no concern in the context of carnival. Because I have always believed that one of the best ways of understanding a genre is through trying to imitate it, I set myself the job of writing a jig, initially with a plan to send it to Mark Rylance at the New Globe under a covering letter outlining my argument that jigs should be revived there. The piece, unfortunately, is fatally flawed, and I have sent neither jig nor letter. But the project is a serious one at a time when the English theatre has lost touch with the people, and I conclude this essay by reference to my own experience as a jig-maker.

These were the conditions I set myself. The language must be modern, but the historical setting may better be Elizabethan. There must be a central clown and a sexual entanglement of some kind. The tunes for the sung dialogue must be familiar, but out of copyright to avoid exorbitant costs. Is it not the case that 'Who's afraid of Virginia Woolf?' had to be sung to 'Here we go round the mulberry bush' because it turned out that 'Who's afraid of the big bad wolf?' would swallow the profits if Albee's play had a long run? As an easy compromise between the modern and the Elizabethan, I chose an anecdote about the fat fool, Jem Cammer, from Armin's *Foole upon Foole*:

There was a Laundres of the Towne, whose daughter used often to the Court, to bring home shirts and bandes, which Jemy had long time loued and solicited, but to no ende, shee would not yeelde him an inch of her maydenhead: now Jemy vowed he would have it all. Well, she consented at last, and to be short, soone at night, at nine a clocke being in the winter, when she knew her mother to bee gon to watch with a sicke body, hee should come and all that night lye with her: Jemy though witlesse, wanted no knauish meaning in this, thought long till it was night. But in the afternoone, the mayde goes up to the Castle, and gathers a great basket of nettles, and comming home strawes them under the bed.

   Night comes, nine a clocke strikes, Jemy on his horse comes riding forward, sets him up and knockes at the doore, she lets him in, and bids him welcome bonny man: to bed hee goes, and Jemy was never used but to lye naked, for it is the use of a number, amongst which number she knew Jemy was one, who no sooner was in bed, but she her selfe knockt at the doore, and her selfe asked who was there, which Jemy hearing was afraide of her mother: alas Sir sayes she, creepe under the bed, my mother comes. Jemy bussled not a little, under he creepes stark naked, where he was stung with nettles: judge you that have feeling of such matters, there he lay turning this way and that way, heere he stung his leg, heere his shoulder, there his buttockes: but the Mayde hauing lockt the doore to him, went to bed, and there lay hee in duraunce (as they say) till morning.[6]

It does not matter, I think, whether the Clown wins or loses in the end, but this anecdote, which Armin maintained as true tale, is good material for a jig. I began with a dialogue between Jem Cammer and 'Alice',

6. *The Collected Works of Robert Armin* (New York and London: Johnson Reprint Company, 2 vols, 1972), vol.1, C3.

setting up the assignation to the tune of 'Tit Willow' (which those who know the problems of copyright in Gilbert and Sullivan would probably advise against). With the entrance of Alice's ferocious mother, the tune changed to 'Molly Malone'. My model was *Singing Simpkin*, so I stuck with 'Molly Malone' for the rest of the piece: another mistake. Much repeated, 'Molly Malone' has a droningly monotonous tune. Jem is driven off by Alice's mother, and a time-lapse is signified by the playing through (I'm not sure which instruments would be best) of a verse of the song. I then introduced a lamplighter to indicate the imminence of night:

> LAMP: Lights out in the city.   *(Sees Alice entering.)*
>   Why, hello my pretty,
>   What brings a young virgin so late to the town?
> ALICE: Before darkness settles
>   I'm gathering nettles
>   To flavour the soup and to perfume my gown.

Jem enters at one of the stage doors, outside Alice's house and therefore unable to see her putting the nettles in (not under) the bed. She opens the door, lets him in, tells him to get undressed while she slips into something more comfortable and exits. There is a noise in the tiring house, and Alice bursts on to the already naked Jem:

> ALICE: Quick Jem, it's my mother!
>   This bit of the other
>   Will end in disaster unless you can hide.
> JEM: Where? How my heart's beating!
> ALICE: Here, under the sheeting.
>   Pretend you're a bolster. Lie still on your side.

The scene that follows involves Alice rushing from side to side (perhaps from stage door to stage door inside the recess on the New Globe stage) to play her mother and herself while Jemmy hides in the bed, where the audience can see and hear him.

> ALICE: *(mother)*   What's happening, Alice?
>   I'm seething with malice
>   That you keep me waiting so long in the
>   street.
> *(herself)*   Oh mother, don't fuss me,
>   There's no need to cuss me.
> JEM: I'm covered in stings from my head to my feet.

36

ALICE: *(herself)*	Lie still!
JEM:	That's not simple;
	I'm one great big pimple.
ALICE: *(mother)*	Was that a man's voice that I heard in
	your bed?
(herself)	No mother, that's silly.
JEM:	I've stings on my willy!
ALICE: *(herself)*	Keep quiet!
JEM:	I'm dying!
ALICE: *(mother)*	I'll cut off his head!
	It's a man! *(herself)* I've repelled him.
(mother)	The scoundrel! I'll geld him!
	I'll go to the kitchen and fetch me a knife!
	(Slams door SL)
JEM:	I'm done for! She'll kill me!
ALICE:	Well, knackered you will be
	Unless you get moving and run for your
	life. *(Exit JEM SR)*
ALICE:	There goes Jemmy Cammer
	With throbs in his whammer.
	He'll not harass me till his stings are
	unstung.
(LAMPLIGHTER emerges from under the bed)	
LAMP:	And what about me, then?
ALICE:	I'm a sucker for he-men!
	Come on, let's get going, the night is still
	young!
(They lead the audience in a wild dance in the yard.)	

This is the kind of thing I would like to see after the first staging of *King
Lear* at the New Globe. Something to turn up the toes of the posh
critics, as the jig turned up Joseph Hall's in 1597:

Now, least such frightfull showes of Fortune fall,
And bloudy Tyrants rage, should chance appall
The dead stroke audience, mids the silent rout,
Comes leaping in a selfe-misformed lout,
And laughes, and grins, and frames his Mimick face,
And justles straight into the princes place.
Then doth the Theatre eccho all aloud,
With gladsome noyse of that applauding crowd.

A goodly *hoch-poch*, when vile *Russettings*,
Are match'd with monarchs, & with mighty kings.
A goodly grace to sober Tragick Muse,
When each base clown, his clumbsie fist doth bruise,
And show his teeth in double rotten-row,
For laughter at his selfe-resembled show.[7]

---

7. Quoted in Andrew Gurr, *Playgoing in Shakespeare's London* (Cambridge: Cambridge University Press, 1987), p. 211.

4

Three Elizabethan Actors

William Knell and the Rigours of Touring

We know very little about William Knell, and are unlikely to learn any more. Because he is associated only with the Queen's Men, he has never attracted the eager beavers of Shakespearean research, and it was not until 1961, when Mark Eccles published his *Shakespeare in Warwickshire*, that details of his death were revealed to posterity. Although it is Knell's death that concerns me here, it required a life like his to bring about a death like his, so what is known should be recorded.

In the first place, then, Knell was still a young man when he was selected to join the Queen's players. If he had not been highly thought of, he would not have been nominated. There was nothing random about the membership of the Queen's Men. Scott McMillin and Sally-Beth MacLean have argued convincingly that the creation of the company in 1583 was the outcome of political deliberation, guided by Sir Francis Walsingham and the Earl of Leicester.[1] There seems to have been a mixture of intentions. Conscious, and a little fearful in the nervous 1580s, of the growing appeal of the London-based companies, Elizabeth I's counsellors hoped to weaken them by plucking out their finest players. More significantly, perhaps, they were concerned to promote the Queen's authority in provincial areas which she rarely visited. (Elizabeth I never travelled further north than Coventry and during the critical 1580s abandoned her royal progresses altogether.) Leicester and, in particular, Walsingham were visionary exponents of the Tudor trade in public relations. The dominant figures of the Queen's Men, wisely chosen to capture public joy, were clowns: John Singer,

---

1. See McMillin and MacLean, *The Queen's Men and their Plays* (Cambridge: Cambridge University Press, 1998), pp. 18–36.

John Lanham, Robert Wilson and, above all, Richard Tarlton. Their mission (or, to speculate closer to likelihood, Walsingham's mission) was to spread the gospel of the Elizabethan settlement: a compliance and a moderation that implicitly linked Protestantism and Englishness. But clowns alone limit a repertoire. They may comment on, but cannot represent, history in action, and since a favoured source for the new drama was English history, there was a need for an actor of stature to play the king or prince for the company, someone to do what Edward Alleyn would do later in the decade for the plays of Christopher Marlowe. The first choice seems to have been John Bentley, but Bentley died at the age of thirty-two in August 1585. It is a fair supposition that Knell replaced him.

The pattern of the Queen's Men's year was emerging by then. From late spring, through summer and the early autumn they toured the provinces, moving to playing places on the fringes of London in late October, and presenting themselves at Court or in the homes of grandees during the Christmas season. Performances were then suspended through Lent, prior to the resumption of touring. It still requires both physical stamina and mental durability to sustain six, seven or eight months on the road, and roads were rougher then. To cover 30 miles (48km) in a day was good going, and the schedule of the Queen's Men sometimes required it. There has been a tendency to assume that their five years of glory ended with the death of Tarlton in 1588, but McMillin and MacLean believe that they remained the country's leading touring company into the new century. Either way, they were at their peak in 1585, when Knell joined them. He must have brought a reputation with him, but we do not know how and where he earned it. On the evidence of a will proved on 17 September 1585 in the name of Henry Knell, Honigmann and Brock wonder whether the family emanated from Bremen,[2] but it is not certain that Henry was William's father or even a relation. The possibility that the Queen's Men's new recruit was the son of an immigrant remains just that, a possibility. The assumption that he specialized in heroic parts is slightly more secure. There is an undated letter to Alleyn which refers to a wager that he could equal Bentley or Knell in any of their roles,[3] and he is again linked with Bentley in Heywood's An Apology for Actors and in Nashe's Pierce Penilesse, but the only role with which he is confidently associated is that of the young King in The Famous Victories of Henry V, and even then on the strength of an anecdote in Tarlton's Jests.

2. E.A.J. Honigmann and Susan Brock, Playhouse Wills, 1558–1642 (Manchester: Manchester University Press, 1993), p. 7.
3. W.W. Greg (ed.), Henslowe Papers (London: A.H. Bullen, 1907), p. 32.

Until Mark Eccles revealed his findings, that was the totality of William Knell. What we now know is that, on 13 June 1587, the Queen's Men were in Thame, near Oxford. Their route before this date is uncertain. They had performed four plays for the Queen's Court at Greenwich over the previous Christmas season, but their programme between then and June has not yet been traced. Uncovered records suggest that they may have proceeded from Thame, more or less immediately, to Abingdon and then to Saffron Walden, Cambridge and Ipswich.[4] If they did, it was without one of their leading actors: Knell was dead. On the evening of 13 June, for reasons unknown, he had drawn his sword and attacked a fellow player called John Towne. The coroner's inquest determined that it was in self-defence that Towne stuck his own sword through Knell's neck. The skirmish took place in White Hound Close and the mortally wounded aggressor was dead within half an hour. Friendships are severely tested and rivalries exacerbated by the enforced proximity and interdependence of theatre tours. There is no reason to suppose that any politics other than theatrical ones motivated the fight. Towne might, of course, have been making advances to Knell's young wife Rebecca, or mocking Knell for his childlessness, or they might both have been drunk. Whatever the buried truth, it was the end of the story for Knell, but not quite the end of the story.

Before 1587 was out, the Queen's Men performed in Stratford. Shakespeare was twenty-three, a little bit younger, perhaps, than the dead actor. Coming up with a needle in the haystack of conjecture (how did Shakespeare break into the theatre?), fond speculators have proposed Stratford's most famous son as the natural replacement for the lost player. This is, of course, an implicit aspersion on the standards of Elizabethan acting companies. Much more interesting, because it is evidence of the way in which the community of players protected each other's interests, is the subsequent history of Rebecca Knell. Having been granted the administration of her late husband's estate in December 1587, she remarried on 10 March 1588. Her new husband was John Heminges, known now as Shakespeare's colleague in the Chamberlain's/King's Men and joint editor of the First Folio of his plays. By him she had several children during a marriage that lasted the thirty-one years until her death in 1619. Heminges' will stipulated that he be buried in the parish church of St Mary Aldermanbury 'as neere vnto my louinge wife Rebecca Heminges who lieth there interred and vnder the same stone which lieth in parte over her there if the same Conveniently may be'.[5]

4. McMillin and MacLean, p. 177.
5. Honigmann and Brock, p. 165.

Augustine Phillips, Company Man

There are few more endearing documents in English theatrical history than the will of Augustine Phillips. It offers us an insider's glimpse into the company spirit that enabled the Chamberlain's Men to survive their transformation into King's Men and to endure as an effective force until the closing of the theatres at the outbreak of the English Civil War. It is dangerous, of course, to judge people by their wills without knowing the circumstances of their place and time. There was a widower in Sheffield, whom I vaguely knew, dying alone but for the daily care of a middle-aged bachelor. Neighbours were shocked to discover, when the bequests became known, that the bachelor received nothing more than an annual season ticket to attend the home matches of Sheffield Wednesday Football Club. Because the dead man had been rich, they decided he was mean, not realizing that Sheffield Wednesday was the most precious thing in his life. Because Phillips' will is generous, I may be deluded in thinking that he was, too; but if so, it is a delusion I shall continue to cherish.

We know nothing for certain about his antecedents, though it is clear from his will that he considered himself a gentleman. Like Shakespeare and other players, he had applied for a coat of arms, but we do not know whether his application was successful. William Smith, pursuivant in the College of Heralds, complained that 'Phillips the player had graven in a gold ring armes of Sir Wm Phillipp, Lord Bardolph, with the said L. Bardolph's cote quartred'.[6] There is no reason to doubt that Phillips claimed kinship with Lord Bardolph, and there is a hint in the naming of characters in Shakespeare's *Henry IV* that his fellow players enjoyed a joke at his expense. There is a Lord Bardolph, albeit a traitorous one, in the second part of *Henry IV*, though his contribution is much less prominent than that of the red-nosed commoner who is one of Falstaff's associates. This may well be an in-house allusion that commentators on the text have missed. Actors enjoy this kind of rehearsal-room secret. A character's name that signified something to the Chamberlain's Men and nothing to the public may well have been a source of trivial but harmless fun. Such allusions are not readily available to posterity. I have, I think, spotted one in Dekker's *Satiromastix* (1601) which Shakespearean sleuths have missed. The play is Dekker's untidy riposte to Jonson's attack on him earlier that year in *Poetaster*. Tucked away in a sub plot, where he is one of the suitors to the widow Miniver, is a character called

6. Quoted in Edwin Nungezer, *A Dictionary of Actors* (New Haven: Yale University Press, 1929), p. 282.

Sir Adam Prickshaft. For three reasons, it seems likely that this was a role designed for Shakespeare to play:

1. Prickshaft is a sexual allusion to the surname Shakespeare.
2. There is a long standing tradition that Shakespeare created the role of Adam in *As You Like It*.
3. It is stipulated in Dekker's text that Sir Adam Prickshaft, like the Shakespeare we see in contemporary portraits, was bald.

It seems unlikely that Phillips played Bardolph in the *Henry IV* plays, but quite likely that the alternatives of treachery and drunkenness represented by the two Bardolphs are a humorous reminder to Phillips of the perils of his social aspirations. If so, he must have taken it in good part: unlike Oldcastle—changed to Falstaff because the powerful Brooke family took exception to the slur on their ancestor—the names remain. The really important point is that Phillips was an active campaigner for the dignity of his profession, one of the first generation to fight for the social status of players. He handled his own affairs with sufficient prudence to enable him, in 1604, to purchase a country estate in Mortlake, not far from Richmond Palace. Andrew Gurr has suggested that the King's Men assembled there, out of reach of the plague, before making the trip to perform at Wilton House, where the new King had taken refuge.[7] This is plausible on two counts: first, that we know that the company was reimbursed for the cost of travel from Mortlake to Wilton; and second, that Phillips was just the kind of man to offer this kind of hospitality to his colleagues.

Phillips' name is first mentioned in the surviving playhouse synopsis of the lost play, *The Seven Deadly Sins*, which was in the repertoire of Lord Strange's Men between 1590 and 1592. He was probably in his early thirties by then, of sufficiently high standing to be one of only two players not required to play more than one part. His casting as Sardanapalus is suggestive of graceful bearing and vocal authority. When the plague hit London uncommonly early in 1593, Lord Strange's Men were well set up to tour the provinces, favouring their patron's home county of Lancashire, but they returned to London in time for the reopening of the playhouses in December. Perhaps because touring had strained company relationships, they were in some disarray and the untimely death of Lord Strange himself, not long after he had inherited the title of Earl of Derby, made dissolution inevitable. Almost certainly Phillips was among the small band of actors who regrouped under the

7. Gurr, *The Shakespearian Playing Companies* (Oxford: Clarendon Press, 1996), p.54.

secure patronage of Henry Carey, Lord Hunsdon. Ferdinando, Lord Strange was linked, rightly or wrongly, with the Catholic cause: Hunsdon was a staunch Protestant and a blood relative to the Queen. As Lord Chamberlain, he was formally charged with overseeing her entertainment at Court. We have no reliable information about the process by which the composition of playing companies was determined, but it is scarcely surprising that the Lord Chamberlain's Men achieved a rapid prominence. They had a nucleus of strong actors and a powerful patron ideally placed to favour them. Phillips was probably a founder-member, along with Shakespeare and the brothers Richard and Cuthbert Burbage. He was certainly one of the five actors (Shakespeare was another) who bought a 10 per cent share in the Globe enterprise in 1599, and he remained a shareholder until his death in 1605.

Sardanapalus is the only role with which Phillips can be uncontestably identified, and it is as second-lead behind Richard Burbage that he is generally placed: Mercutio and Bassanio while he was still comparatively young, Cassius and Claudius in his middle age. There is good reason to picture him as a representatively versatile performer, one who could sing and dance, play more than one musical instrument, fence expertly and, in his youth at least, perform those 'feats of agility' which were the stock-in-trade of Elizabethan professionals. He was also bold enough, even when Will Kemp was in the company, to act in a jig of his own devising: 'Phillips his gigg of the slyppers' was entered in the Stationers' Register on 26 May 1595. No text survives, but farcical footplay is implied by the title. I do not know whether this was a unique example of a 'straight' actor invading the territory of the clown, but it is the only one we have. He seems to have been able to manoeuvre terms without arousing animosity. It was his allowed authority within the company that brought him to the brink of personal disaster in February 1601, when he negotiated with the Earl of Essex's party the notorious revival of *Richard II* at the Globe. The play, with its contentious abdication scene, was manifestly a political hot potato as Elizabeth I approached her dotage, and even if Phillips was unaware that the Earl of Essex was planning a military coup of some sort, it is hard to believe that he took the Earl's money in utter innocence, though that is what he protested at Essex's trial. He was an actor, though, and he got away with it, but I doubt that he got away with it *because of* his acting. The company had more friends at Court than Essex had, and Phillips must have been fairly confident that a token innocence would be enough to protect him and his colleagues. Shakespeare, who was after all the author of the play and whose instinct for self-preservation was stronger, had probably skipped town.

It is an attractive feature of Phillips' recorded responses to cross-examination that he made no attempt to share the blame for the *Richard II* enterprise with his fellow actors. He belonged to a community and had no inclination to betray it. A profound engagement with his fellows is, as I have already implied, the distinguishing feature of his will. Eleven are named as legatees, and one of them is of particular significance. I refer to the mysterious Lawrence Fletcher, who had been part of the King's troupe in Edinburgh, before James VI of Scotland became James I of England, too. Knowing the disfavour with which English society greeted James' Scottish favourites, scholars have often argued that Fletcher was imposed on the King's Men as part of the deal that gave them royal privilege, that they accepted the imposition with bad grace, and that Fletcher never acted with them. If that is so, Phillips' will is anomalous. He lists gifts of thirty shillings to his 'fellowes' William Shakespeare and Henry Condell and to his 'servaunte' Christopher Beeston (in that order), and of twenty shillings to his 'fellowes' Lawrence Fletcher, Robert Armin, Richard Cowley, Alexander Cook and Nicholas Tooley (also in that order). No distinction is made, or implied, between Fletcher and the others. The richest gifts, 'a boule of siluer of the valew of ffyue poundes apeece', are reserved for his executors, John Heminges, Richard Burbage and William Sly. I am unsure what the nature of Beeston's service was. Within a decade, Beeston would become a theatrical power in his own right, but he may, in 1605, have been assisting Phillips in some private business venture, as well as acting, or he may have been overseeing his household in Mortlake. This reference in Phillips' will has encouraged an assumption that Beeston began his theatrical career as Phillips' apprentice, but the will deals separately with 'my Late Aprentice', Samuel Gilburne, and 'my Aprentice', James Sands. Gilburne, still in the early stages of his life as an actor, is left forty shillings and 'my mouse Colloured veluit hose and a white Taffety dublet A blacke Taffety sute my purple Cloke sword and dagger And my base viall'—precious costumes, weapons for stage-fighting and a costly musical instrument. Sands, still indentured as an apprentice actor, receives forty shillings and 'a Citterne a Bandore and a Lute'.[8]

We have no better evidence than this will, dated 4 May 1605 and proved nine days later, of the terms of theatrical apprenticeship in the developed Elizabethan theatre. Phillips clearly had hopes that Sands would establish himself as a musician and that Gilburne would inherit the kind of role that he himself had played. Above all, though, the will exemplifies the intricate network of Elizabethan theatrical connections, an intricacy reflected in Phillips' own domestic circumstance. Through

8. Phillips' will is printed in Honigmann and Brock, pp. 72–75.

the first of his mother's four marriages he was stepbrother to Thomas Pope, a fellow member of the Chamberlain's Men in its first years. His sister was married to Robert Goughe, who joined the King's Men soon after James I renamed the company. The apprentices were brought up as members of the household, surrogate sons in a family of daughters and fully sons in Phillips' other family, the Chamberlain's/King's Men. Thirty years after Phillips' death, Cuthbert Burbage remembered him as one of four 'deserving men' (the others were Shakespeare, Heminges and Condell). It is easy to see what he meant.

Will Kemp: Look at the Fat Man Dancing

Kemp was not a company man. He was a man of sudden departures, one of those people who meets a crisis with a change of scene. They are not the easiest of friends, but they have an enviable independence and the appearance of undentable self-confidence. There is a record, dating from the visit of the Earl of Leicester's players to Ipswich in 1580, of a payment of sixpence for 'carrying a letter to Mr Kempe'. This may be our man: the East Anglians had a justified reputation for independent thinking, and Kemp was certainly in Lord Leicester's service in the Netherlands in 1585, as part of the showy alternative Court through which the Earl displayed his grandeur. Display was Leicester's delight, and his entourage included fifteen actors and twelve musicians to embellish it. When the actors left the Hague for England, they were paid £12 for services rendered, and there was a separate payment of £1 to 'William Kemp the player'. He was a solo artist already, perhaps a notional jester to 'King' Leicester as Tarlton was to Queen Elizabeth at about this time.

Between December 1585 and Leicester's death in 1588, Kemp's itinerary has only two fixed points. At Amersfoort in the spring of 1586, he earned five shillings by leaping into a ditch for the amusement of the Earl and a princely guest (anyone can leap into a ditch, of course, but there is no easy way of getting paid for it), and from June 1586 he was diplomatically engaged as one of six English 'instrumentalists and tumblers' at Elsinore. Once again he was singled out from the other five on the Elsinore payroll for September 1586: 'Wilhelm Kempe, instrumentist, got two months' board money for himself and a boy named Daniel Jones'.[9] His five colleagues progressed from Elsinore to Saxony, but we have no evidence that Kemp was with them there. He had left a

9. Nungezer, p. 216.

month before them, perhaps with Daniel Jones in tow: a peculiar double act of man and boy paying their way across Europe with music and mime.

It is probable that Kemp was back in England by the time Leicester died, since he had already an established reputation as a clown by 1590. Perhaps he had joined the company patronized by Lord Strange. He was certainly one of Strange's Men in June 1592, when he featured in a new play called *A Knack to Know a Knave*. Once again, though, he was allotted a self-contained episode, 'Kemp's applauded merriments of the men of Gotham in receiving the King into Gotham'. There is no indication here of a renunciation of solo status, so that it is almost a surprise to find him, with Shakespeare and the Burbage brothers, among the founder-members of the Lord Chamberlain's Men in 1594. Thomas Pope and George Bryan, who had been among the Elsinore musicians, were also in at the start of this famous company, but the two who would emerge as stars during the early years at the theatre and on tour were Richard Burbage and Kemp, a tragedian and a clown.

Kemp is likely to have been in his late thirties in 1594, and it is during his time with the Chamberlain's Men that we have our firmest grip on him. We know that he was Peter in *Romeo and Juliet* and Dogberry in *Much Ado about Nothing;* we can reasonably suppose that Launce was added to the former text of *The Two Gentlemen of Verona* to accommodate his talents and that Launcelet Gobbo in *The Merchant of Venice* was the hyperactive 'son' of Launce; and we have the confidence to nominate Costard as his part in *Love's Labour's Lost*. These are generally roles that play into the hands of a man who prefers to rehearse separately and to improvize his way out of trouble. Bottom is more significantly integrated into *A Midsummer Night's Dream*. If the Chamberlain's Men trusted Kemp with his creation, it can only have been because he wanted it.

And then there is Falstaff. David Wiles has argued that he was Kemp's.[10] If so, it might have to be seen as the last straw in the fragile interrelationship of the company soloist and pluralists like Augustine Phillips. Falstaff is a role in which a selfish actor can overwhelm lesser talents. What we know is that Kemp left the Lord Chamberlain's Men in 1599, before they had fully launched themselves in their new playhouse, the Globe, but after he had paid his share of the costs involved. This was an extraordinary occurrence, the sort of thing that would saturate gossip columns in modern newspapers, and yet we have nothing but surmise to account for it. It may have been the direct outcome of a quarrel; it may have been Kemp's indignant response to someone's suggestion that his style was too downmarket for the new project; it may

10. D. Wiles, *Shakespeare's Clown* (Cambridge: Cambridge University Press, 1987), pp. 116–35.

simply have been that, after five years with one group, he was restless. But the question that sticks in the throat of a theatre historian is, 'what about the jig?'.

What I have briefly outlined above is a man's progress from solitary specialism through specialism on the fringes of a company to specialism within a company, terminated by a sudden departure which throws cold water on the whole idea of progress. When he joined the Chamberlain's Men, Kemp was already the leading English exponent of the jig. He wrote them, starred in them, rewrote them and starred in them again. Tarlton's jigs had been built around words and song; Kemp's were built around words and dance. He was carnal, not intellectual. In order to understand a long-dead performer's physical impact, we have to rely on textual hints or the evidence of contemporary comments and anecdotes. There is also the problem that concepts of size and shape are not historically fixed. It is not, then, certain that Tarlton was thickset, Armin dwarfish and Kemp fat. It is nonetheless sufficient for my purpose that Wiles has reached the conclusion, after a compilation of available evidence, that Kemp was 'a large man' with a 'remarkably solid physique'.[11] Let us call him fat; he is out of reach of protest. What engages me is the curious theatrical power of the fat man who dances daintily.

There is a personal history in this. At some time in my boyhood I attended a London theatre to watch a musical. I think it was *Blue for a Boy*, I know that Richard Hearne (then better known as Mr Pastry) was in it, but what I remember is Fred Emney Junior dancing. I have made no attempt to verify dates because the vagueness surrounding the central memory is the whole point. Emney was a ton of a man in a loud suit and total control of a monocle. He entered smoking a cigar and was very soon dancing in company with Richard Hearne. I think there was a pram centre stage and that the dance was somehow addressed to it. I know that I was peripherally conscious of Hearne, but fixed on Emney. There was such a discrepancy between the weight of the body and the bird-light feet. J.C. Trewin records Emney's entry in the 1940 revue *All Clear*, swung down from the flies in the guise of a barrage balloon, with monocle and cigar.[12] The monocle and cigar were trademarks, but the dancing was pure skill. Hearne's dancing was probably just as skilful, but I scarcely noticed it. My response to the double act of Kemp and Richard Cowley (who created Verges to Kemp's Dogberry in what may have been a classic thin man/fat man duo) in a jig would probably have

11. Wiles, pp. 105 and 106.
12. J.C. Trewin, *The Turbulent Thirties* (London: Macdonald, 1960), p. 131.

been the same. In such a context, Kemp and Emney are weights, Cowley and Hearne makeweights.

It might be argued that the fascination of the fat dancer falls into the Dr Johnson trap: 'a woman preaching is like a dog walking on its hind legs: it is not done well, but we are surprised to see it done at all'. But I don't think so. The dance *is* done well, and that is the source of enchantment. Kemp and Emney are not isolated cases: there is a long theatrical history which I am only beginning to encounter. William Rowley, for example, who belonged to the next generation of clowns after Kemp, was fat. Although he is best remembered now as Middleton's collaborator in *The Changeling* and other plays, he was much more famous in his own time as a performer. He was Plumporridge in Middleton's *Inner-Temple Masque*, and the Fat Bishop in *A Game at Chess*. What also seems likely is that the attractively active Cuddy Banks in *The Witch of Edmonton* was written for, and perhaps by, him. So far as I know, Rowley has not yet been confirmed as the author of any jigs, but he certainly performed in many. He may, of course, have made comic capital out of the fact that he was a maladroit dancer. In that respect jigs were permissive: a clumsy fat man in a woman's dress would invite raucous guffaws. But most professional clowns take pride in the skilled simulation of ineptitude. The eighteenth-century actor John Harper is a fine example. Later renowned for playing Falstaff without padding, he first made his name with a drunken-man dance at Southwark Fair in 1715. The dance continued to be called for long after Harper had established himself in the legitimate theatre—as Sancho Panza, Sir Tunbelly Clumsy, Sir Epicure Mammon and Ursula the pig-woman in Jonson's *Bartholomew Fair*. Having seen him act, audiences still wanted to see him dance. Virtuosity has always given pleasure, and Harper's nickname of 'Plump Jack' was a token of admiration, not mockery. The same is true of Roscoe Arbuckle, known as 'Fatty' from the day in 1913 when Mack Sennett began to promote him. Arbuckle was a 19 stone (120kg) plumber's mate at the time, and it was the combination of his 'butterball appearance and bouncing agility'[13] that made him a star of the silent screen. A visible disparity is at the heart of the attraction—the body that bears down on legs that lift up. Oliver Hardy, who played Kemp to Stan Laurel's Cowley, had a comparable quality. Dancer's feet beneath a beer-barrel body. I think it was in homage to Hardy that the burly Barry Stanton developed the mincing walk-cum-dance that made his Lucio in the 1974 *Measure for Measure* at Stratford remarkable. When a fat man dances, gravity is on trial, and the effect is oddly thrilling.

13. Kenneth Anger, *Hollywood Babylon* (London: Arrow Books, 1986), p. 21.

For reasons that have everything to do with prejudice, it is not the same with fat women. They may sing, but if they dance it is for the raucous amusement of fans of Benny Hill. Amy Caddle, who performs under the name of Amy Lamé, makes the point for me in her *Gay Man Trapped in a Lesbian's Body* (1994):

> For this performance I was searching for a size 22 flamenco dress—as a lesbian Don Quixote, a flamenco dress is absolutely essential. So I went to one of the foremost costumiers in London. I walked into the shop—I was looking pretty glamorous that day I must say—and asked the shop assistant if he had any flamenco dresses. He asked me what size. I responded proudly, '22' and he said, 'Oh it's for you!'. He escorted me to the flamenco dress department, showed me a flounce or two and said, 'Sorry, none in your size. These costumes are for dancers'.

Lamé's shrugging conclusion is that 'after all, fat girls aren't supposed to be dancers, or models, or performers, or people'.[14] Patriarchy's double standard flourishes in the aesthetic arena still. I have in my mind a confusion of images—the camera pans along a line of slim ballet dancers in tutus until it suddenly chances on a fat one (compulsory laugh!). She is probably a man in drag. In an Elizabethan jig, she was necessarily so. As the featured clown, Kemp would not have played a woman's part, but he might well have donned a dress to dance his way out of a sticky situation. It would still have been a fat man dancing, though. There was no attempt at female impersonation in the Elizabethan jig: parody released laughter more quickly. Kemp was always a crowd pleaser. The last certain sight we have of him is in February 1600. He is no longer a Chamberlain's Man, and anyway the playhouses are closed for Lent. He is a solitary performer again: a solo artist and self-publicist. So he announces his intention to dance from London to Norwich—and he does it. Not in the high style of London's theatrical élite, but in the traditional garb of a morris dancer. It is probably better to leave him there rather than to clutch at the straws of biographical continuity. He was, after all, doing what he did best—dancing.

14. Quoted in Bruce Bayley, 'The Queer Carnival', unpublished PhD thesis at the University of Exeter, 2000, p. 99.

5

A Note on Elizabethan Rehearsal

Plays were purchasable commodities in the Elizabethan theatre. They cost a theatre company six or seven pounds. Working playwrights were not inclined to write what they could not market: they made their plays to the measure of the actors. There is no lost store of unperformed drama; the system made no allowance for it. We have to remember that the task of the newly professional theatre companies was not to *select* from a national repertoire but to *create* one, and to create it at a time when the audience demanded novelty and the long run was unthought of. The supply of bright young men with the aptitude to produce five acts to order, the so-called University Wits, was plentiful, but even so it was insufficient to meet the increase in demand. A second group of playmakers emerged from the theatre itself: working actors with a knack for turning stories into plays. The best of this second group was Shakespeare, which is presumably why Robert Greene singled him out for abuse; but Greene was not to know, when he attacked the 'upstart crow' in his *Groatsworth of Wit*, that Shakespeare would become a sharer in the most successful of London's theatre companies. He was afraid of being elbowed out of the market by writers of lesser knowledge but greater know-how. Greene died in 1592 and has been fairly consistently underrated ever since, so perhaps he had a point. His best plays were written for companies that folded or, as in the case of the Queen's Men, sacrificed their hold on posterity by concentrating on provincial touring. It was in and for London that the production line of the new drama was established.

Because he was an active member of the company for which he wrote exclusively, Shakespeare is exceptional. We do not know what sort of arrangement he had with the Chamberlain's Men, but his income was not dependent on his writing alone. If it had been, he would have averaged more than two plays per year and involved himself in many more collaborative projects. The general position will be clearer if we consider it from the point of view of a freelance dramatist, one of the many in the theatrical circle of the Admiral's Men at the Rose in the 1590s. He has an idea for a play—about, let us say, Robin Hood—but he is not going to write anything until he has had a word with his closest friend among the actors. Is it the kind of thing the Admiral's Men might be interested in right now? If the answer is no, the play never gets written. If the answer is yes, he will write down a brief plot—a skeletal outline of the story—and return it to his actor-friend, Richard Jones, say. Jones will now assess the merits of the plot with his senior colleagues. If they reject it, once again the play never gets written. If they accept it, they pay our playwright £2 commission, with a further £4 promised on prompt delivery of the manuscript. I don't know how long they gave him, but I doubt whether it was much more than a month, which is why he generally looked for help from one or two collaborators. The simple way was to divide up the episodes of the plot and share them out. The actors, except in the rare case where one of them was involved in the writing, now briefly took a back seat while the commodity was in production.

The physical appearance of the completed manuscript (the authors' 'foul papers') depended on the compositional methods adopted by the playwrights. The company's active engagement with it may have begun with a reading. If so, it was probably the authors who read it out. This is a custom hinted at in Act Two of *Histriomastix*, when Posthast gives his colleagues a taste of his new play, 'The Prodigal Child'. He has only 'two sheets done in folio', and there is a limit to the number of people who can read over his shoulder. A single copy is not of much use for a reading by a multiple cast, nor is there any reason to assume that all playwrights wrote a clear hand, rarely crossed out, and never employed inserts. The final payment would have followed a satisfactory reading or the submission of emendations called for by the actors. Now the manuscript belonged to the company, but it was not yet of any use to them. Two full copies had to be made, three if the Revels Office could not be relied on to return the copy delivered there for approval or censorship. This was a job for specialist scribes, who may or may not have been expert in theatre practice. Some errors in transcription are inevitable, and if the first fair copy served as copy for the second fair copy, further errors, now at two removes from the original manuscript, may well be enshrined in what has survived as the authoritative text. The next mechanical task was the one that mattered most to the individual actors. Someone had the job of cutting up one of the fair copies, assembling in the right order the speeches belonging to each character, supplying each new speech with a brief cue (this was a wearisome job, and it is not surprising that the cues were generally very short indeed—

as little as two words, with no mention of the speaker of the cue lines), and pasting them up in the form of a scroll. The actor's 'part' was not an abstract entity but a physical object, to be held in his hand until it had been deposited in his memory.

Not only is the laboriousness of the whole exercise obvious, but also its fragility. With one of the new manuscripts in fragments preparatory to pasting, or in the process of pasting itself, a speech may be lost, or inserted out of order, or given to the wrong character. Another (*the* other?) manuscript must be propped open nearby for checking. And even when the part has been given out, a careless actor may lose it—in which case it will have to be copied out all over again. Once committed to memory, the parts must be collected and stored: the play is, after all, subject to revival with a new cast, and that would involve a redistribution of parts. The tendency has been to assume that the responsibility for all this lay with the company's 'book-holder', but we have no authoritative information and no names. But one way or another, the parts reached the actors and the process of rehearsal, as we would naturally suppose, was ready to begin. We are immediately confronted, though, with further uncertainties. How were rehearsals constituted? Who ran them? At what time of day did they take place? Where? How long did any single rehearsal last? How much rehearsal was required for a five-act play? What was the normal time lapse between the first rehearsal and the first performance? *Was* there a normal time lapse or were decisions taken according to the exigencies of the theatrical moment? And before we can address such questions, we have to determine what constitutes reliable historical evidence.

There are two particularly famous examples of performance practice among Shakespeare's dramatic fictions: 'The Mousetrap' in *Hamlet* and 'Pyramus and Thisbe' in *A Midsummer Night's Dream*. The professional players who arrive unannounced in Elsinore are prepared to pluck the old play of 'The Murder of Gonzago' from their repertoire, and to insert in it a sixteen-line speech, in time for a performance 'tomorrow'. Hamlet's bizarre request ruffles them not a jot, despite the fact that they are to play before the highest audience in the land. It is fair to suppose, since the city company clearly stands 'in house' for the Chamberlain's Men, that English professionals would similarly have accommodated a royal command. Performances were adaptable within a framework of convention. Peter Quince's amateur group has four days to mount 'Pyramus and Thisbe' for the Duke's Athenian court. We see the distribution of the parts, ranging in size from Bottom's thick scroll to the much thinner ones of Starveling and Snout (and none at all for Snug, who must roar extempore). The play, when we eventually see it, is very short, but this is, of course, a dramaturgical joke. Shakespeare has shrunk a full-length tragedy so as not to exhaust the laughter, and the rehearsal period has been compressed along with it. There is not much to help us here. Nor is there in the decision of the players in *Histriomastix* to announce for next Friday a play that has not yet been written, since the author's purpose is satirical. The rehearsal scene in *Histriomastix* degenerates almost immediately into mere bickering. If we are going to make use of evidence drawn from plays, we need something firmer to balance it on, and that something may be provided by the enigmatic document generally known as Henslowe's *Diary*.

I will take a particular example, but the *Diary* furnishes many that are comparable. On 29 September 1598, just one week after the duel in which Ben Jonson killed Gabriel Spencer, thereby depriving the company of a leading actor, Dekker and Drayton delivered to the Admiral's Men the manuscript of a play which Henslowe records as *The first Civil Wars of France*. It was staged about five weeks later, on 4 November 1598. A modern repertory theatre would revel in a five-week rehearsal period, but the Admiral's Men never aspired to such luxury. As we have seen, there was much to be done before the actors received their parts. Neil Carson has calculated that two weeks was normally allowed for the conversion of a playhouse manuscript into a form workable by actors.[1] That would bring us to 13 October, still three clear weeks before the opening of *Civil Wars*, but on 21 October the Admiral's Men staged the premiere of a different new play, *Pierce of Winchester*, in the authorship of which the busy Dekker also had a hand. (He is known to have worked on as many as six plays at a time.) Until 21 October, then, *Pierce of Winchester* must necessarily have taken precedence over *Civil Wars*. Given the likelihood that the company was spared the task of performing one new play in the afternoon and rehearsing the next one that evening, we can confine the Admiral's Men's work on the text of *Civil Wars: Part One* to the period between the morning of 22 October and the morning of 4 November 1598. Take away two Sundays, on which formal rehearsal would be taboo, and they were left with twelve days. Take away the afternoons, during all of which the actors would have been involved in performances of other plays in the repertoire and, assuming a non-stop working day of twelve hours, there remains a maximum of 108 hours to mount *Civil Wars*. (I am allowing for three hours per day lost to performances.)

The mathematics are quite tidy, but the sum is a fictional one. There is no such thing as non-stop work in any theatre. What is more,

1. Carson, *A Companion to Henslowe's Diary* (Cambridge: Cambridge University Press, 1988), p. 76.

rehearsing on an open-air stage during late October and early November evenings is an improbable proposition. Apart from the cold, how would they have lit themselves? Candles were costly items. I have to assume that there was an indoor rehearsal room somewhere—in a chamber in the jointly managed neighbouring Rose brothel, perhaps—but I doubt that very much time was actually spent there. When did the actors learn their parts? When, indeed, did the actors receive their parts for *Civil Wars*? It would be placing precious documents in crazy jeopardy to give them out on the eve of the opening of *Pierce of Winchester*. The best time, surely, would have been immediately after that premiere. We know, from a document dated 7 April 1614 (once among Henslowe's papers but now lost), that the actor Robert Dawes 'shall and will at all times during the said term duly attend all such rehearsal which shall the night before the rehearsal be given publicly out'.[2] That sounds like sensibly established routine at the end of a working day, an end which coincides with nightfall (i.e. earlier in late autumn than in summer). We too readily forget the significance of darkness in a city without much artificial light.

Here, then, is my first proposal: that the parts for *Civil Wars* were distributed on the stage of the Rose at about five o'clock on the evening of 21 October 1598. Once he had his part, the first responsibility of an Elizabethan actor was to take it to a private place and learn it. It was a bare document, remember, carrying the character's name and columns of speeches punctuated by brief cues. Unless he was a leading actor, there was certainly more than one such scroll. As a possession, outside the context of a performance, a part declared little about the action and a lot about reactions. Decoding it came more easily to experienced actors than to novices. Even so, the material layout of the part must have had some bearing on the nature of performance in the Elizabethan play-houses. The lonely memorizer was dependent on dramatic conventions as a guide to his reading. His intuitive embodiment of the language allotted to him carried him towards conventional gesture in response to powerful stimulus. Vocal inflection was something he had also to decipher, much as a skilled musician might practise a part in isolation from its place in the totality of the orchestration. If our Admiral's Man was lucky, he might have been able to share some of his learning with an appropriate colleague, or even two, but the hidden imperative of the distribution of parts to working actors was 'get on with it!'. The peremptory need was to know the social status of the character represented by the scroll. A courtier's response to a stimulus was as physically

---

2. G.E. Bentley, *The Profession of Player in Shakespeare's Time* (Princeton: Princeton University Press, 1984), p.48.

distinct as it was vocally from a servant's, and the actor might very well find himself cast as both servant and courtier in the same play. Always in Elizabethan drama, the pecking order of power is crucial to the communication of the narrative. An actor whose style of performance distorted the pecking order, who stood too close to the King or failed to dominate the underling, would not last long in professional company. There was no time to rehearse that kind of routine business. Its practice on the stage was no more than a heightened form of its practice in daily discourse. A well-written part gave a well-versed actor virtually all the information he needed to perform his responses.

The 108 hours I have allowed as a fictional maximum for rehearsal is cut to forty-eight if you take out the evenings, and cut further if the demands of playhouse business are taken into account. Thomas Dowton, who probably had a leading role in *Civil Wars*, may also have been chiefly responsible for its purchase and was evidently in charge of its production. On 8 October, and again on 11 October, he received advances from Henslowe 'to bye divers things for the play called the first syvell wares of france'. This is evidence of pre-rehearsal preparation, designed to smooth the passage of the play when its turn comes. It was not trivial expenditure. The combined sum of Henslowe's advances came to £10—almost twice as much as Dekker and Drayton received for the play. Without doubt, most of the money went on material for costumes. They, too, carried vital information about the relative status of the enacted characters, and were a theatre company's most precious possession. The Dawes contract mentioned above stipulates a fine of £1 for missing a performance and £40 for walking off with (or in) a playhouse costume. But Dowton's job was not complete by the time rehearsals for *Civil Wars* began. There were properties to assemble, costumes to fit and emergencies to deal with. The chances of clear and concentrated rehearsal time in excess of twenty-four hours seem to me negligible: and you cannot hope to go systematically scene by scene through a five-act play in that time. The Admiral's Men did not expect to. We do not know whether the whole piece was ever run through before the first performance. Perhaps on the morning of the same day?

There was nothing unusual about the schedule for the month of October 1598. Through her detailed examination of documents connected with the Rose, Carol Rutter has discovered that a new play every two weeks was what the Admiral's Men looked for.[3] Dekker and Drayton presented them with a second part of *Civil Wars* on 3 November 1598

---

3. Rutter, *Documents of the Rose Playhouse* (Manchester: Manchester University Press, 1984), p. 3.

(it opened on 9 December), and a third part on 30 December. By the end of the year they had £18 to share between them, and the Admiral's Men had the new commodities they coveted. Not that they always got what they wanted, but the shows had to go on regardless. There was a period of ten weeks in 1595 when they gave fifty-seven performances of twenty different plays, four of them new.[4] I have read the arguments that Elizabethan actors had phenomenal memory systems; I am even prepared to go along with them; but it is out of the question that all the actors were normally word-perfect. One of the fascinating mysteries of the Elizabethan stage is its prompting system. There was nowhere (or nowhere sensible) for a prompter to position himself unobtrusively, unless in the balcony at the back of the De Witt stage. Are we to believe that the actors were so expert at 'fribbling' their way out of trouble that they had no need of a prompter? If so, that was no longer the case in the 1630s, or Richard Brome would not have had his Lord Letoy single out among his household players:

> . . . one, that never will be perfect in a thing
> He studies: yet he makes such shifts extempore,
> (Knowing the purpose what he is to speak to),
> That he moves mirth in me 'bove all the rest.[5]

I have, in an earlier essay, referred to the significance of 'knowing the purpose'. The point I am making here is that Lord Letoy finds exceptional the capacity of this erring actor to 'fribble through, and move delight'. Lesser actors would surely need a prompt. Can it be that the prompter was always on stage with the actors, and that his presence was so much taken for granted that there is no contemporary reference to it? There is no mention of line rehearsals either. It might be argued that they, too, were matters of routine, but I doubt it. It seems to me certain that Elizabethan plays were originally staged in a manner that would seem shockingly rough-and-ready to a modern audience, and that the business of rehearsal was strictly confined. But confined to what?

Let us return to the morning of 22 October 1588: the first time the actors have assembled with the play fully cast and the parts distributed. Dekker or Drayton may be in the playhouse, but Dowton is the man in charge. The object is not what we would see as rehearsal, but a systematic testing of the play's logistics and its special requirements. Does Richard Jones have the opportunity and time to make the necessary

4. Rutter, p. 91.
5. Brome, *The Antipodes*, II.ii.16–19.

costume change? Do all the actors know who they are in each scene, and whom in particular they are addressing? Where are the awkward elisions? What special effects are needed (they must be marked in the prompt-book)? Which are the tricky scenes to stage (mark them down for later rehearsal)? It is, in a sense, what we might call a walk-through, and it takes as long as it takes (provided that is not more than three mornings). Now the actors can get ready for the afternoon performance, and then disperse about their business—after receiving the rehearsal calls for the next day. Most of the scenes require no rehearsal. Positioning on the platform stage is conventionally determined by status, and the conventions also take care of the actors' fundamental job of responding appropriately to the stimulus of the central action. Where there are massed entries, precedence follows the pecking order. Low-life characters, particularly those associated with the specialist clown, never rehearse in public. When the day of performance arrives, their important engagement will be with the audience, and their scenes are generally separated off in such a way as to allow private exploration if anyone is so conscientious, or so persuasive, as to arrange it. It is only the exceptional scenes that call for morning rehearsal in the second week: no company, certainly not the King's Men, would wait for inspiration at the first performance to work out how to hoist the dying Antony onto Cleopatra's monument.

I have based my argument on the Admiral's Men, and there is no guarantee that Shakespeare's company operated according to the same sort of schedule. But it is unlikely, given the prolonged competition between these two leading groups, that their customs were radically opposed. My assumption is that audiences neither expected nor witnessed perfection, that the actors knew they were at stretch to hold separate in their heads the words they were due to speak today from the broadly similar ones they spoke yesterday and the subtly different ones they should be speaking tomorrow, and that a prompter's intervention normally got the performance back onto its rails. Not invariably, though. There was always the possibility that his promptings might be overruled in the heat of the moment by an actor who considered himself beyond the range of the law of averages. Part of the spectators' excitement, part of the raw, present-tense thrill of the Elizabethan theatre was to watch actors operating at their wit's end and, by a timely provocation, push them over the edge.

Tiffany Stern's *Rehearsal from Shakespeare to Sheridan* will have been published by the Clarendon Press before this book appears. She very kindly sent me page proofs of her chapter on Elizabethan rehearsal practices, and this brief essay would be incomplete without some reference to her scholarship. Hers is, after all, the first full investigation of the history of English rehearsal, and it provides a corrective commentary on some of my reflections. It is not my intention to provide a summary of a chapter which deserves to be read in full, but I should record two of her distinctive proposals. Firstly, that the Elizabethan prompter was placed 'behind a curtain that divided some part of the tiring room from the stage' (p. 96), and secondly, that each actor's individual preparation was complete before there was ever a general rehearsal (p. 70). The most radical of Stern's proposals concerns the status of a play's first performance on the London stage. Elizabethan actors, she proposes, were reluctant to commit themselves to rehearsal until the first audience had demonstrated the play's capacity to 'take' (p. 93). What we may see as the substantive text was the one settled on *after* the 'trial' performance before a first-day audience that came knowingly as 'triers'. She argues that 'the cueing system allowed players to act a play with knowledge only of their own parts, and therefore made it possible to put on productions with minimum preparation' (p. 66). Stern's conclusion is that, apart from group sequences like 'songs, dances, sword-fights, and slapstick', the norm was a single general rehearsal before the first performance (p. 76); but she does not rule out the possibility that there was more extensive rehearsal if the play had proved itself, and that a general rehearsal in the presence of the Master of the Revels might have been a routine requirement before a successful play was deemed suitable for performance at court.

Part Two

ACTORS AND ACTING
IN THE
EIGHTEENTH AND NINETEENTH
CENTURIES

6

Bigamy and Theatre

If we make the calculation in percentage terms, British monarchs have been more prone to bigamy than British actors. Henry VIII and George IV were bigamists certainly, Edward IV almost certainly, and William IV all but. Monarchs, though, were protected by the law whilst actors were vulnerable to it, so that the incidence of bigamy in the theatrical profession has more to tell us about the attitudes and anxieties of society at large. And there was, particularly before Lord Chancellor Hardwicke cajoled his Marriage Act through Parliament in 1753–54, much to be anxious about, whether you were a young person in love or a concerned parent. What follows is a preliminary listing of the kind of material that might appear in a fully researched account of the incidence of bigamy in the British theatre. It is my belief that such an account would demonstrate that the notoriously immoral stage was no more immoral than the society which nurtured it.

Bigamy was made a felony in England in 1603, as part of the canon law. As was usually the case, the poor and illiterate felon would hang, whilst those sufficiently educated to be able to read the 'neck-verse' (normally the first verse of Psalm 51—in Latin) could plead benefit of clergy and escape with a branded thumb. The Bigamy Act and the reiteration of the indissolubility of marriage that followed it in 1604 were assertions of the Church's authority over an immensely important aspect of domestic life, but this authority was radically challenged during the Protectorate. Puritans, many of whom had suffered in the often corrupt Consistory Courts, moved swiftly to place the administration and registration of marriages in secular hands. The muddle that followed the restoration of the monarchy in 1660, then, is scarcely surprising. Canon law tried to reclaim *all* the power that it had lost to common law, and regained *some* of it. The outcome was a shambles. 'It is fair to say', Lawrence Stone concludes, 'that before 1753, marriage was to a considerable extent out of the control of either church or state'.[1] The

1. Stone, *Road to Divorce* (Oxford: Oxford University Press, 1990), p. 11.

position was such that, as will become clear, many people were uncertain whether or not they were legally married. Worse still, perhaps, it was beyond the means of all but the privileged and wealthy to escape a bad marriage—and that remained the case, despite the palliative effects of the 1857 Divorce Reform Act, until the introduction of a legal aid system after World War I. As Stone goes on to say, 'England thus endured the worst of all worlds, largely lacking either formal controls over marriage or satisfactory legal means of breaking it'.

Consider, for example, the different 'Restoration' fates of Mary Moders and Hester Davenport. Moders, daughter of a Canterbury chorister, was about seventeen in 1660, either already, or soon to be, married to a shoemaker's apprentice called Stedman. The couple had had two children, neither of whom survived infancy, before she decided that life had more to offer and left home. To begin with, she went no further than Dover, where she met and married a surgeon named Day. Her reasons were probably mercenary, and she had evidently spent most of Day's savings before being arrested and tried for bigamy. Stedman, for whatever reason, did not travel to Dover for the trial and the case was dismissed for lack of evidence. It is quite possible that there was no formal registration of either marriage, since verbal contracts had been recognized during the Protectorate. Moders, pondering no doubt on her own marketability, embarked for Holland en route for Cologne. It was probably there that she developed her self image as a distressed German princess, in which character she presented herself in London in early 1663. The performance was sufficiently convincing to allure the rich, young (and foolish?) John Carlton, who rushed into a marriage with his German princess in March of that year. Too late to prevent the marriage, Carlton received a tip-off, and Moders found herself on trial for bigamy again, but the Dover pattern repeated itself. Neither Stedman nor Day appeared to give evidence, and gullible Londoners were quickly ready to give credit to her fantasy. An obscure playwright called Holden dashed off a play, and William Davenant cashed in on this new cause célèbre by signing Moders up to play herself in *The German Princess*. The move paid off, and from April to June audiences flocked to the Duke's Playhouse. Taking sides for or against Moders was part of the fun. Pepys went at least twice, telling his *Diary* on 7 June 1663: 'My Lady Batten inveighed mightily against the German Princess, and I as high in defence of her wit and spirit; and glad that she is cleared at the Sessions.' The story has a disenchanting end. Moders was only briefly an actress before returning to the better-paid jobs of confidence-trickster and courtesan. She was eventually transported to Jamaica for stealing a tankard from a Covent Garden tavern. She had spirit, though. After two years in Jamaica, she tricked her way on board a London-bound ship, was spotted in London by a former gaoler of hers, and executed on 2 January 1673 for the capital offence of violating her transportation order. I do not know whether the scurrilous epitaph carved on her grave in St Martin's churchyard is still legible. It read:

The German Princess, here against her will,
Lies underneath, and yet, oh strange, lies still.

She is one of many women to have exploited for her own ends the law's difficulty in verifying contract marriages; but there were even more women who were its victims. Hester Davenport was one of them.

Davenport first attracted the attention of London's starved theatre-goers, when she played Roxalana in the 1661 revival of Davenant's *The Siege of Rhodes*. Aubrey de Vere, Earl of Oxford and a widower in his forties, was the most persistent of her many admirers, but Davenport did not fall easily. To work out what actually happened, we have to rely on the reports of contemporaries with an eye for scandal—the Comte de Gramont and the Baroness d'Aulnoy—and the facts are too slippery to count as 'true history'; but they are, in that respect, images of the wedding business. To persuade Hester Davenport into his bed, the Earl showed her a signed contract of marriage and followed it up with a scene that belongs to drama. He and Hester went through a wedding ceremony, she in good faith and he cynically, in which the minister and one of the witnesses were disguised musicians of the Earl's household. Hester's witness was a fellow actress who was probably not in the plot, but could be paid off later. According to the Baroness d'Aulnoy, the new 'bride' was woken next morning by a peremptory 'husband': 'Wake up Roxalana, it is time for you to go'.[2] Possibly, but who was in the room to hear it? For her part, Davenport considered herself married to the Earl of Oxford; she bore him a son in 1663 and was still signing herself 'Hester Oxford' when she made her will. Almost certainly, in her own eyes, she *was* married to him, and this despite the fact that he had taken as his second wife (to Hester this would have seemed a third, and a bigamous, marriage, but she could never have proved it) Diana Kirke, a famous beauty not noted for her virtue. That was in 1673. By the early 1680s Lady Diana was cuckolding the Earl with the charismatic courtier Henry Sidney, but there was never any suggestion of divorce. Parliament sanctioned only two divorces between 1660 and 1700, and only sixteen

---

2. Quoted in Antonia Fraser, *The Weaker Vessel* (London: Mandarin, 1993), p. 482.

between 1660 and the 1753 Marriage Act.[3] The Earl of Oxford's humiliation continued until his death in 1703. Only then did Davenport herself
contemplate marrying, and when she did so it was as Dame Hester,
Dowager Countess of Oxford.

Contract marriages and decoy weddings were not a new invention of
the late seventeenth century, of course. There is a famous theatrical
example of the first in Shakespeare's *Measure for Measure* and of the
second in Jonson's *Epicoene; or, The Silent Woman,* and scores more in
the surviving texts of the era. But the authority of the canon law is there
flouted, not doubted. And the Bigamy Act of 1603 was unambiguous.
Bellafront is warned to take heed of 'the last statute of two husbands'
after her apparently bigamous marriage to Scudmore in Act Five of
Nathan Field's *A Woman Is a Weathercock* (*c*.1609), and this was a
matter on which public opinion sided with the law. The securing of
inheritance was (and is) the fundamental concern guiding all legislation
on marriage, and it is among the crimes of patriarchy that the interests
of the wife were always secondary in the eyes of the law until well into
the twentieth century. An abused or disaffected woman's only financially
secure escape from a bad marriage was widowhood, or even, when the
husband was stubbornly long-lived, murder. Thomas Arden of Faversham
was indirectly a victim of the laws governing marriage, and his death in
1551 is exceptional only because of the play it inspired.

Post-Restoration drama was the major contributor to public debate
about the laws governing, in particular, clandestine marriage. G.S.
Alleman, on the strength of a survey of 241 comedies written between
1660 and 1714, has concluded that over a third of them (91 to be
precise) feature clandestine marriage.[4] Nor was there any falling off after
1714. Because it involved a formal ceremony, clandestine marriage was
invested, certainly for its participants, with a spiritual solemnity lacking
from a straightforward verbal or written contract. That, presumably, is
why the Earl of Oxford chose to 'reassure' Hester Davenport with his
cynical charade. But its practice was cloaked in materialism. For the
young couple, it might offer, variously, an escape from parental authority,
an urgent response to pregnancy, or simply privacy. There was no
reading of the banns, no pre-nuptial gossip, no awkward questions. This
was the decisive factor for the young provincial actor, Roger Kemble,
when he fell in love with his manager's daughter, Sarah Ward. On 6 June

---

3. The list of the 127 husbands who successfully sued for divorce between 1660 and
   1800 can be found in Allen Horstman, *Victorian Divorce* (London: Croom Helm,
   1985), pp. 16–18.
4. Alleman, *Matrimonial Law and the Materials of the Restoration Drama* (Wallingford,
   Penn., 1942), p. 82.

1753, while Hardwicke's Act was on its way to becoming law, he and his teenage bride sneaked off ('eloped' would probably have been Sarah's choice of word) to Cirencester to tie the knot, knowing that Sarah's father would not have approved. They were inadvertently preparing the conditions for a theatrical dynasty that would include in the next generation Sarah Siddons and John Philip Kemble, and that, though attenuated, shows no sign of ending. The legality of clandestine marriage was a subject of rancorous debate before the 1753 Act. Hardwicke's keenest parliamentary antagonist, Henry Fox, had notoriously married in secret Georgiana Lennox, one of the lively daughters of the Duke of Richmond. His Whiggish defence of the liberty of the people was not, then, entirely disinterested, but he became a popular hero of the pamphlet war that raged around Hardwicke's Bill, and it was a clause inserted to pacify him that provided a loophole for secret lovers for over a century.[5]

An essential precondition for clandestine marriage was mobility—the capacity to escape from the local parish—and touring actors were among the most mobile members of the population. But marriage is one thing and bigamy at least two: the point here is that the more clandestine a wedding ceremony, the harder it is to verify. The preservation of secrecy was essential to a serial bigamist like Major-General Robert 'Beau' Feilding (1651–1712). When, on 25 November 1705, Feilding married for money the sixty-four-year-old Duchess of Cleveland (better known, from her days of dalliance with Charles II, as Lady Castlemaine), he neglected to tell her that he had married (also for money) someone else two weeks earlier. He was actually too busy making love to the Duchess's granddaughter to bother much about either of these wives at the time. As for the oddly splendid Teresia Constantia ('Con') Phillips, a 'career' rather than simply a serial bigamist, her publication in three volumes in 1748–49 of an *Apology for the Conduct of Mrs. Teresia Constantia Phillips* did more than any legal argument to advance the passage of Hardwicke's Act.[6] So far as I have been able to discover, the acting profession provides no cases as sensational as hers, but it does offer a few historical examples as footnotes to the work of Lawrence Stone and others. My limited purpose is to draw attention to a few, some famous, some little known.

5. See Stone, p. 129, for details of the 'Lord Holland Clause'.
6. For fuller accounts of Feilding and Phillips, see Lawrence Stone, *Uncertain Unions and Broken Lives* (Oxford: Oxford University Press, 1995).

James Quin (1693–1766)

Quin never married, but his successful stage career and considerable charm made him a welcome bachelor guest in high society. He was the son of a lawyer and a grandson of a former Lord Mayor of Dublin, but notoriously reticent about his upbringing. The reason for that reticence has emerged only recently. Quin's uncommonly (for a lawyer) unworldly father had accepted Elizabeth Grindzell's word that she was a widow, and it was only after their marriage that it emerged that her first husband was still alive and working as a shoemaker in Shrewsbury. Legally, then, Quin was a bastard, and it was on that ground that an Irish uncle and cousin contested the terms of his father's will. Quin never inherited the estate that was surely his by right, if not by law.

Constantine Boone (fl. 1710–20)

I have to confess that Constantine Boone's claims to theatrical provenance are slender. He/she was exhibited as an hermaphrodite at Southwark Fair until, in 1719, she was convicted of both bigamy and fraudulent marriage. (She married as a woman.) Sentenced to the pillory, she was more leniently treated by the pelting crowd than were most convicted felons.

Susannah Cibber (1714–66)

Susannah Cibber was not, strictly speaking, a bigamist, though she might just as well have been so far as her reputation was concerned. Born into the musical Arne family, she had rashly married Theophilus Cibber in 1734. Theophilus was a fiery actor, more dangerously volatile off stage than on it. His rapid advancement in the London theatre owed something to his talent, but more to the reputation of his father, Colley Cibber, who had recently signed over his interest in the Drury Lane playhouse to his son and was relishing his appointment as Poet Laureate in comparative leisure. By 1737 Theophilus, who was short on emotional stamina and long on ambition, was out of love and in debt. It seemed to him expedient to secure the services of his financial benefactor, William Sloper, by 'selling' his young wife to him. The unorthodox trio spent the summer together in a villa Sloper had rented in Kingston. Such accommodations were not infrequent, but Cibber had made a fatal miscalculation. Sloper was not the rake he had taken him for. Having fallen in love with Susannah, he remained constant until her untimely death, despite the fact that he had already a wife (a widow with whom he had made an arranged marriage ten years before, when he was twenty) and two sons. By the summer of 1738 Susannah was carrying Sloper's child, and unhappy when her husband insisted on repeating the previous year's *ménage à trois*, this time in Burnham. They put up with Cibber for a month and then sent him packing. His furious response, in September 1738, was to abduct her and, in December, to sue Sloper for 'assaulting, ravishing and carnally knowing Susannah Maria Cibber . . . at several Periods of Time . . . and divers Days . . . Whereby the Plaintiff lost the Company, Comfort, Society and Assistance of his Wife to his Damage of £5000'. The money was of greater concern to him than Susannah, but Sloper was ably defended by William Murray, the future Lord Mansfield and one of the century's finest legal minds. The case was sufficiently sensational for Murray to make his reputation by it. There was no doubt of Sloper's guilt under the law, but the jury stipulated damages of only £10. When the prurient public interest had subsided, Susannah Cibber and William Sloper resumed their pattern of intermittent cohabitation, bigamists both in all but name, and soon to be parents too. Society, though, looked askance at Susannah for the rest of her life. If, as a pious Roman Catholic, she prayed to Saint Uncumber, the patron saint of women who wish to be rid of their husbands,[7] her prayers remained unanswered until 1758, when Theophilus Cibber drowned in a storm on the Irish Sea.

Mary Hamilton (fl. 1740–50)

Mary Hamilton is another back-door entrant to the list. She owes her place in it to the inventiveness of Henry Fielding. In plays, novels and pamphlets, and as a magistrate, Fielding regularly exposed the inadequacy of the marriage laws, most eccentrically in the fictionalized documentary of *The Female Husband* (1746). This pamphlet was based on a 1746 case of fraud in Taunton. Mary Hamilton, a transvestite who had set up in business as a Doctor Charles Hamilton, had married a certain Mary Price, but was arrested after the young wife had publicly declared that her 'husband' was a woman. The court heard that 'after their marriage they lay together several nights and that the said pretended Charles

7. Known variously as Saint Uncumber, Saint Livrade and Saint Wilgefortis, she was the daughter of a King of Portugal, who ordered her to marry the King of Sicily. In hopes of avoiding the marriage, she prayed to be made unattractive, and was rewarded with a moustache and beard.

Hamilton . . . Entered her body several times, which made this woman believe at first that the said Hamilton was a real man'.[8] Not surprisingly, there was much interest in Somerset, where Mary Hamilton was publicly whipped in four towns and imprisoned for six months. The *Bath Journal* of 22 September 1746 inflamed the story further by reporting a rumour 'that she has deceived several of the fair sex by marrying them'. Mary Price is, in fact, the only recorded victim of the quack doctor, but it was out of rumours of pluralism that Fielding fashioned *The Female Husband*, which contrived simultaneously to feed a taste for pornography, to take a swipe at lesbian perversion and to alert the reading public to the perils of bigamy whilst marriage laws remained so ill-defined.

Hardwicke's Act effectively put an end to contract marriage in England, and narrowed the options on clandestine marriage; but English law was not operative in Scotland or Guernsey. One of the Act's by-products, then, was the century-long prominence of Gretna Green (731 couples married there in the peak year of 1854), and the less-publicized matrimonial option of a sea-crossing to Guernsey. If Hardwicke's assault on clandestine marriage had been wholly successful, there would have been no market for the great Drury Lane hit of 1766, *The Clandestine Marriage*. The play's authors, George Colman the Elder and David Garrick, must surely have had in mind the great society scandal of 1764. They were, after all, close acquaintances of one of the participants. William O'Brien had been a leading member of Garrick's company at Drury Lane since 1758, particularly admired as a gentleman comedian. He was known to have a female following, but it seems to have taken everyone by surprise when he disappeared from the theatre after the performance on 3 April 1764. Four days later, at St Paul's Church in Covent Garden, he married Lady Susan Fox-Strangways, niece to Hardwicke's old adversary, Henry Fox (now Lord Holland), and, until her elopement and unannounced marriage, a girl of impeccable credentials with an entrée to the highest society in the land. Garrick was only too aware of the likely repercussions. Writing from Italy to his friend the Duke of Devonshire, he promised that 'the imprudent Step of Lady S.S. has sorely vex'd me; I always thought she had a foolish liking for ye Drama, & ye dramatis personae, but I could not have imagin'd, yt the flesh wd have overpower'd her Spirit, when there was a good

8. Quoted in Lynne Friedli, 'Passing women', in G.S. Rousseau and Roy Porter (eds), *Sexual Underworlds of the Enlightenment* (Manchester: Manchester University Press, 1987), pp. 238–39.

understanding to have help'd in the Struggle—'tis a most deplorable Business indeed!'.[9]

There was nothing bigamous about O'Brien and Lady Susan—the marriage lasted for fifty-one years—but the match changed both their lives. He left the stage and she the social whirl. For a while, in fact, her shame faced family arranged for them to set up home in America. They would return to England in the 1770s to live in genteel semi-seclusion in Dorset. For the last forty years of her life (1787–1827), Lady Susan kept a journal (as yet unpublished), which might usefully be read as a companion piece to the novels of Jane Austen. The suspicion lingers, though, that it was her pride that sustained a marriage that ended much as it began—secretly. There were other actors whose clandestine marriages were not so innocent.

West Digges (1720–86)

Details of the life of Digges are not easily verified, but if he went through a marriage ceremony with George Anne (or Georgiane) Bellamy in Dublin in 1761, he hid the fact that he was still married to a Mary Wakeling. Between whiles, he had fathered six children on the actress Sarah Ward. It may have been to cover his tracks that he adopted Bellamy's name for his performances at Edinburgh in 1762, though Scotland anyway was a different country with marriage laws of its own. Even a touring actor as well known as Digges might hope to avoid trouble by taking an engagement north of the border. Bellamy was far from immaculate herself. The six-volume *Apology* (1785) that she wrote in poverty, after squandering fortunes, is kept afloat by self-pity. Even so, she was probably unfortunate in her liaisons. She might have hoped for marriage as the outcome of her long relationship with Henry Fox's financial adviser, John Calcraft, but he too concealed for many years the existence of a wife in Grantham.

Samuel Reddish (1735–85)

Reddish played leading roles with Garrick at Drury Lane from 1767 until Garrick's retirement in 1776; thereafter he fell out of favour and his services were dispensed with in 1778, when his memory began to fail.

9. *The Letters of David Garrick*, ed. David M. Little and George M. Kahrl (Cambridge, Mass.: Harvard University Press, 1963), vol.1, p. 419.

He had married a minor actress in 1767, and some accounts suggest that she was still alive when he was married again, this time to the widowed mother of the future politician, George Canning (1770–1827). It may be that he had forgotten his first wife: he certainly spent his last years in a York asylum, a little too early, unfortunately, to benefit from the humane regime of the York Retreat.[10]

George Frederick Cooke (1756–1811)

Cooke's many marriages, like most of the rest of his life, seem to have been associated with alcohol. He hoped a wife might help to limit his consumption of it. Broadly speaking, he was wrong. There are two recent, scholarly biographies of Cooke—by Arnold Hare and Don Wilmeth—but even they have been unable to work out how often he went through some form of wedding ceremony. What seems clear is that the latest Mrs Cooke was not expected to wait for the death of the previous one. The first can be traced on playbills dating from Cooke's seasons on the Lincoln circuit in 1773–75, but her name is unknown. A second, also nameless, acted with him in the north of England from 1784–86. A third (there may have been others in between) was Alicia Daniels, and we know something of her. She and Cooke were first in company on the Manchester circuit in 1792, when she was only fifteen, but it was not until 1796, at St Peter's Church, Chester, that they were married. Evidence of the secrecy of the ceremony comes from the proceedings at Doctors Commons in May 1801, when Alicia success-fully sued for annulment according to the provisions of the 1753 Marriage Act 'for the better preventing of Clandestine Marriages': she had been under twenty-one at the time (Cooke was forty) and the parents had not given consent. So far as we know, Cooke's next wife was Sarah Lambe, whom he married in St Andrew's Church, Edinburgh on 21 September 1808, and who seems to have disappeared from his life within a year. She was not consulted when, in October 1810, he took the momentous decision to tour the theatres of America. With the Atlantic between him and the law, he would marry for the last time in New York in the early summer of 1811. It can only be assumed that the mysterious Mrs Behn knew what she was taking on, and we have the word of Cooke's first biographer, William Dunlap, that she remained 'a faithful

10. For details of the innovative moral therapy at the York Retreat, see Roy Porter, *Mind-Forg'd Manacles: a history of madness in England from the Restoration to the Regency* (Cambridge, Mass.: Harvard University Press, 1987), pp. 222–28.

and affectionate nurse to the day of his death'.[11] Alcohol addiction
ensured that it would not be a long stint.

Margaret Cuyler (1758–1814)

Cuyler was a courtesan first and an actress second. She took her
surname from a Captain of the 46th Foot, and may have married him.
If so, her marriage to Dominic Rice of Gray's Inn on 21 February 1778
was bigamous. There is no evidence that she took it particularly
seriously. The fact that, in her years of decline, she was a beneficiary of
the Drury Lane Actors' Fund suggests that theatre people liked her, but
she seems to have been an indifferent actress whose starring roles were
confined to routs and masquerades.

John Hatfield (1759–1803)

The career of this notorious philanderer and bigamist is tied to the
theatre only by a reference in Wordsworth's *Prelude*. Having married and
deserted an illegitimate daughter of the Duke of Rutland whose dowry
he had squandered, he was released from a debtor's prison in
Scarborough through the good offices of Michelli Nation, a romantic
Devonian who had observed him through his prison window. They were
married on 14 September 1800, the day after his liberation. After two
years with his second wife, Hatfield had again run up debts that he had
no hope of paying. He took refuge in Keswick, where he proclaimed
himself brother of the third Earl of Hopetoun and won the love of Mary
Robinson, beautiful daughter of the landlord of the Fish Inn in
Buttermere. They married by special licence on 1 October 1802, and
Mary was already pregnant by the time that Hatfield's true identity was
discovered. Once again he made a run for it, getting nearly as far as
Swansea before being captured. He was eventually tried in Carlisle on a
string of charges, two of which—forgery and impersonation—were
capital offences. He was hanged just outside Carlisle on 3 September
1803. Wordsworth had been among his many prison visitors, and was
reminded of Hatfield when he saw a play in London only a short while
later:

11. Quoted in Arnold Hare, *George Frederick Cooke* (London: Society for Theatre
    Research, 1980), p. 187.

> a Story drawn
> From our own ground, the Maid of Buttermere,
> And how the Spoiler came, 'a bold bad Man'
> To God unfaithful, Children, Wife, and Home,
> And wooed the artless Daughter of the hills,
> And wedded her, in cruel mockery
> Of love and marriage bonds.[12]

Wordsworth goes on to shape his 'Mary of Buttermere' into an icon of feminine guilelessness. My chief regret is that I have been unable to trace the play he saw, but there were very many like it throughout the nineteenth century.

Dorothy Jordan (1761–1816)

The most popular comic actress of her day never married, though she was twice a wife in all but name. She belongs in this list by virtue of the fact that her experiences contextualize bigamy at a time when attitudes to marriage made actresses peculiarly vulnerable. She lived in the well-founded hope of marrying the wealthy barrister Richard Ford, by whom she had three children, and was, from 1791 to 1811, effectively the wife of the Duke of Clarence, by whom she had ten more. Both men dithered and procrastinated over the question of marriage, meanwhile committing Jordan to a life of concubinage. Though a reasonably fond father, the Duke was no supporter of the rights of women. He was generally a sleeping member of the House of Lords but when, in 1801, a Mrs Addison carried a divorce suit (on the grounds of her husband's incestuous adultery with her married sister) to parliament, he roused himself into vehement opposition. Jordan might have glimpsed her own future in his outraged eyes. She died in poverty, much too soon to see the Duke crowned William IV. Somehow, whilst finding time to bear and care for fourteen children (her first had been the product of a casual seduction by her Dublin theatre manager), she had maintained a busy schedule on the London and provincial stages. It can have given her no comfort, as she lay dying meanly in Paris, that she had been loved by two 'husbands' who did not need to marry her.

12. Wordsworth, *The Prelude*, Book 7, ll.321–6.

Anna Maria Crouch (1763–1805)

As a young singer on the Dublin stage, Anna Maria Phillips was ardently pursued by John Philip Kemble, but she was in love with the son of an Irish peer with whom she planned an elopement to Scotland. The plans were thwarted by contrary winds on the Irish Sea, and the man she married in early 1785 was Rollings Crouch, a midshipman in the Royal Navy. The marriage did not survive her brief liaison with the future George IV in 1791, but her husband had been, since 1787, a complacent member of a *ménage à trois* with his young wife and the famous tenor, Michael Kelly. It was as Kelly's acknowledged concubine that Mrs Crouch spent the rest of her short life. Their convivial hospitality was a famous feature of London's theatrical scene. Rollings Crouch had meanwhile contracted a bigamous marriage with an heiress. Contemporary gossip maintained that it was the first Mrs Crouch who warned him that the father of the second Mrs Crouch had discovered the crime and was intent on taking action. Crouch and his new wife took flight to France, where they remained until after Anna Maria's death.

Charlotte Deans (1768–1859)

Deans, an otherwise obscure strolling actress, published her *Memoirs* in Wigton in 1837.[13] She was the daughter of a Wigton attorney, disowned by her family after eloping in 1787 with a strolling actor called William Johnston. Her father took no further action, though he must have known that, by the terms of the 1753 Act, he could have had the marriage annulled. Charlotte was still a minor, but evidently a wilful one, with strength of body as well as mind. During the years of incredibly strenuous touring, predominantly in Scotland and Cumberland, she bore seventeen children, some by Johnston and some by her second husband, another strolling actor called Deans. She was not a bigamist (Johnston had died in 1802 and her marriage to Deans was solemnized in Workington in 1803), but he may have been—by Scottish law. The *Memoirs* record an incident in the small town of Culgaith, when 'a young lady from Scotland attended by two soldiers in a post chaise, claimed him as her husband, and required him to accompany her'. Charlotte and other members of the theatre company had the wit to warn off the soldiers with a threat of reporting them for desertion, and the *Memoirs* conclude

---

13. A facsimile was republished by Titus Wilson, Kendal, in 1984. I bought my copy in Brantwood, John Ruskin's former house by Coniston Water.

that the importunate woman 'must have been badly advised to proceed from Scotland without some certain document with which she might assert her claims'.[14] It was, in many instances, the lack of documentation that provided bigamists—of whom Deans might have been one—protection from the law.

Junius Brutus Booth (1796–1852)

It was sheer confidence in his own genius that inspired Booth to challenge Edmund Kean's London eminence in 1817. The story of his downfall does not belong here, but the story of his wives does. Adelaide Delannoy, whom Booth married in London in 1815, was Belgian. Two of their children had died in infancy and Booth's London career was in jeopardy when he fell in love with a Covent Garden flower girl. It was with Mary Ann Holmes, not Adelaide Booth, that he embarked for America in May 1821, four months after going through some kind of marriage ceremony. The majority of Booth's acting career belongs to America, where he and Mary Ann brought up those of their ten children who survived infancy. They included America's greatest nineteenth-century actor and Abraham Lincoln's assassin. Unable to control his drinking when away from home, and subject to fits of suicidal madness, Booth was comparatively peaceful at home, comfortably distant from his Belgian wife. But Adelaide's surviving son emigrated to join his father, and his mother heard through him of her husband's second family. From 1846 to 1851, both in America and from London, she fought for a formal divorce and a financial settlement. Even in Maryland, America's divorce laws were more liberal than England's. In April 1851 Adelaide won her claim for both, and on 10 May 1851 Junius Brutus Booth married Mary Ann Holmes for the second time.

I have listed a handful of examples of marital confusion during the century that divided Hardwicke's Act from the Divorce Reform Act of 1857. The manifest defects of the present law had led to the setting up of a Royal Commission on Divorce in 1850. In the years that intervened between its establishment and the introduction of the parliamentary bill, there was much talk about the universal availability of divorce, but the Palmerston government had no intention of extending it to the poor. The 1857 Act brought to an end the authority of parliament and the Church over the granting or withholding of divorce, investing it instead

14. Deans, *Memoirs*, pp. 44–45.

in a secular Matrimonial Causes Court, but the cost of access remained prohibitive to all but the rich and privileged. If, as I suspect, there was a decline in theatrical bigamy in the nineteenth century, that owes little to the 1857 Act. There was, on one hand, a greater efficiency in the registration of marriages and, on another, a growing willingness simply to cohabit, as Michael Kelly and Mrs Crouch had at the opening of the century. Most significantly, the 1790s saw the introduction of a change in the statutory punishment for bigamy. Until then, actors, by virtue of their literacy, could have pleaded benefit of clergy. The new penalty for bigamy, though, was seven years transportation without benefit of clergy. There was still criminal scope for fearless fraudsters like John Hatfield, but actors, and in particular actresses, were not so easily deceived. I conclude this brief survey with two strange cases dating from the late nineteenth century.

Dion Boucicault (1820–90)

Not much is known for certain about Boucicault's first marriage. His wife was French, a widow some years older than her ambitious young husband. They married in Lambeth in 1845, and she was dead by the late summer of 1848. Lurid stories circulated about their starting off together on a climb in the Alps and his returning alone, but they lack much conviction. In 1850 Boucicault became an unofficial writer-in-residence for Charles Kean at the Princess's, where he formed a relationship with Kean's ward, Agnes Robertson (1833–1916). Kean disapproved, and the couple took ship for America. It is not clear whether Boucicault and Robertson thought of their embarkation as an elopement, but they went through a marriage ceremony in New York in 1853. Honing his skills as an entrepreneur, Boucicault billed his young bride as 'The Pocket Venus' in a series of his own plays, which they toured across America. They had six children, but the marriage was a troubled one and, in 1873, Agnes returned to England with a grievance. Her husband was openly consorting with his leading lady, Katherine Rogers. She would later claim that he was the father of Rogers' child. There was an informal separation, but no written agreement. Boucicault continued to divide his theatrical life between England and America until, in 1885, he took his company to New Zealand and Australia, himself still playing, in his mid-sixties, the energetic role of Conn in *The Shaughraun*. It was in Sydney on 9 September 1885 that he married Louise Thorndyke, a twenty-one-year-old actress in his company. In defence, and at the risk of burdening his children with the stigma of illegitimacy, he claimed that his New York marriage to Agnes Robertson had no legal status. Agnes decided to sue for divorce and the suit was finally granted in 1889. The status of Boucicault's marriage to Louise Thorndyke remains unclear, but there is no doubt that she considered herself his wife and, until her death in 1956, his widow.

Charles Coghill (fl. 1860–90)

My only source for Coghill's story is the *Random Reminiscences* of the amateur playwright and *soi-disant* wit Charles Brookfield. And despite Brookfield's confident claim that Coghill was 'one of the very best actors of our time',[15] I have so far been unable to trace any other reference to him. According to Brookfield, Coghill was with an English touring company in America, 'a good deal broken by the life he had led, for to every ordinary form of self-indulgence he added the habit of taking drugs and anaesthetics'. It was about 1885, and Coghill had been accompanied as far as New York by his devoted wife. She did not, however, join him on the tour, and 'I think it was in Pittsburg [sic] that the shattered but still impressionable Charles met a girl, young, beautiful, and good, with whom he fell desperately in love'. Within a few days, and (Brookfield says) with the father's agreement, the pair were married. But almost at once the fact of his previous marriage was discovered, and Coghill was brought to trial in Pittsburgh. The decisive witness for the prosecution was his English wife. 'What is your name?' asked the prosecuting counsel. 'Katharine Anne Rivers', she replied. (There was certainly a well-established theatrical family called Rivers.) 'You are the wife, are you not, of the prisoner at the bar?' ' No ... I lived with him for many years as his wife, but we were never married.' It was perjury, but the American court had no documentary evidence with which to expose it. Coghill, like the guilty husband in Agatha Christie's *Ten Minute Alibi*, was given his freedom for the price of his wife's reputation.

15. Brookfield, *Random Reminiscences* (London: Thomas Nelson, 1911), pp. 246–50.

7

David Garrick

Alive in Every Muscle

The career of David Garrick is the most extraordinary single episode in the whole history of the English theatre. That might still be the case if he had confined himself to acting, but I doubt it. Actors are usually too preoccupied with the theatre to make much impact outside it: Garrick got everywhere. But the Garrick phenomenon dates from his first anonymous appearance as Richard III at the unlicensed playhouse in Goodman's Fields on 19 October 1741. Arthur Murphy, who wasn't there at the time, was not greatly exaggerating when he reported that '[f]rom the polite ends of Westminster the most elegant company flocked to Goodman's Fields, insomuch that from Temple Bar the whole way was covered with a string of coaches'.[1] The vitality of the young actor, his expressive features and vivid eyes, were the talk of the town. But it was more than that. What might have been mere novelty was felt to be actually *new*.

Against what theatregoers had come to expect of tragedians— something like the lofty expression of human passions in the manner of a slowly moving Poussin canvas—here was a man who dared to portray Richard III in his particularity. Fumbling for definitions, audiences were gripped by a sense that 'real life' had entered the theatre: soon they would be agreeing that this young man embodied in performance the scope of the sympathetic imagination. In that first season they could see him in comedy too, as Clodio in Cibber's *Love Makes a Man* and as the fatuous Bayes in *The Rehearsal*. But only those in the know realized that the new idol was also the author of the two-act farce, *The Lying Valet*, first staged at Goodman's Fields on 30 November 1741, and destined for durable popularity. The plot was French but the language was Garrick's, as was the title role of the mendacious Sharp. It was always his acting rather than his writing that singled him out. As a dramatist, and as an adapter of old plays, he served the taste of the time; as an

---

1. Murphy, *Life of David Garrick* (London, 1801), vol.1, pp. 25–26.

actor he was startlingly innovatory. And he knew he was. Five weeks after his London debut, he wrote to his brother in Lichfield: 'I have the Judgment of the best Judges (Who to a Man are of Opinion) that I shall turn out (nay they Say I am) not only the Best Trajedian but Comedian in England'.[2]

Theatrical taste does not, of course, change unless there is something in the culture that demands it. It was Garrick's good fortune that attention was now being focused on the theatre more than it had ever been. The cult of *The Beggar's Opera* in 1728, followed by Fielding's aggressively newsworthy activities at the Little Theatre in the Haymarket, had alerted the Walpole government to the capacity of drama to sting, and the reaction had been the Licensing Act of 1737. Whatever a government tries to suppress or control is looked at with renewed interest. And the seeds were already there. The industrious Aaron Hill's journal *The Prompter* (1734–36) had asserted the worthiness of theatre as a subject of study, and his regularly rehearsed complaints about the moribund state of acting at the patent houses make him a kind of John the Baptist preparing the way for Garrick. In the sixty-sixth number (June 1735), for example, he bemoaned 'the puffed, round mouth, an empty, vagrant eye, a solemn silliness of strut, a swing-swang slowness in the motion of the arm, and a dry, dull, drawling voice that carries opium in its detestable monotony'.[3]

This was an attack on, among others, James Quin, then the leading tragedian at Drury Lane. Quin was intelligent and sociable, but a victim of the gourmandizing habit of his era. The bulk that served him in Falstaff might have made him risible in tragedy had it not been for his on-stage dignity. It is often said by careless historians that he 'chanted' verse, but there is no evidence that that verb was being literally used by his contemporary critics. The reference is to a mode of delivery that amplified the passions in accordance with the rhetorical standards of the post-Restoration stage. It was a speaking style established by Thomas Betterton, one which enabled Betterton himself to continue playing heroic roles into his old age without evident incongruity. We cannot be sure that he was as universally admired as Colley Cibber assumes in his *Apology*: Cibber was Betterton's press agent before such a role was invented. We can, however, say that Quin's audience was more critically alert than Betterton's, and that his right to pre-eminence had already been challenged before Garrick made his debut. One joke given currency

2. *The Letters of David Garrick*, ed. David M. Little and George M. Kahrl (Cambridge, Mass: Harvard University Press, 1963), vol.1, p. 32.

3. *The Prompter*, (ed.) W.W. Appleton and K.A. Burnim (Cambridge, Mass.: Harvard University Press, 1966), p. 85.

was that Quin walked in blank verse. I would be surprised if Charles Macklin failed to spread that one abroad. He and Quin had a troubled relationship at Drury Lane: among the few things they had in common was the fact that they had both killed fellow actors and that neither admired the other's acting. It must have mortified Quin to be playing Antonio in *The Merchant of Venice* on 14 February 1741 when Macklin created his iconoclastic Shylock, no mere comic butt but a man of feeling. Beside Quin's measured cadences, Macklin's speaking style was startlingly natural, and audiences, though a little bemused, were stirred. Not so Quin. At the end of the season he left for Dublin, where he performed to admiring audiences until February 1742.

So Quin was not in London when Garrick, who had been spending in Macklin's company time stolen from his job as a wine merchant, carried the revolution a significant step further. Legend has it that, when he saw Garrick act for the first time, Quin's comment was, 'if this young fellow be right, then we have been all wrong'. More certainly, he compared the new cult with that of George Whitefield, the charismatic Methodist preacher: 'Garrick is a new religion; Whitefield was followed for a time; but they will all come to church again.' Garrick's bold response was a doggerel squib:

> *Pope Quin*, who damns all churches but his own,
> Complains that Heresy infects the town;
> That *Whitfield-Garrick* has misled the age,
> And taints the sound religion of the Stage;
> "Schism!" he cries, "has turn'd the Nation's brain,
> But eyes will open, and to Church again!"
> Thou Great Infallible, forebear to roar,
> Thy Bulls and Errors are rever'd no more;
> When Doctrines meet with gen'ral approbation,
> It is not *Heresy*, but *Reformation*.

Garrick always found it difficult to curb his tongue when people criticized him, and it is more to Quin's credit than his that the rivalry never opened up into enmity, and that it culminated attractively in friendship. But the older actor had the sense to resist attempts to test audience responses through open competition. While Garrick was at Drury Lane in the seasons from 1742 to 1745, Quin was at Covent Garden. Having reached the age of fifty in 1743, he negotiated with John Rich to reduce the number of his performances, and began seriously to cultivate his social interests in Bath: 'the cradle of age', he called it, 'and a fine slope to the grave'. It was not until 14 November 1746 that Rich manoeuvred the old and the young pretender onto the same stage. The play was Rowe's *The Fair Penitent*, and the experience for the teenaged Richard Cumberland in the audience was a thrilling one. Sixty years later he recalled Garrick as Lothario, 'young and light and alive in every muscle and in every feature', bounding onto the stage to confront Quin's 'heavy-paced Horatio'. 'It seemed as if a whole century had been stept over in the transition of a single scene.'[4] If there ever was a genuine battle, Quin had lost it well before 1746. His last years on stage were spent in Garrick's shadow. By 1762, Garrick was writing to his brother about the company of strolling players that had recently visited Lichfield: 'We in Town are Endeavouring to bring the Sock & Buskin down to Nature, but *they* still keep to their Strutting, bouncing & mouthing.'[5] So quickly had the revolutionary become the voice of the establishment.

If 'Nature' meant the same thing from age to age, or if it ever meant anything concrete and singular, there would be no problem in coming to terms with Garrick's acting. Quin was artificial, Garrick was natural—full stop. But Garrick was Diderot's paradigm of artifice and 'nature' was less a concept in the eighteenth century than overwhelmingly a subject of enquiry. The shift in taste that was a precondition of Garrick's rapid assimilation into the London theatre was already observable in other art forms. The hold of Kneller's grand style in painting had been loosened in 1732 by the extraordinary success of Hogarth's *A Harlot's Progress*, much as the hold of Italian opera had been in 1728 by *The Beggar's Opera*. There was a cultural quest, part of the new Hanoverian patriotism, for native British art: forms that would reflect the British virtues of industry and independence and that made themselves available to the newly vocal bourgeoisie. George Lillo's *The London Merchant* had been a surprise success in 1731: a prose tragedy pitched in a sombre key, but implicitly respectful of trade and of the streets where 'ordinary' people lived. Cityscapes were no longer confined to the Mall or the grander reaches of the Thames. Joseph Van Aken painted Covent Garden Market in the late 1720s. Hogarth places the first of his *Four Times of the Day* sequence (1736) in a corner of Covent Garden, and Balthasar Nebot presented it in panorama in 1737 (in several versions, to meet demand). In the year of Garrick's debut, Samuel Richardson published *Pamela*, and transformed almost at a stroke the conduct and subject matter of the novel. Three years later Joseph Highmore painted his famous, and intrinsically theatrical, sequence of twelve scenes from *Pamela*. I select these examples—there are many others—to display the

4. *Memoirs of Richard Cumberland* (London, 1806), pp. 59–60.
5. *Letters*, vol.1, p.367.

new artistic interest in 'the way we live now'. In the long run, however resistant to the tide the patent theatres may have been, it was an interest that had to be picked up by actors.

In broad artistic terms—they are terms usefully harnessed by Alan Hughes in a sequence of articles in *Theatre Notebook*[6]—the shift in acting style matched the shift in painting from the baroque to the rococo. There is great variety in the English painters who have, at various times, been listed under the rococo label. What they express in common, either directly or mediated by Gravelot, is the influence of Watteau. In place of the poised but generally static baroque compositions of Van Dyck and Kneller, they delight in plenitude and motion. Ronald Paulson has captured a group of them in the highly theatrical act of providing paintings to decorate the Vauxhall Gardens project of Jonathan Tyers: Hogarth, Francis Hayman, George Lambert, Richard Yeo, Gravelot himself:

> To 'recover nature' the English rococo provided it with a shape and a subject: the present time, the ordinary place whether city or country, the ordinary person, and certainly the forthright approach. Hogarth had already dramatized one form of this development in his *Harlot's Progress* and another in his *Rake's Progress*. His artist friends, decorating houses or pleasure gardens and painting stage designs or landscapes, were reacting to the new mode by replacing cherubs and satyrs with squirrels and foxes, abstract designs with oak and laurel leaves, or assemblies of gods with . . . swinging, dancing rustics.[7]

It is no belittling of rococo art to say that it involves a reduction of the baroque scale, but it is in the different invitation it offers to the viewer that it impinges most directly on the theatre. We stand *below* a baroque painting, whose aspiration is always upwards towards the unknowable. With Watteau, and even more with Hogarth and Hayman, we stand face on. The perspective is our perspective. That remains true even if, as in much of Canaletto or in Zoffany's delightful picture of the Garricks picknicking alfresco at Twickenham, we are looking down on the view. The looking down is not an expression of superiority: it is simply where we have to be to see what we see. What rococo represents is a different way of looking at the world: the way that was Hogarth's and Fielding's from artistic conviction and Garrick's out of a fundamental naivety that was proof against acquired sophistication.

6. Hughes, *Theatre Notebook*, vol.41, nos.1, 2 & 3 (1987).
7. Paulson, *Hogarth* (New Brunswick, NJ: Rutgers University Press, 1992), vol. 2, p. 73.

1. Francis Hayman, The Wrestling Scene from *As You Like It*: the perspective is our perspective.

It is impossible to recover the effect on Garrick's acting of his friendship with Hogarth, but difficult to evade a sense of its profundity. That Hogarth 'staged' his paintings, boxed them inside a proscenium arch that coincides with the frame, is unmistakable. In a draft of *The Analysis of Beauty* he writes that 'my Picture was my Stage and men and women my actors who were by Means of certain actions and express[ions] to Exhibit a dumb shew'.[8] The model for Hogarth's pursuit of the 'modern moral subject' had been provided by Addison and Steele in their *Spectator* papers. The very title of this vastly influential journal links it with the theatre at the same time as it celebrates the human capacity to observe and learn. Paulson has directly compared the systems of 'visual mnemonics' which first Hogarth and then Garrick developed. Observation was the key to it. It enabled Hogarth virtually to dispense with a sketch book. Instead, he would store the shapes and details of his visual experience in his memory, so that 'be where I would with my Eyes open I could have been at my studys so that even my Pleasures became a part of them, and sweetned the pursuit'.[9] Garrick's mnemonic technique, suggests Paulson, his 'observing and committing to memory regional accents, gestures, and phrases as he "sauntered" about London', is strikingly similar to the one Hogarth used for his graphic compositions.[10] One of Garrick's party pieces was to mimic, with extraordinary accuracy, the manners and mannerisms of fellow guests or people in the public eye, and he would entertain children with bird imitations. But the important point of the comparison with Hogarth is the way in which their memories stored images and the discrimination with which they selected and applied what was of value in the store. 'Rococo', writes Alan Hughes, 'is comic in spirit, not Aristotelian comedy where men are "worse", but the high comedy of daily life', and he finds an explanation for Garrick's success in both tragedy and comedy in his natural tendency to bring the two genres closer together.

It is a point which can be sustained by reference to Garrick's own comments. Finding French tragic actors too rigid, he suggested that 'there must be *comedy* in the perfect actor of tragedy', and to Charles Bannister, pining for comic roles, he said, 'you may humbug the town some time longer as a tragedian, but comedy is a serious thing'.[11] These are *obiter dicta* that link the actor Garrick to the painter Hogarth, but they give a misleading impression of a coherent acting theory. Elsewhere you will find Garrick arguing for the old rigidities. The passions have no

8. See Paulson, vol. 1 (1991), p. 46.
9. See Paulson, vol. 1, p. 106.
10. Paulson, vol. 2, p. 249.
11. See Mrs Clement Parsons, *Garrick and His Circle* (London: Methuen, 1906), p.78.

place in comedy, nor laughter in tragedy, for example.[12] Fame came to him so much more quickly than it did to Hogarth that he had neither time nor need to formulate an aesthetic. There is no 'analysis of acting' to balance the *Analysis of Beauty*, but his admiration of Hogarth's work is an essential part of any understanding of Garrick's ethos. Among the actor's treasured possessions were not only the Hogarth portraits he commissioned but also *The Wedding Banquet* and what may well be Hogarth's finest work, the four paintings in *The Election* sequence. A letter to his brother George, written in July 1763 at an early stage of the protracted grand tour that he and his wife had embarked on, hopes anxiously that 'Charles has taken care of Hogarth's Pictures, if ye Sun comes upon them they will be spoilt'.

If, as I assume, the reference is to the recently bought *Election* paintings, it suggests that Garrick had the uncommon discrimination to recognize the finest pieces in his large art collection. Artists were prominent among his friends, and he knew how much, in a worldly sense, he owed to Hogarth in particular. It was the impact of Hogarth's vast painting of him as Richard III, and in particular the popularity of the prints taken from the engraving in July 1746, that confirmed his supremacy on the London stage. Not only that: it was this painting above all that verified the worthiness of acting as a subject of study. For the rest of the eighteenth century, artists were busy about the theatre. The walls of the Garrick Club are today coated over with some of the products. Garrick, who never afterwards underrated the value of paintings as publicity, was himself the subject of more than 200 portraits, in and out of role. Almost inevitably, the idea of himself caught on canvas at a dramatic high point infiltrated his acting.

The alliance of painting and acting had been a subject of aesthetic debate at least since the publication of Jonathan Richardson's admired *Theory of Painting* (1715). In the theatre, he argued, we see a hybrid of literature and painting, 'a sort of moving, speaking pictures'. But acting has the disadvantage of transience and of not representing things truly. The actor is not Julius Caesar, whereas the painted image is a true projection of the artist's imagination. The argument has its flaws, and Hogarth exposes some of them in *The Analysis of Beauty*, but what is of particular interest there is Hogarth's confrontation of the loss to portraiture of those very qualities of 'Deportment, words, and actions' which are the stuff of theatre: 'We will therefore compare subject[s] for painting with those of the stage'.[13]

12. *Letters*, vol. 2, p. 478.
13. Quoted in Richard Wendorf, *The Elements of Life* (Oxford: Clarendon Press, 1991), p. 177.

2. William Hogarth, Garrick as Richard III: 'alive in every muscle'.

There is a similar sentiment in Gainsborough's lament that the portraitist can have no recourse to voice or action: 'only a face, confined to one View, and not a muscle to move to say here I am, falls very hard upon the poor Painter who perhaps is not within a mile of the truth in painting the Face only'.[14] Hogarth made no secret of the difficulties he had in capturing Garrick on canvas, because of the actor's notorious mobility of expression. Which was the 'true' face of Garrick? This is less significant in the Richard III painting, since Garrick is there partly transformed into a representative figure of English history, than in the portraits. It was almost impossible for the hyperactive Garrick to 'sit' for an artist. There are, however, two intriguing letters in which the actor seeks to marry his art to that of a painter. The painter in question was Francis Hayman, whom we have already seen at work on the Vauxhall Gardens project and whose charming rococo interpretation of the wrestling scene from *As You Like It* may have been a trial design for that project. (It is now in the Tate Gallery.) Hayman was a convivial man, whom Garrick knew as scene painter, friend and, now, established artist. Hogarth's Richard III sparked an interest in large-scale illustrations of scenes from Shakespeare which would culminate in the ambitious Boydell Gallery, but Hayman was planning six Shakespearean pictures even as Hogarth was completing his canvas towards the end of 1745. He turned to Garrick for advice, and the actor provided it—lavishly.

These are his thoughts on the appropriate subject from *King Lear*:

> Suppose Lear Mad upon the Ground with Edgar by him; His Attitude Should be leaning upon one hand & pointing Wildly towards the Heavens with his Other, Kent & Fool attend him & Glocester comes to him with a Torch; the real Madness of Lear, the Frantick Affectation of Edgar, and the different looks of Concern in the three other Characters will have a fine Effect; Suppose You express Kent's particular Care & distress by putting him upon one Knee begging & entreating him to rise & go with Gloster.[15]

Lear was, perhaps, Garrick's finest part in tragedy, and there seems little doubt that the tableau he here formulates for Hayman represents his own production vision. It is focused and full of feeling, an encapsulation of a whole scene, a singularity in variety. Garrick is trying to see acting through the eyes of a painter, and the result is not easily distinguishable

14. Wendorf, p. 176n.
15. Letters, vol. 1, p. 53.

from baroque history painting. The second letter, written in August 1746, with the popularity of the Hogarth engraving of Richard III at its height, is about *Othello*, a play in which Garrick's physique made him vulnerable to ridicule. Quin famously observed of his performance as Othello, 'There was a little black boy, like Pompey, attending with a tea-kettle, fretting and fuming about the stage, but I saw no Othello'. (The Pompey reference is to the second plate of *A Harlot's Progress*.) In this letter, it is the actor who dictates to the painter, pointing out that the scene he has selected has been wrongly neglected by 'the Designers who have publish'd their Several Prints'. It is the moment when Emilia reveals to Othello the truth about the handkerchief:

> The back Ground you know must be Desdemona murder'd in her bed; the Characters upon the Stage are Othello, Montano, Gratiano & Iago. Othello (ye Principal) upon ye right hand (I believe) must be thunderstruck with Horror, his Whole figure extended, wth his eyes turn'd up to Heav'n & his Frame sinking, as it were at Emilia's Discovery. I shall better make you conceive My Notion of this Attitude & Expression when I see You; Emilia must appear in the utmost Vehemence, with a Mixture of Sorrow on Account of her Mistress & I [think] should be in ye Middle: Iago on ye left hand should express the greatest perturbation of Mind, & should Shrink up his Body, at ye opening of his Villany, with his eyes looking askance (as Milton terms it) on Othello, & gnawing his Lip in anger at his Wife; but this likewise will be describ'd better by giving you this Expression when I see You.[16]

The determination to *show* Hayman the image of Emilia and Iago is implicitly an assumption that the actor carries in his body more than the painter can carry in his imagination. But the letters to Hayman are clear indications, not only of the gestural characteristics of Garrick's acting in tragedy but also of his utter confidence in the dignity of his profession. If we follow the implications of the canvases he envisioned, Garrick's *King Lear* was staged as a baroque history-play and his *Othello* as a contorted conversation piece. It is as if he is asking Hayman to take the production photographs for display in the foyer.

Garrick's acceptance into the artistic world of his age had an enormous and lingering impact on the status of the theatre, and his interaction with Hogarth was the central feature of that acceptance. Before Hogarth made the eccentric, and decidedly risky, decision to

---

16. *Letters*, vol. 1, pp. 82–83.

paint a scene from *The Beggar's Opera* (1728–29) and to follow it up with 'Falstaff Examining His Recruits' (1729–30), 'there was no tradition of [painting] group scenes on a stage, or of actors playing in a Shakespeare play',[17] and it was the picture of Garrick as Richard III that initiated a new tradition of reading great actors as works of art in their own right. Had Garrick been as pompous as he was ambitious, his acting would surely have suffered. In the event, though, his participation in the artistic debates of the mid-century was only one facet of the social energy that was, even more than Boswell's, his distinguishing characteristic. Unlike a few of his fellow actors (John Laguerre, William Parsons, Alexander Pope, John Bannister), he was not himself a painter. I doubt whether he had the patience to paint. But he bought pictures and prints, landscapes as well as figures, and immersed himself in what Mary Ann Caws has called the 'architexture' of his era.[18] His wife, because she was Lord Burlington's ward when he courted her, brought him into direct contact with one of the wealthiest artistic patrons of the age, and there was some aping of the Earl's Palladian taste in the approach he took to his Hampton estate. Few men of Garrick's stature have been so prone to give themselves away. 'It is my utmost pride and ambition', he wrote to Lord Lyttelton, 'to deserve the kind thoughts of the great and the good'.[19] It was, too! In 1753 he was even contemplating buying an estate in Derbyshire, near to Chatsworth House, the home of his friend the Marquis of Hartington.

However, it is in describing what he is looking for that he betrays his unthinking adherence to the Burlington school of landscape gardening: 'I own I love a good Situation prodigiously, & I think the four great Requisites to make one are, Wood, Water, Extent, & inequality of Ground.'[20] Keeping up with the Burlingtons was one of the incentives that turned Garrick into a connoisseur, and he was always more a follower of artistic fashion than a leader of it. Arthur Murphy had Garrick wickedly in mind when he wrote the character of Drugget in *What We Must All Come To* (1764): 'I won't have anything in my garden that looks like what it is.' Because he was wealthy enough to indulge a taste that was not consistently his own, Garrick was always vulnerable to such sneers. But it is noteworthy that his friendships with painters, from Hogarth to Reynolds, were more secure than his friendships with literary men. He brought painting and acting into unaccustomed alignment, and in doing so reflected the aesthetic sensibility of his age.

17. Paulson, vol. 1, p. 160.
18. Caws, *The Eye in the Text* (Princeton: Princeton University Press, 1981).
19. *Letters*, vol. 2, p. 765.
20. *Letters*, vol. 1, p. 193.

It is quite clear that Garrick, particularly in tragedy, was far from anything we would now recognize as 'natural'. Macklin, whose views were more advanced and whose training of actors was more systematic, would invite his pupils to speak lines as they would in real life, and then adapt the mode of delivery for the theatre by heightening it. The whole framing of the action on the eighteenth-century stage declared artifice, and Garrick placed himself within the frame. But there is ample evidence that contemporary audiences recognized reality in his performance. Fielding's famous account of Partridge's reaction to his Hamlet, in Book 16 Chapter 5 of *Tom Jones*, is a more complex exploration of the Garrick effect than has generally been recognized, one which takes account of both theatrical space and theatrical time. Mrs Miller, her youngest daughter, Tom Jones and Partridge are, we should note, in the cheap seats, up in the first row of the gallery at Drury Lane. 'Partridge immediately declared it was the finest place he had ever been in'. He has seen strolling players 'in the country', but never been in a theatre. For him the initial impact is all pictorial. The stagehand who lights the upper candles after the first music is 'the very picture of the man in the end of the common-prayer book before the gunpowder-treason service': the Ghost in his strange dress is 'like what I have seen in a picture'. But everything changes when Garrick's Hamlet confronts the Ghost. Partridge 'fell into so violent a trembling, that his knees knocked against each other'. What has just happened on stage has broken the pictorial illusion, and it takes Partridge a moment to recover from the shock:

> . . . I know it is but a play. And if it was really a ghost, it could do one no harm at such a distance, and in so much company; and yet if I was frightened, I am not the only person . . . You may call me coward if you will; but if that little man there upon the stage is not frightened, I never saw any man frightened in my life.

In retrospect, Partridge is unimpressed: 'I could act as well as he myself. I am sure, if I had seen a ghost, I should have looked in the very same manner, and done just as he did'. Claudius is another matter altogether: 'he speaks all his words distinctly, half as loud again as the other. Anybody may see he is an actor'. Dr Johnson, of course, found Garrick's response to the Ghost excessive and by implication vulgar. We have Lichtenberg's account of the actual gestures that followed Horatio's 'Look, my Lord, it comes':

> At these words Garrick turns sharply, at the same time staggering back two or three steps, his knees giving way under him;

3. James McArdell, after Benjamin Wilson, Garrick as Hamlet: 'if that little man there upon the stage is not frightened. . .'.

his hat falls to the ground, and both his arms, the left most noticeably, are stretched out almost to their full length, his hands as high as his head, the right arm bent more with its hand lower, and the fingers apart; his mouth is open: thus he stands rooted to the spot, with legs apart, but no loss of dignity, supported by his friends who are better acquainted with the apparition, and

who are afraid lest he should collapse. His whole demeanour is
so expressive of terror that it made my flesh creep even before
he began to speak.[21]

It is Garrick's delineation of fear that eats into Partridge and
Lichtenberg. For them, if not for Johnson, Garrick was 'good at fear'.
Benjamin Wilson painted him in the pose Lichtenberg describes, and it
was one he held for long enough to ensure that onlookers would register
it. The same is true of the fear/horror freeze we see in Hogarth's *Richard
III*. Eighteenth-century audiences expected a display of multiple passions
in tragedy, and Garrick's special skill was in the grace and rapidity with
which he moved his face and body from one passionate configuration to
another one. Bertram Joseph has rightly identified the progress from the
sudden 'start' to the 'fine attitude', and the risk of indulgence: 'His
strength in pantomime led him into the temptation not only to start
when it was not really necessary but to contrive transitions . . . in which
he could trap applause by the virtuosity of his swift change of stance and
attitude—his expression and tone of voice changing at the same time'.[22]
The significance of the passions to the performance of tragedy is one of
the few aspects of eighteenth-century acting to have been well treated by
modern scholars.[23] I have nothing to add to the work already done on
this. The crucial point, if we are to come to a just estimate of Partridge,
of Lichtenberg, or of the general reception of Garrick in his own time,
is that a skilful tragedian could transmit *real* passion through physical
and vocal conventions. Garrick's theatre was realistic *as theatre*.

The appeal of the 'new' in Garrick's acting is poorly represented by
attempts to link it to naturalness. What he did (his body was a more
reliable instrument than his voice) on stage was felt by the audience to
be appropriate. A key text is provided in Pope's 'Essay on Criticism':

> Expression is the Dress of Thought and still
> Appears more decent as more suitable.

Pope's concern with suitable *language* is echoed by Garrick's concern
with suitable *action*. That which suits is 'decent', well dressed, appro-

21. M.L. Mare and W.H. Quarrell, *Lichtenberg's Visits to England* (Oxford: Clarendon
    Press, 1938), p. 9.
22. Joseph, *The Tragic Actor* (London: Routledge and Kegan Paul, 1959), p. 112.
23. See, for example, Alan Hughes in the last of the three *Theatre Notebook* articles cited
    in note 6, George Taylor, 'The just delineation of the passions' in Kenneth Richards
    and Peter Thomson (eds), *The Eighteenth-Century English Stage* (London: Methuen,
    1972), and Shearer West, *The Image of the Actor* (London: Pinter, 1991).

priate to its context. 'Propriety' was a key term in his own dictionary of acting. This is why it is so important to our understanding of Garrick's popularity to see him in his whole social and artistic setting. He had a gift for doing the right thing, for accommodating his behaviour to his company. In normal circumstances Drury Lane under his management was as convivial as he himself was. The qualities of energetic relaxation and contained expressiveness are nicely caught in Lichtenberg's summary:

> No actor ever needed less elbow-room for effective gesture. His way of shrugging his shoulders, crossing his arms, cocking his hat, or putting it on and taking it off—in short, whatever he does—is so easily and *securely* done, that the man appears to be *all right hand*. His intelligence is ubiquitous throughout every muscle of his body.[24]

The perception of Garrick as 'all right hand' is very informative. It describes natural grace, certainly, but also a self-discipline that came from an understanding of his own body. The choreographer Jean Georges Noverre credited Garrick with giving him the confidence to tell a story through dance. There was also the admired precision of his facial expressiveness and the mobility of his features. 'Il est naturellement singe', was Friedrich Grimm's verdict, and Shireff, the deaf and dumb miniaturist, saw Garrick's face as a language.

None of the attempts, contemporary or modern, to account for the unique estimation in which Garrick's acting was held is quite satisfactory. As I have tried to show, this is because they have been too confined to the stage. The mid-century shift in the attitude to the 'reader' has been referred primarily to the work of Hogarth and Fielding.[25] Garrick, too, invited an active participation from a wider audience. The theatrical application of reader-response theory is a particularly complex one, but the direct address of Garrick's numerous prologues and epilogues invites it. His stamina and his appetite for personal engagement were unnerving. His sobriety and the early hours he kept disconcerted many of his company at Drury Lane, and his seasonal schedule of rehearsal, business correspondence and negotiation and social engagements was constantly taxing. Even in society, he was a compulsive entertainer. Joshua Reynolds quite fondly noted his 'desire for popular applause' and

24. Quoted in Parsons, p. 65.
25. See, for example, Murray Roston, *Changing Perspectives in Literature and the Visual Arts* (Princeton: Princeton University Press, 1992), pp. 172–89.

4. John Finlayson, after Johann Zoffany, Garrick as Sir John Brute: 'all fuss and bustle'.

his tendency to prepare himself for any occasion 'as if he was to act a principal part'. He also wryly noted that Garrick 'never came into company but with a plot how to get out of it',[26] but that appearance owed more to the quantity of Garrick's business interests than Reynolds realized. It relates to the most commonplace criticisms of Garrick's acting—that there was too much *bustle* about it. Charles Reade has an amusing version of it in his novel *Peg Woffington* (1852), when the 'old school' Colley Cibber derides the new man:

> . . . This Garrick's manner is little, like his person, it is all fuss and bustle. This is his idea of a tragic scene . . . 'Give me another horse!' Well, where's the horse? Don't you see I'm waiting for him? 'Bind up my wounds!' Look sharp now, with these wounds. 'Have mercy, Heaven!' but be quick about it, for the old dog can't wait for Heaven. Bustle! Bustle! Bustle!

Garrick's ease was complemented by an intensity of nervous energy that he displayed openly only in comedy. Zoffany's painting of his

26. Reynolds, *Portraits*, ed. F.W. Hilles (London: Heinemann, 1952), pp. 86–87.

beskirted Sir John Brute laying about him with a stick captures it finely. Mary Nash associates Susannah Cibber's delight in partnering him on stage with an 'energizing, virile impulse',[27] which was generally sufficient to compensate for his smallness of stature. I conclude with a striking image of Garrick, strung taut between the demands of the worlds on stage and off it. It comes from Robert Baker's Introduction to his *Remarks upon the English Language* (1779).[28] Baker was a keen theatregoer and a stickler for etiquette. Hence his complaint:

> Garrick ought not to be Garrick until the scenes hide him. Instead of this, Mrs Woffington and he took it into their heads long ago, how serious soever the part were that they were playing, to trip off the stage with a bridled head and an affected alertness. If one had a mind to be ill-natured, one might suppose this was in order to give the spectators an idea of the liveliness of their private character. Mrs Cibber was sometimes guilty of the same fault; but Mrs Pritchard never was.

Garrick (Peg Woffington, too) could never be entirely contained by the theatre whose artistic status he elevated. That is the whole point about him.

27. Nash, *The Provoked Wife* (London: Hutchinson, 1977), p. 182.
28. See John Levitt, 'London actors in the 1740s–1760s—the evidence of Robert Baker', in *Theatre Notebook*, vol. 52, no.2 (1998), pp. 111–14.

8

Summer Company
Drury Lane in 1761

It is a tendency of theatre history to record the successes and the singular disasters of the past, whilst consigning the merely mediocre to oblivion. One effect is to deprive success of its context and even of its extraordinariness. The danger is that we are snared into accepting Shakespeare and the Chamberlain's/King's Men, Garrick's Drury Lane or Irving's Lyceum as the historical norm rather than recognizing the exceptional achievement that they represent. It is no easy thing to harmonize conflicting histrionic temperaments over a period of years whilst, at the same time, gratifying the public taste without a significant lowering of your own artistic standards. Certain compromises are inevitable: they can be seen in the repertoire of the Elizabethan Globe almost as clearly as at the Hanoverian Drury Lane and the Victorian Lyceum. But great theatre companies have always created around them an urge to emulate, and ineffective emulation pays its own homage to greatness. It is the purpose of this chapter to contextualize Garrick's managerial genius by exploring a project that aimed to emulate him, and might have succeeded. Historical parallels could be found in Worcester's Men in Elizabethan London or in Wilson Barrett's challenge to Irving at the end of the nineteenth century.

The Drury Lane season of 1760 to 1761 came to an end with a performance, on 4 June 1761, of *Henry VIII*. It was billed as a Benefit for Decayed Actors. The King was played by the largely forgotten Astley Bransby, Wolsey by the loyal William Havard, and Queen Katharine [*sic*] by Hannah Pritchard. Garrick was not in the cast, but he took the opportunity to deliver an 'Address to the Public'. He was not to know that this was the halfway point in his management of Drury Lane, but he knew well that the original articles of agreement between himself and his fellow manager James Lacy had duly expired and that, now in his mid-forties, he must either retire from management or recommit himself to it. His immediate plan was to recuperate over the summer, mostly in his country house in Hampton where any thoughts of retirement would

97

soon dissipate. The coming season would open in September with a series of revivals, but Garrick had to ensure that they were fully cast. Competition from Covent Garden, always an irritant, was uncommonly threatening in this particular September, because the month would see both the wedding of the new King to Charlotte of Mecklenberg-Strelitz and their subsequent coronation, and both the Theatres Royal would be expected to stage their own versions of these royal occasions. John Rich had a better eye for theatrical spectacle than Garrick, who determined, at least, to have accuracy on his side. In July, he wrote from Hampton to the Reverend Thomas Birch to ascertain where he might find 'the best printed Forms of the Kings Marriage'.[1] Garrick and Lacy at Drury Lane and Rich at Covent Garden had already achieved a level of prosperity that most past and future managers of the Patent Houses would wonder at, but constant vigilance remained a condition of success. It was Garrick's reward that his summers were no longer given over to performances in Dublin, nor in any of the other provincial centres where lesser members of his company could earn star billing as 'of the Theatre Royal, Drury Lane'. Summer was his off-season, as it was for most of the fashionable members of his regular audience. It was a time for visits to and with the well-connected, for touring on the continent, or for entertaining friends in rural retreats. The two Theatres Royal were generally closed for refurbishment or for the regular attempts to increase capacity without overstraining budgets. But, in the summer of 1761, this was not the case with Drury Lane. Instead, it became the site of a peculiarly promising experiment, and that is the subject of this chapter.

The initiators of the experiment were Samuel Foote and Arthur Murphy, by any reckoning among the best playwrights of the mid-century. Murphy had made his London debut as an actor at Covent Garden in 1754, but without distinction. He was no longer acting by 1761: at the age of thirty-three he was training for the law. Foote, though, was one of the outstanding 'personality' actors of this and any age. His greatest gift, in box office terms, was to create and exploit scandal and controversy, often by imitating in solo performance people in the public eye.

Foote was forty-one years old in 1761, an established maverick who rarely lost an opportunity to promote his own talent for mimicry, not least of Garrick, who was sadly sensitive to it. In the long run, Foote's carelessness about his friends would contribute to his downfall and Garrick, whilst not openly hostile, was inclined to watch his back when

---

1. *The Letters of David Garrick*, ed. David M. Little and George M. Kahrl (Cambridge, Mass.: Harvard University Press, 1963), vol. 1, p. 341.

Foote was in the same room. Add to this the fact that the relationship between Garrick and Murphy was, as we will see, under stress in 1761, and it seems likely that it was through Lacy, rather than Garrick, that Foote and Murphy arranged to lease Drury Lane from the middle of June through to early August. The basis of the agreement was that the company would perform on the evenings of Monday, Wednesday and Friday and that Foote and Murphy would each provide three new plays for a season of original comedy with a company of actors small enough not to represent too severe a financial burden. The interest to us is the composition of that company, and its randomness as a representative portrait of the summer activity of actors on the ceaseless quest for a more assured income. In the event, according to Genest, Foote and Murphy shared a profit of £600. If so, Foote was lucky. Murphy fulfilled his part of the bargain by writing *The Old Maid* (in two acts), *The Citizen* (in three acts) and *All in the Wrong* (in five acts). Foote provided nothing new at all, though his *The Minor* was revived for single performances on 21 July and 7 August. It may reasonably be argued that the promise of the season was barely fulfilled—certainly it had no successor—and that may have been because of its inherent weaknesses. It is these weaknesses that will emerge from an exploration. But I begin with its strengths, the chief of which, on the face of it, were Foote and Murphy themselves.

Foote brought to the summer company the immediate notoriety of *The Minor*, which had been a controversial success at Drury Lane throughout the 1760–61 season. Written primarily as a vehicle for his own versatility, the play featured Foote as the Methodist bawd Mrs Cole, as the mimic Shift and *in propria persona*. It was the creation of the outrageous Mrs Cole that caused most of the furore and that led to the involvement of the Lord Chamberlain. Modelling his gestures on those of a well-known Covent Garden bawd called Jennie Douglas, and decking his large body in a voluminous dress and his head in a bonnet, Foote made Mrs Cole a comic grotesque of hypocrisy. She is only tangentially involved in the plot, but she opened the way for some wicked ridicule of the Methodist movement as a whole and of George Whitefield in particular. Whitefield 'possessed the inborn gift of preaching to the nerves',[2] and was, when *The Minor* was first staged, gathering converts to his tabernacle in the Tottenham Court Road, a scattering of actors among them. It amused people to claim that the great Peg Woffington had warmed her last days (she died in March 1760) before the cleansing fire of Methodism, and the Covent Garden comedian Ned

2. Mrs Clement Parsons, *Garrick and His Circle* (London: Methuen, 1906), p. 245.

Shuter was seen at the Tabernacle almost as often as at its neighbouring taverns. Garrick is said to have credited Whitefield with the capacity to move any audience to tears simply by the way he pronounced 'Mesopotamia'. The Countess of Huntingdon was the most distinguished of his many adherents, and one of the most vociferous in condemning *The Minor*.

Outraged audiences are the best publicity a play can have. Such was the impact in 1760 of the Drury Lane production that Rich felt bound to stage it at Covent Garden too, with the young Tate Wilkinson mimicking the mimic. The rival performances were a feature of the London stage in November and December 1760 until, with typical bravado, on 18 December Foote crossed to Covent Garden to reclaim his roles from Wilkinson there. He was back with the Drury Lane cast on 22 December. For a number of years, Foote had been on the lookout for a summer theatre in London; the Little Theatre in the Haymarket was generally available, and would become indelibly associated with him from 1762 until his contrived disgrace in 1776. But the Little Theatre was taken in the summer of 1761, and it was probably this fact that pushed Foote into his alliance with Arthur Murphy. Murphy was Irish, a Catholic and, by 1761, a campaigning journalist as well as a trainee lawyer. He had written several plays for Drury Lane since the appearance there of his two-act farce, *The Apprentice*, in January 1756, most recently *The Way to Keep Him*, which opened in its extended five-act form, with Garrick as Lovemore, on 10 January 1761. But the friendship of Murphy and Garrick, though it blew hot at times, blew very cold at others. Whatever the two men actually thought of each other in general, the playwright Murphy resented the control of the manager Garrick over the selection of his plays for performance. In early 1760 Garrick had rejected Murphy's first draft of *The Man Does Not Know His Own Mind* (it was eventually staged, as *Know Your Own Mind*, at Covent Garden in 1777, only to be eclipsed by Sheridan's *The School for Scandal* at Drury Lane), and the rejection still rankled. Murphy had something to prove when he teamed up with Foote in the summer of 1761. He was also seeking the patronage of the Earl of Bute, formerly George III's tutor and now a power in the land. In the confused politics of the mid-century, he was simultaneously aligned with the dissident Whig, Henry Fox, whom he had supported against Pitt the Elder during the Seven Years War, and with the Tory interest favoured by the new King and spearheaded by Lord Bute. As Fox's journalistic supporter, he had edited *The Test* in 1756–57, as Bute's he would go on to edit *The Auditor* in 1762. He was brave, or foolhardy, enough to declare in *The Auditor* his opposition to the people's hero, John Wilkes, who was by some way the least respectable of Garrick's many friends. Foote was no respecter of persons (his habit of addressing aristocrats by their surnames offended Dr Johnson); Garrick, though friendly with many of the leading Whig aristocrats, was cautious in his politics; Murphy used politics in an openly self-seeking way, thus making himself vulnerable to partisan hostility in the theatre as well as outside it.

During the summer months of 1761, Garrick's plans for reducing Drury Lane's reliance on Murphy were already forming. The great success of *The Jealous Wife* during the 1760–61 season offered the prospect of further collaborations with the more congenial and much less cantankerous George Colman. With intimations of his fall from grace at Drury Lane, Murphy had more at stake in the summer season than Foote, but there were two particularly dangerous threats to his continuing relationship with Garrick, neither of which he felt able to escape. The first was the political involvement on which his future prosperity might depend; the second was his mistress.

Foote was not, I suspect, much engaged in the pursuit of actors for the summer company. He belonged to the tradition of the solo clown, who could act with anybody because nobody could act with him. Murphy, on the other hand, had everything to gain from a strong ensemble; everything, that is, except the continuing affection of the eighteen-year-old Ann Elliot. She was at best a courtesan, at worst a prostitute when he met her in about 1760, and he would continue to labour on her behalf until her early death in 1769. To begin with, though, he took on the task of preparing her for the stage, hoping to engage Garrick's interest. It was probably about her that Garrick wrote from Hampton on 22 June 1761:

> I have consider'd the Young Lady's Merit, with all the Care that I am Master of, & now send You my Sincere Thoughts upon ye Matter: It is with some reluctance that I Enter into this disagreeable part of my office, as I fear that my Sentiments will not correspond with the Lady's Inclinations.
>
> She does not appear to Me to have a Genius for ye Stage— She may be made decent, but will never, I doubt, arrive at any Excellence. Her Powers are weak, Her Voice is indifferent, Her pronunciation Erroneous, & her Face more form'd to create Passion, than to Express it—In short, were I to advise the Lady, I should certainly dissuade her from appearing at all—However, Sir, if her Heart is fixd upon it, We will give her a Tryal, & a very fair one—but it will be impossible for Us to give ye Lady any Sallary for what little she may do the approaching Season, & we must be quite at Liberty to Engage her, or Not, for the

101

Winter afterwards—

Our Company is so Overloaded, that unless one of great
Merit should arise, Every addition to us will be an Incumbrance.[3]

The letter is the contorted product of a manager under pressure, but it
is scarcely a triumph of diplomacy. Murphy's infatuation is patronized
(Ann Elliot's face is, after all, formed to create passion), but Garrick's
only concession is to offer her the chance of playing bit parts for no
money during the 1761–62 season at Drury Lane. After receiving such
a letter, Murphy can hardly have maintained confidence in his influence
over Garrick. All he could hope was to prove him wrong. Ann Elliot
would have her chance when *The Citizen* opened on 2 July, but Garrick
was then a guest of the Duke of Devonshire at Chatsworth House.
There is no evidence that he attended any of the summer performances
at Drury Lane, and no likelihood that he would have changed his mind
about Ann Elliot if he saw her as Maria in Murphy's farce. Critical
response to her acting was warm, but never ecstatic, and Maria remained
a favourite role until she took her leave of the London stage in 1767. By
then, she had succeeded the opera singer Anna Zamperini as mistress of
the King's brother, the Duke of Cumberland. Murphy, to his credit, was
one of the executors of her will and a battler for her right to the money
she claimed to be in possession of at her death. She was not, however,
in the cast of *All in the Wrong*, which opened on 15 June, and which was
the most significant contribution to the summer season. It is that play,
and the actors who created it, that best indicates the potentiality of the
season and that offers us a snapshot of the London stage at its
eighteenth-century peak.

All in the Wrong is a marriage play, written by a bachelor with a legal
interest in the after-effects of Hardwicke's 1753 Act of Parliament.
Murphy's plays habitually place the institution of marriage under scrutiny,
and though *All in the Wrong* is a comedy, it is not a frothily jolly one. It
covers the events of a crowded day which begins with the exposure of
the excessive jealousy of the married Sir John Restless, whose haste to
jump to unjustified conclusions is shared by the yet unmarried Beverley.
The whole business of the play is to bring them to a recognition that,
having been all in the wrong, they must endeavour in the future to be all
in the right, and Beverley, in the final speech, is addressing the audience
as well as the on-stage assembly: 'we will make it our business, both you
who are married, and we who are now entering into that state, by mutual
confidence to ensure mutual happiness'.

3. *Letters*, vol. 1, pp. 340–41.

The first Sir John Restless, playing way below his actual age, was Richard Yates, who was born around 1706. He had been at Drury Lane since 1742, primarily deployed as a low comedian, but really the supreme example of a theatrical jack-of-all-trades. He had run his own booth at Southwark and Bartholomew Fairs where he developed a sequence of one-man shows, could turn his hand (and feet) to Harlequin, offered entr'acte entertainments as both singer and dancer, and was the kind of manager's delight who took on anything that was asked of him. Too much, probably. He had a reputation for forgetting his lines. He was, though, a proud professional, and had been upset by Charles Churchill's sneering comments in *The Rosciad*, published on 14 March 1761 and greedily read by a gossip-hungry public:

In characters of low and vulgar mould
When nature's coarsest features we behold,
When, destitute of ev'ry decent grace,
Unmannered jests are blurted in your face,
Then Yates with justice strict attention draws,
Acts truly from himself and gains applause.
But when to please himself or charm his wife,
He aims at something in politer life;
When, blindly thwarting nature's stubborn plan,
He treads the stage by way of gentleman,
The clown who no one touch of breeding knows
Looks like Tom Errand dressed in Clincher's clothes.

Sir John Restless gave Yates an opportunity to prove his capacity as 'something in politer life', and it might have been this that tempted him to join the summer company. Within a month of the last performance on 8 August 1761, he would open at Bartholomew Fair (on 1 September) a recitation 'enlivened with several entertaining Scenes between England, France, Ireland, and Scotland, in the diverting personages of Ben Bowling, an English Sailor; M Soup-Maigre, a French Captain; O'Flannaghan, an Irish officer; M'Pherson, a Scotch officer', but he was ready at Drury Lane on 5 September for the opening performance of the new season, when he played his familiar role of Peachum in *The Beggar's Opera*. A theatrical diehard, Yates remained active well into the 1780s, and may have been as old as ninety when he died in 1796. According to a 'friend', who visited him during his last years in Pimlico, his death was the result of 'a fit of rage at being unable to obtain eels for dinner'.

Beverley, the juvenile lead, was created by William O'Brien, a handsome young actor whom Garrick had recruited for Drury Lane in

1758 to replace Henry Woodward. Like Murphy, O'Brien was an Irish Catholic. He may have been, and seems to have believed he was, distantly related to the O'Brien who was created Viscount Clare in the seventeenth century, but his own father was a fencing master who had trained his son in swordplay. The duel between O'Brien as Laertes and Garrick as Hamlet was greatly admired, but O'Brien's natural home was in the gentlemanly roles in comedy. Despite his excessive jealousy, Beverley is an endearing character, and a grateful one for an actor who delights to charm. It would not have stretched O'Brien, whose promising career was brought to a sudden end in 1764 when he eloped with Lady Susan Fox-Strangways, thus becoming nephew by marriage to Murphy's patron, Henry Fox. (See above Chapter 6.) In the context of the summer company, though, it is of interest that O'Brien had already expressed to Garrick his support for Murphy in the matter of *The Man Does Not Know His Own Mind*. There may have been an element of national solidarity in this alliance. What seems clear is that O'Brien had confidence as well as charm. He was an asset to the summer company: one of those actors who shines brightly for a while and then vanishes.

Although, according to Benjamin Victor, who in 1761 began to establish his reputation as a historian of the English stage, *All in the Wrong* 'was excellently well acted in all its parts', there were only two other actors of real quality in the original cast. The first of these was Mary Ann Yates, second wife of the Richard Yates who created the role of Sir John Restless. Much younger than her husband, she was probably thirty-two or thirty-three in 1761, and had been a regular member of Garrick's company since 1756. Both Murphy and her husband had coached her during her novice years, and both survived to see her recognized as London's leading tragedienne in the years between the retirement of Hannah Pritchard in 1768 and the rise of Sarah Siddons. By 1761, she was already a commanding woman, though not yet the major force she appears in Robert Edge Pine's striking portrait of her as Medea (1770). Garrick valued her acting but considered her too temperamental: she thought him unsympathetic and took exception to the speed with which he insinuated his personal opinions into the public press. Given the chance, she gave always as good as she got. James Harris may have been hinting at a known theatrical tension when he wrote that 'for everything that was nervous, various, elegant and true in attitude and action, I never saw her equal but in Garrick, and forgive me for saying I cannot call him her superior'. Belinda, the character she played in *All in the Wrong*, is a lively heroine, beloved of Beverley for the very quality of independence that fuels his jealousy. It was only in later years, and then more out of circumstance than necessity, that Mrs Yates became fixed in tragedy. O'Brien and she were well matched in 1761. She was not, however, an easy colleague. Her health (or was it, as Garrick suspected, her temperament?) had been a problem in the 1760–61 season at Drury Lane, and performances of *All in the Wrong* were suspended for most of July due to her indisposition. The audience admired her too much to accept a substitute. What Murphy and Foote thought is not recorded. They probably had to tread warily with both Mrs Yates and her husband, who had no adequate reason to associate themselves with any kind of anti-Garrick murmurings in the company. Their presence was too valuable to the summer enterprise to be put at risk.

The remaining actor of quality was Thomas Weston, son of an undercook in George II's kitchen. At the age of twenty-four, though, Weston had not yet acquired the reputation that would make him a favourite in the gallery. In *All in the Wrong* he played a cameo role as Beverley's servant, Brush. More significantly, he was required to act every night of the season, always in minor parts, and it was probably word of mouth that encouraged Garrick to employ him for the 1761–62 season at Drury Lane. As a young unknown, Weston had good reason to join the summer company, and was probably its chief beneficiary. His acting of Scrub opposite Garrick's Archer in *The Beaux' Stratagem* would, in the 1770s, come to be recognized as one of the finest comic turns of the period. It was described in detail by Georg Christoph Lichtenberg:

> While Garrick sits there at ease with an agreeable carelessness of demeanour, Weston attempts, with back stiff as a poker, to draw himself up to the other's height, partly for the sake of decorum, and partly in order to steal a glance now and then, when Garrick is looking the other way, so as to improve on his imitation of the latter's manner. When Archer at last with an easy gesture crosses his legs, Scrub tries to do the same, in which he eventually succeeds, though not without some help from his hands, and with eyes all the time either gaping or making furtive comparisons. And when Archer begins to stroke his magnificent silken calves, Weston tries to do the same with his miserable red woollen ones, but, thinking better of it, slowly pulls his green apron over them with an abjectness of demeanour, arousing pity in every breast. In this scene Weston almost excels Garrick by means of the foolish expression natural to him.[4]

4. Quoted in G.W. Stone Jr and G.M. Kahrl, *David Garrick* (Carbondale: Southern Illinois University Press, 1979), p. 484.

5. William Dickinson, after Robert Edge Pine, Mrs Yates as Medea: 'nervous, various, elegant and true in attitude and action'.

Weston's mature reputation was built on his ability to excite laughter whilst seeming entirely unaware of it. He had a very expressive face and a peculiar air of obliviousness which contemporaries found irresistibly funny. There was nothing funny, though, about the addiction to drink which killed him before he was forty.

No playbill for *All in the Wrong* has yet been found, and the only other role that can be confidently ascribed is that of Lady Restless. Hannah Haughton was about forty in 1761, and had been playing secondary roles at Covent Garden and Drury Lane for more than twenty years. She had, for example, been Regan to Garrick's Lear in the 1760–61 season at Drury Lane. It was widely known that she had worked to overcome a lisp on the way to her modest success, but in general, and unusually for an actress at a time when the press was avidly snapping for trifles of thespian infamy, she seems to have kept her private life private right through to her retirement from the stage in 1764, and there was some surprise when the will, proved after her death in 1771, revealed that she was the mother of five surviving children. The father of at least one of them was Major-General William Keppel, whose aristocratic family would not have approved his connection with an actress. I do not know of any particular reason for Haughton's participation in the summer company, but if she had little to gain by it, she also had little to lose.

We have the names of the actors who made up the rest of the cast, but not the parts they played. It is a logical assumption that the Mr Miller, who was billed as a 'Gentleman, first appearance on any stage' played Beverley's friend Bellmont. He probably paid for the privilege of appearing at Drury Lane, and Bellmont is the least Murphy could have given him in return. He is one of the younger generation whose plans for married happiness are blighted by paternal interference.

Sir William Bellmont has his mind set on Belinda as wife for his son, and it is part of the play's intention to show that parents, too, must learn from experience. Sir William was probably entrusted to Robert Baddeley, already a specialist 'old man' despite the fact that he was only twenty-eight. Baddeley would not have relished being jockeyed into what is essentially a utility role, but there were compensations for him in the season's other plays. He had begun his adult life as a cook, may even have been Foote's cook for a while, but Garrick had taken him into the Drury Lane company for the 1760–61 season, and allowed him a shared benefit night on 11 May 1761. He was at the beginning of a long career, and Foote in particular had reason to appreciate his talents. As Sir William Wealthy in *The Minor*, Baddeley had first shown his quirky quality as a 'foreigner' struggling with English pronunciation. Although he is generally remembered as the creator of the Jewish Moses in Sheridan's *The School for Scandal* (1777), that was only one of many parts specially created by playwrights to exploit Baddeley's adroit mangling of the English language. His own life story became a cautionary tale on the dangers of clandestine marriage after his elopement in 1764 with the beautiful eighteen-year-old Sophia Snow. As Mrs Baddeley she came to rank high among the leading courtesans of the age, famous for her

107

satin boudoir and a domestic staff numbering eight, three men and five women. Tate Wilkinson gives a sensational account of her subsequent addiction to laudanum and her death in abject poverty.[5] She had charm, though; enough to incite Garrick's brother George to challenge Baddeley to a duel for his neglect of her in 1770, the year in which Arthur Murphy would negotiate a legal separation (not a divorce, of course) for his former associate.

Baddeley probably gained a little by his work for the summer company, more anyway than the remaining members of the cast. Clarissa, Beverley's sister, Belinda's friend and Bellmont's sweetheart, offers nothing to an actress. The role was probably created by one of the two Misses Ambrose who have been faintly preserved in history with one initial and no Christian name between them. They seem to have been the daughters of a Portuguese Jew and an English mother, who married a Covent Garden prompter after her first husband was executed as a spy during the War of Jenkins' Ear. The initial ('E') belongs to the younger one, whose subsequent theatrical career rose as high as Regan in *King Lear*, but no higher. The nature of the Marquis of Hertford's interest in her is uncertain. Green-room gossip accorded to the elder Miss Ambrose, after 1761, a colourful amatory life involving two Irish peers, a hatter and a lesbian frolic with an unnamed French lady.

Mary Cokayne, whose theatrical life was almost exclusively devoted to playing maids, was Tippet if Miss 'E' Ambrose was Tattle, and Tattle if she was Tippet. A long-term member of the Covent Garden company (1753–71), this was her first recorded appearance at Drury Lane. Also in the cast was Helen Johnston, who had created the servant role of Toilet in *The Jealous Wife* at Drury Lane on 12 February 1761, and whose ruddy complexion may have encouraged Murphy to write in the unnecessary Marmalet. Miscellaneous servants are essential to the social comedies of the eighteenth and nineteenth centuries, and the livelihood of actresses like Cokayne and Johnston depended on them. Henry Marr, probably the original Robert, was a resentful male equivalent. Tate Wilkinson calls him 'one of the worst actors that ever exhibited in theatre or in barn',[6] and it is something of a mystery that Garrick put up with him at Drury Lane for so long. If we can rely on Wilkinson, Marr was not at all grateful:

> I remember old Mar [*sic*], from his inveteracy to Garrick, for not giving him principal characters, always said, the very sound of

5. Wilkinson, *The Wandering Patentee* (York, 1795), vol. 2, pp. 151–53.
6. Wilkinson, vol. 2, p. 55.

Manager put his frame into a ferment.—If when he fed the ducks in St James's Park, any one of the feathered race was peculiarly alert, and swallowed more than the others, he would vociferously roar out! 'O damn you! you are the Manager'.[7]

The last character to appear in *All in the Wrong*, and the last in our putative cast, is Belinda's father who, like Sir William Bellmont, has to learn to relinquish control of his child's future happiness. Thomas Dibble, who acted under the stage name of Davis, was about thirty in 1761, and already an expert on bad marriages. But for lack of precise information, he would certainly have figured in my account of known bigamists. In 1795, at the end of a life which Tate Wilkinson sees as the height of dissoluteness, he was being tended by his fourth or fifth wife. It was most likely through Foote that he was invited to join the summer company, having made an impression as the gambling Loader in *The Minor*, and it was probably during the season that he began the association with Thomas Weston that led the two of them into a disastrous combination of drink and theatre management. 'I do attest', wrote Wilkinson in 1795, 'that thirty years ago (save the blemish of an eye) he was a handsome man—but now, O! ye gods! How fallen! How changed!'.[8]

The Foote/Murphy company was a particular one, but sufficiently typical to provide us with a background to the sort of job Garrick did year by year, and to help us to measure his achievement. It was, of course, unusual for a single playwright to carry as much responsibility as Murphy did during that Drury Lane summer. To complete the story of the season, I should comment on the performances in which Murphy was not directly implicated. To begin with, then, there was always speciality dancing as part of the programme: Master Rogie and Miss Capitani in a 'Pantomime Dance', Miss Scott in a hornpipe. Foote, though he wrote nothing new, appeared as Young Philpot in Murphy's *The Citizen*, and summoned up *The Minor* on 21 July to cover the absence of Mary Ann Yates. Extraordinarily, the allusions to Methodism still caused a stir, although the Duke of Devonshire, Garrick's close friend and the Lord Chamberlain responsible for the licensing of plays, had bowed to pressure from Lady Huntingdon and others. Among the lines cut were Mrs Cole's from Act One, when she is torn between praising the salvationary Mr Squintum (Whitefield had a squint) and providing Sir George Wealthy with a bedmate. I quote them here as evidence of Foote's mischievous talent:

7. Wilkinson, vol. 3, p. 17.
8. Wilkinson, vol. 1, p. 77.

There had I been tossing in the sea of sin, without rudder or compass. And had not the good gentleman piloted me into the harbour of grace, I must have struck against the rocks of reprobation, and have been quite swallowed up in the whirlpool of despair. He was the precious instrument of my spiritual sprinkling.—But, however, Sir George, if your mind be set on a young country thing, tomorrow night I believe I can furnish you.

Foote's dislike of Methodism was social, not theological. Methodists were 'enthusiasts', and enthusiasm had a dampening effect on the witty conversation piece of which he believed himself a master. But other people saw more sinister implications. When Alexander Jephson published his *Friendly and Compassionate Address, To all serious and well disposed Methodists* in 1760—the year of *The Minor*—it was to charge Methodism with the political crime of levelling, for teaching denial of the riches of the world. It was because the issues were serious, not because Foote was, that *The Minor* was the year's sensation. There is no substance to the satire, nor any centrality. In fact, like *All in the Wrong*, at its only serious level *The Minor* is a marriage play. Here, too, the fathers must learn to leave the final choice of spouse to their children; and whilst this is a familiar feature of comedy, it would be a mistake to ignore the new poignancy it acquired after the 1753 Marriage Act. Foote and Murphy, both bachelors, were entering consciously into a weighty public debate.

One other piece was included in the repertoire of the summer season, though I have the feeling that neither Murphy nor Foote thought well of it. The author, Richard Bentley, was the son of a famously polemical scholar, and was a scholar in his own right. He was not, however, a dramatist. That *The Wishes* was staged at all was straightforwardly the result of political pressure. So far as I know, it has not been published, and my account is entirely dependent on contemporary reports, above all on a manuscript in the collection of Lord Waldegrave at Chewton Priory. It is there stated that Garrick and John Rich had both rejected it early in 1761, that the playwright Richard Cumberland, who was Bentley's nephew, then took the manuscript to Lord Melcombe who carried it to the Earl of Bute who showed it to George III who 'sent Bentley £200 and ordered the new summer company to play [it]'.[9] Murphy was in no position to reject any request that carried the *imprimatur* of Lord Bute, let alone of the King, but Foote evidently refused to deliver the prologue's servile flattery of George III and Bute.

9. Quoted in G.W. Stone, Jr. (ed), *The London Stage*, Part 4, vol. 2 (Carbondale: Southern Illinois University Press, 1962), p. 877.

He did not, however, obstruct the performance of an epilogue (authorship unknown) which satirized Garrick: 'not very kind on his own stage', commented Horace Walpole in the letter he wrote to George Montagu the day after the play's 27 July premiere. Cumberland, who had anonymously published a pamphlet attack on Garrick on 25 July, was deeply embroiled in the whole murky proceeding; one of many examples of the spats with playwrights dotted through Garrick's managerial career. Walpole's letter gives a comic account of the first-night audience, with Bentley and his wife 'perked up in the front boxes', and in a stage box Lady Bute, Lord Halifax and Lord Melcombe: 'I must say the last two entertained the house as much as the play.' Walpole considered 'the whole very ill-acted'—scarcely surprisingly if it had been got up in a resentful hurry—but, having heard Bentley read the play, he had no very high hopes for it: 'It turned out just what I remembered it, the good parts extremely good, the rest very flat and vulgar'.

It is difficult to know what Bentley was trying to do. The cast list belongs to *commedia dell'arte* by way of English pantomime: O'Brien as Harlequin, Baddeley as Pantaloon, Ann Elliot as Columbine, Dibble/Davis as Pierrot, Weston as the Doctor, and Foote in the role of Distress, a poet. But Bentley's literary pretensions aimed higher than pantomime. A tolerant, if sometimes bemused, audience was suddenly aroused to hissing fury in Act Five when Harlequin was hanged in front of their very eyes. Was Bentley trying to kill pantomime? If so, the audience refused to let him. The facts are not entirely clear, but it would seem that further performances (there were five in all) were permitted on condition that the gibbeting was cut. One way and another, *The Wishes* was a sour addition to the season.

The story of the project concludes with an epilogue involving Garrick and Murphy. If I read it correctly, Garrick was disgruntled about many aspects of the summer programme, and Murphy, with the epilogue to *The Wishes* a recent memory, was acting disingenuously when he wrote to the manager on 16 September 1761 to ascertain Drury Lane's plans for his three plays, as well as for the revised *The Man Does Not Know His Own Mind*. Garrick's guarded reply confirmed his impression that *The Citizen* and *The Old Maid* were due to take their place as afterpieces in the 1761–62 season, contradicted Murphy's assumption that he himself wished to play Sir John Restless in *All in the Wrong*, complained about Murphy's refusal to allow the playhouse scribe to copy out parts in preparation for staging his farces, and kept open the option on the new comedy. He concluded, 'I have neither Seen You, or heard from You, till the Receipt of yr Letter, but have heard from others, that You are in another Interest, which indeed I could not, nor can I now, account for'.[10] The probability is that Murphy, all too aware of the offence he might have given to Garrick, was in duplicitous negotiation with Covent Garden, but currently stymied by John Rich's terminal illness and the uncertain position of his successor, John Beard. Both manager and playwright were playing for time. In response to a second letter from Murphy, Garrick protested that his co-manager James Lacy had been misrepresented:

> As to his saying that I should appear in Mr Yates's character, there must be some mistake between you, for he denies his having said to you that *I would play Yates's part*: he told you, in conversation, that *All in the Wrong* ought to have been acted in the winter, originally with us, and that I should have done Yates's part; but that he made no stipulation for my taking the part upon the revival of the Comedy.[11]

This is Garrick standing on his dignity as a great actor: it is one thing for such a man to create a role and another thing altogether for him to take it over at second hand. The dispute rumbled on in a mist of crooked talk until 17 December, when Garrick reported to George Colman in secret relief that 'Mr Murphy has at last declar'd off with us, & in a Letter to Obrien says, that he has been so great a loser by ye Managers of Drury Lane that he can never more have any dealings with Us—Wish Me joy my dear Friend, but Keep this to yrSelf for Many Weighty reasons'.[12] It was not until 1768 that Murphy would next have a play staged at Drury Lane. He was, for a while at least, the real victim of the 1761 summer season that ought to have been his path to glory.

10. *Letters*, vol. 1, p. 345.
11. *Letters*, vol. 1, p. 346.
12. *Letters*, vol. 1, p. 349.

9

Edmund Kean versus
John Philip Kemble

'We wish we had never seen Mr. Kean', wrote Hazlitt in the *Examiner* on 27 October 1816. 'He has destroyed the Kemble religion and it is the religion in which we were brought up.' Hazlitt was writing just over two years into a debate about acting whose ferocity has never since been equalled and for which the only precedent in England can be found in the critical response to the London debut of David Garrick in 1741. Garrick did more than anyone to make acting a focus of high cultural concern, and both Kemble and Kean were his beneficiaries in that respect. But the conflict over the relative merits of the school of Garrick and the school of Quin was tame when compared to the bloody battles between Keanites and Kembleites. To be sure, Quin was past his best by 1741, but so was Kemble by 1814, when Kean made his sensational Drury Lane debut as Shylock. Battle-scarred after the Old Price riots of 1809, he had only just returned to Covent Garden after a two-year absence. Dates are interesting here. Conscious of the occasion, Kemble selected for his comeback on 15 January 1814 his favoured role of Coriolanus. Twelve days later Kean came out in Shylock. There was thirty years' difference in their ages (Kemble was born in 1757 and Kean in 1787), and they had never met. I have found no record of their ever meeting during Kean's years of fame, and must assume that that was by Kemble's choice. Perhaps a kind friend warned him that they were even more incompatible socially than they were artistically.

However, by the sheer coincidence of theatrical programming in the second half of January 1814, a confrontation of styles that might have developed too slowly to generate much controversy acquired immediately a sensational dimension. London's newspapers were in a particularly excitable condition at the time. Despite the rout of his army at the Battle of Leipzig in October 1813, Napoleon had refused to accept defeat and the outcome was uncertain. The Duke of Wellington, already a hero to a natural Tory like Kemble, was advancing cautiously in the vicinity of Bayonne, but it was not until after Waterloo that the English press would confidently ascribe to him a military genius to rival Napoleon's. The old anxiety lingered, fuelled by the sophisticated group of 'unpatriotic' Whigs who continued to tout their admiration for the 'little Corsican'. The advent of Kean was as welcome a cultural distraction as the simultaneous publication of a new narrative poem by Lord Byron. *The Corsair* sold 10,000 copies on the day of its publication and vied with Kean for attention in the London periodicals through February 1814. Byron, who never disguised his admiration for Napoleon, was unreliably a Whig. His own bias in the Kemble/Kean controversy is revealed by a jotting in his journal, dated 19 February 1814:

> Just returned from seeing Kean in Richard. By Jove, he is a soul! Life—nature—truth—without exaggeration or diminution. Kemble's Hamlet is perfect;—but Hamlet is not Nature. Richard is a man; and Kean is Richard.[1]

It is a comment pitched exactly where the quarrel was pitched, and where, to a large extent, it is pitched still, but the intention here is to restore that quarrel to its neglected political frame. The setting of Kean against Kemble was not the design of either actor but of a politically partisan press. Kemble was a Tory favourite and Kean was innocently adopted as the Whig candidate for the office of supreme tragedian.

Not that innocence is a quality readily associated with Kean, whose dissipation led many people (women especially) to despair and himself to an early death. But he laid no claim to political insight. Naturally antagonistic, sometimes to the point of paranoia, he resented any authority that opposed him. His instincts were probably sufficiently egalitarian to carry his sympathies towards the Whigs, however tarnished their defence of liberty, and away from the Tories, advocates of pacification through privilege. But Kean was wildly inconsistent. He would claim to be the love child of Charles Howard, Duke of Norfolk (he called his first son Howard and his second Charles), would send his surviving second son to Eton, lease a large house in fashionable Clarges Street as soon as he could afford it, and invite the cream of society to dine there. He even purchased an estate on the Isle of Bute. But these, surely, were the convulsive responses of a man who had spent the first quarter of his life in abject poverty. Modern pop stars do the same kinds of thing when propelled into sudden fame, and some of them are as willing as Kean might have been to parade their social consciences by attending smart

---

1. Leslie A. Marchand (ed.), *Byron's Letters and Journals*, Vol. 3 (London: John Murray, 1974), p. 244.

parties at the invitation of prominent public figures. Kemble, by comparison, was a model of political consistency. Brought up and educated as a Roman Catholic when the Exclusion Laws still bit and when it was not uncommon for Whigs to accuse Tories of being secret Catholics and Jacobites, he exhibited throughout his managerial career a loyalty to George III that might have been sycophantic if it had not been so conventional. James Boaden, his friend and first authoritative biographer, claims that Kemble knew nothing of politics and never read a newspaper.[2] It is a claim that puts me in mind of the poster in a Devon village shop during the run up to County Council elections: 'Keep Politics out of Local Government: Vote Conservative'. Had Kemble worn his heart on his sleeve, his career at Drury Lane under the feckless management of the Whig playwright and politician, Richard Brinsley Sheridan, would have been a constant, rather than an occasional, nightmare. As it was, their most serious clash came after Kemble, without consulting Sheridan, cancelled the performance at Drury Lane on 25 January 1793 as a sign of sympathy and an emblem of mourning for the beheaded Louis XVI of France. Kemble was much more successful than Kean at maintaining his relationship with members of the aristocracy, not least because he knew how to get drunk *with* rather than *before* them.

Party politics fuelled the debate over the relative merits of Kean and Kemble, but its long-term interest is aesthetic. It remained, and perhaps remains, active long after their deaths. The broad terms of the argument have already been encountered in Byron's *Journal*. Kean was direct, compellingly human, hot; Kemble was remote, superhuman, cool. It could also be fairly deduced, though Byron does not say as much, that he recognized blemishes in Kean's performance—it lacked the finish of Kemble's Hamlet. 'The distinctive characteristic of Kemble's acting was finish', wrote the nostalgic William Robson,[3] who reviled the memory of Kean as much as he relished the memory of Kemble. Byron also points us down two of the most notorious cul-de-sacs in the whole history of debates about acting. Kean was 'natural' and internally *feeling* ('By Jove, he is a soul!'), whereas Kemble, by implication, was artificial and a representer of feeling through external signs. This is uncomfortable territory, but we cannot avoid it without ignoring every contemporary contribution to the debate. In retrospect, we can say confidently that neither Kean nor Kemble would have looked natural to us, and this is not simply because conversational and behavioural habits—the whole conduct of social discourse—have changed. The great new actor has

2. James Boaden, *Memoirs of the Life of John Philip Kemble* (London, 1825), vol. 2, p. 76.
3. William Robson, *The Old Playgoer* (London, 1846), p. 37.

always been seen as more natural than the great old actor. In the theatre of 1814, particularly in the realm of tragedy, 'Nature' as Byron used the word meant 'recognisable passion'. Hamlet is 'not Nature' because he disguises his passions. Richard III *is* 'Nature' because his passions are transparent. Kean is natural by virtue of the fact that he channels Richard's passions to the audience. There is not much to be added on that score, beyond a recognition that Kemble would have considered some of Kean's vocal and physical mannerisms vulgar and that it was these same mannerisms that some of the audience found startlingly natural.

The matter of 'feeling' is more complex. To play a passionate scene effectively, the actor must be feeling something, but does he feel *for* the audience, *with* the audience, *like* the audience or *for* the character, *like* the character, *in* the character? This was an old debate, soon to be reactivated by the posthumous publication of Diderot's *Paradoxe sur le comédien* (1830). The paradox is that the actor, however fully and convincingly he expresses the feelings of the character he plays, does not himself share those feelings. The expression may give the appearance of reality, but it is artifice that creates the expression. It was not necessary to have read Diderot in order to take sides in the theatrical quarrel between nature and art on the battlefield of tragedy. Not all of the combatants shared Diderot's metaphorical vision. He saw in the actor a representative image of humanity under pressure from circumstance. Kembleites and Keanites pitched their tents parochially, either in Covent Garden or in Drury Lane. In the long run, though, it is Diderot's vision that matters. Actors can, some do, speak to us with uncommon command on behavioural issues of uncommon magnitude. That is why the quarrels over the relative merits of Kean and Kemble mattered at the time and matter still. How much *real* feeling is necessary if *simulated* feeling is to be convincingly portrayed? Many a politician and even more adulterers have come to grief over the answer to that question.

At one level the debate was about the nature and scope of human character at a time when the subject was under peculiar scrutiny in every branch of the arts. Shakespeare provided the acid test for actors, and the scholarly Kemble was always alert to critical opinion. He was in general agreement with Whateley's *Remarks on Some of the Characters of Shakespeare's Plays* (1785), which argued that individual character is the product of the interplay between a predominant principle of behaviour and some few discernible subsidiary traits. His own preparation, before undertaking a new role, aimed to determine the leading passion that would give overall shape to his portrayal. The detailed 'points', which audiences expected of any leading actor, were brought into harmony with Kemble's generalizing conception. It was an intelligent reading of Shakespeare, but not a subtle one. Believing that all human behaviour is explicable, Kemble set about explaining it. His Macbeth, though not among his finest roles, is exemplary. Whateley had identified in Macbeth the type of a coward; Kemble went so far as to publish his disagreement in a pamphlet, *Macbeth Reconsidered* (1786), which he revised for publication in June 1817, to coincide with his retirement from the stage. By close reference to the text, he there argues that it is Macbeth's constant courage ('intrepidity' is his preferred word) that leads him from virtue into crime. That is how Kemble played him. But a more general clue to his method is provided by a sentence approaching summary:

> The characters that Shakspeare [*sic*] draws, are human creatures; and however their peculiarities may individuate them, yet they are always connected with the general nature of man by some fine link of universal interest, and by some passion to which they are liable in common with their kind.[4]

Sir Joshua Reynolds held comparable beliefs about portraiture. Whilst recognizing the difficulty of 'marking' the individual subject, he rested the excellence of portrait painting 'more upon the general effect produced by the painter, than on the exact expression of the peculiarities or minute discrimination of the parts'.[5] More tellingly from the actor's view, Reynolds asserts that it is the whole, rather than the parts, that gives to the work of art its 'true and touching character'.[6] There is no doubt that Kemble aimed to touch the hearts of his audiences (Kean's approach calls for a more vigorous verb) by presenting sympathetic portraits of Shakespeare's tragic heroes. There is more doubt that he framed himself consciously in a tradition of neo-classical portraiture. That reputation was initially foisted on him by reviewers who thought of theatre pictorially, and who liked to display their knowledge of the visual arts. James Boaden's busy biography of Kemble is punctuated with flattering pictorial analogies, some of which chillingly present his subject as if he were a piece of statuary. Kemble was, as actors must be, very aware of his appearance—not only of his graceful physique and handsome head, but also, crucially, of the pictorial potential of actors significantly grouped and isolated on the plane of the stage. (He has credible claims

4. Kemble, *Macbeth and King Richard the Third: an essay in answer to remarks on some of the characters of Shakespeare* (London: John Murray, 1817), p. 166.
5. Reynolds, *Discourses on Art*, ed. Robert Wark (New Haven: Yale University Press, 1975), p. 200.
6. Reynolds, p. 193.

JOHN PHILLIP KEMBLE.

In the Character of Cato.

Taken from a Bust by J. Gibson Esq of Rome

London Printed & Published by N Chater & Co. 23 Fleet St.

Feb 20 1823.

6. M. Gauci, lithograph after a bust by J. Gibson, Kemble as Cato: static and clean-cut according to contemporary perceptions.

as a forerunner of the modern director.) But the tendency to adopt statuesque poses came comparatively late, and our readiness to visualize him arrested centre stage as if modelling for Michelangelo owes more to Thomas Lawrence than to truth. Lawrence's portraits of Kemble, in and out of role, are immensely grand, but they have verified for history a view of his acting that plays into the hands of his detractors. They give

118

us a glimpse, though, of a distinctly idealizing approach to character. At a time when history painting was rated above all other kinds, Kemble may have pictorialised himself as history in an honest quest for the sublime.

Kean was luckier in his painters as well as his critics; lucky, at least, not to be misrepresented by anyone as accomplished as Lawrence. The famous likeness, attributed to George Clint, of Kean as Sir Giles Overreach is all fire. It is also, appropriately perhaps, unfinished. However fine Kean was at moments, no one has claimed that he was fine all through a play. The decisive point, though, is the one made by G.H. Lewes:

> . . . all defects were overlooked or disregarded, because it was impossible to watch Kean as Othello, Shylock, Richard, or Sir Giles Overreach without being strangely shaken by the terror, and the pathos, and the passion of a stormy spirit uttering itself in tones of irresistible power.[7]

The charismatic actor is forgiven, sometimes even enjoyed, for lapses that are inexcusable in one who has based his reputation on consistency. Lewes, who never saw Kemble and who was in his teens when Kean died, did not feel excluded from the debate because he believed that '[t]he greatest artist is he who is greatest in the highest reaches of his art'. His implicit verdict, based solely on his boyhood witnessing of Kean in action, is 'no contest':

> Who can ever forget the exquisite grace with which he leaned against the side-scene while Anne was railing at him, and the chuckling mirth of his 'Poor fool! what pains she takes to damn herself!' It was thoroughly feline—terrible yet beautiful.

It is evidence of a theatrical taste that Regency audiences would bequeath to the Victorians that Kean's finest Shakespearean roles, particularly in the versions in which he played them, were the most overtly melodramatic: Shylock, Richard III, Othello, Nahum Tate's King Lear. Only once, and then briefly in January 1820 in a foolhardy attempt to outshine the rising star of William Charles Macready, did he make the mistake of following Kemble's Roman nose into Coriolanus. To his admirers, Kemble was every inch a Roman: Kean had neither the

7. Lewes, 'Edmund Kean' in *On Actors and the Art of Acting* (London: Smith, Elder & Co., 1875), pp. 1–11.

7. George Clint, Kean as Sir Giles Overreach: 'thoroughly feline—terrible yet beautiful'.

temperament nor the stature for the role. Where Kemble built slowly and deliberately towards a dramatic climax, Kean relished every occasion for climactic display. His Othello was not slow-burning but volatile throughout. The passion might burst out at any moment; and whether or not that is 'right', it was evidently right for him. Very few actors in history have excelled in Othello, and Kean was certainly the smallest of them. When Covent Garden put up Junius Brutus Booth, who had modelled himself on Kean and nursed a fervent desire to rival or outdo him, Kean manoeuvred the Drury Lane management into hiring him to play Iago. On 20 February 1817 Othello annihilated Iago over three hours of savage combat. It was unwarrantable, but magnificent.

There was never any dispute about the quantity of feeling that Kean put into his performances. It was the quality that was questioned. Was the feeling the character's or Kean's? Was it appropriate to the drama as a whole? How much of truth was sacrificed to effect? These were not the questions asked about Kemble. '[I]n every part', wrote the admiring William Robson, 'he was a *gentleman*. . . . In the scene with Lady Anne, he wooed as if he were endeavouring to win a *lady*; Kean, on the contrary, made it a joke between himself and the audience, and would hardly have deceived a cookmaid.'[8] It is a less appealing view of Kemble and a more endearing one of Kean than Robson would have wished. We have lost the taste for elegance and gentility. But Kean's sudden descents into the colloquial could seem gratuitous even to his admirers. Lewes concedes that he was 'fond, far too fond, of abrupt transitions—passing from vehemence to familiarity, and mingling strong lights and shadows with Caravaggio force of unreality'. Robson stays closer to home for his painterly reference to an actor whom he considered vulgar: not Caravaggio, but George Morland, lover of low life and painter of pigs and donkeys.[9] If ever there was an English actor capable of inciting the audience to rebel against the class system it was Kean, who tried unsuccessfully to elbow his way up the ladder instead. There was always danger in what he did. Byron sensed it in comparing Kean to his own Corsair (lines 223–26):

> There was a laughing devil in his sneer,
> That raised emotions of both rage and fear;
> And where his frown of hatred darkly fell,
> Hope withering fled, and Mercy sigh'd farewell!

The point is a serious one. The Byronic hero, from Childe Harold through to Lara, fascinated and disturbed at least two generations. Dark-eyed and smouldering (like Kean), he was also the doomed possessor of forbidden knowledge, at once repelling and attracting. He had arisen from Byron's own encounters with Gothic novels, but never until the first two cantos of *Childe Harold* were published in March 1812 had he been introduced into Regency society. Byron identified Napoleon with his charismatic heroes, and would lament his lonely exile on Elba in stanza 52 of the third canto of *Childe Harold*, since

8. Robson, p. 38.
9. Robson, p. 117.

Quiet to quick bosoms is a Hell,
And *there* hath been thy bane; there is a fire
And motion of the Soul which will not dwell
In its own narrow being, but aspire
Beyond the fitting medium of desire.

According to Thomas Colley Grattan, what Napoleon was to Byron, Byron was to Kean: 'They were each, on their several stages, acting the self-same part—straining for the world's applause, not labouring for their own delight.'[10] It was one thing to represent aspirations 'beyond the fitting medium of desire', as Kean did supremely, but quite another thing to pursue them, as Kean did to his detriment. He became, to some extent, the deluded victim of Byron's fictional projection of Napoleon. By no means the only one (the Russian poet Lermontov was spectacularly another, and Emily Brontë's Heathcliff a fictional version), but the only one who was a famous actor. Kean has often been portrayed as the embodiment of the Romantic quest for the self-justifying self. Alexandre Dumas *père*'s play *Kean* (1836) started the trend three years after its subject's death. But Kean was no more a true Romantic than Byron was. They were both egotists, both actors of invented selves in a London that first adulated and then rejected them—and both preferred the classics of literature to the radically new. Byron, though, had more personal resilience because he was less easily deluded and much funnier.

Kemble had already been projected into fiction, as Dorriforth in Elizabeth Inchbald's novel, *A Simple Story* (1791). Dorriforth is a Gothically gloomy young man whose portrayal, mingled intriguingly with that of the Byronic hero, would contribute to Charlotte Brontë's creation of Mr Rochester in *Jane Eyre*. Because so much attention has been paid to their Shakespearean characters, there has been a distorting neglect of the significant place of Gothic melodramas in the repertoires of both Kemble and Kean. It can be easily shown that their Shakespearean strengths were complementary rather than competitive. Kemble was considered a fine Hamlet, a tame Macbeth and Richard III, a surprisingly inept Romeo (the 'tender passions' were outside his range), impossible as Othello, unrivalled as Brutus and Coriolanus. Kean was an acceptable Hamlet, too small for Macbeth, too malevolent for Romeo (the tender passions were outside his range, also), too fidgety for Brutus and Coriolanus, unrivalled as Richard III, Othello and Shylock. When they strayed into uncongenial territory, they were both generally condemned.

10. Quoted in Raymund FitzSimons, *Edmund Kean: fire from heaven* (London: Hamish Hamilton, 1976), p. 117.

It is in the Gothic drama that they can most straightforwardly be compared and contrasted. Even a critic as hostile to Kemble as Leigh Hunt generally was acknowledged his excellence in 'characters that are occupied with themselves and with their own importance'.[11] It was Kemble who persuaded contemporary theatregoers that Cumberland's *The Wheel of Fortune*, the younger Colman's *The Mountaineers* and Benjamin Thompson's adaptation of Kotzebue's *The Stranger* were great plays. Penruddock, Octavian and the Stranger are men injured by circumstance, isolated and misunderstood. They represent threatened humanity striving to maintain dignity in adversity. Theirs are not grand passions, but immediately recognizable ones. As Thompson's Stranger, recalls Boaden, '[Kemble] bore a living death about him'.[12] The plots are contrived, the dialogue emptily portentous, but the characters Kemble played, swathed in gloom as they certainly were, were as real to audiences as the characters in Ann Radcliffe's novels were to their entranced readers. These Gothic embroideries had already been absorbed into melodrama by the time Kean reached London, but it was as Octavian in *The Mountaineers* on a November evening in 1813 that he sufficiently impressed the acting manager of Drury Lane to win himself the offer of the engagement that would change his life. This is a Gothic tale in its own right. Kean's four-year-old elder son lay dying in a Dorchester lodging house while his father acted the role of Colman's misanthrope-with-a-heart-of-gold. It was not a part in which he would challenge Kemble during his years of fame at Drury Lane, but Colman's *The Iron Chest* furnished him with one of his most admired roles. There is a savoury slice of theatre history here. *The Iron Chest* had been first performed at Drury Lane on 12 March 1796, with Kemble in the role of Sir Edward Mortimer. For whatever reason—the actor's dislike of the play, his overdosing on opium, his dressing-room mixing of opium and alcohol—the performance was a fiasco, and Colman wrote a vitriolic preface to the second edition. He had a point. The play, a dramatization of all that is least interesting in William Godwin's polemical novel *Caleb Williams*, was shrewdly tailored to contemporary taste—and by a master-tailor. Kean would certainly have known the history before agreeing to the revival of *The Iron Chest* on 23 November 1816, and his angry competitiveness increased his determination. Hazlitt was one in an audience shaken to the core by a tour de force of Gothic anguish:

---

11. George Rowell (ed.), *Victorian Dramatic Criticism* (London: Methuen, 1971), p. 10.
12. Boaden, vol. 2, p. 215.

The last scene of all, his coming to life again after his swooning at the fatal discovery of his guilt, and then falling back after a ghastly struggle, like a man waked from the tomb, into despair and death in the arms of his mistress, was one of those consummations of the art, which those who have seen and have not felt them in this actor, may be assured that they have never seen or felt anything in the course of their lives, and never will to the end of them.[13]

Such are the ruses that debaters resort to. If Kean's Sir Edward does not make you feel deeply, you are incapable of deep feeling. A Kembleite response might be: if you can be taken in by that kind of emotional trickery, you lack discernment (but could the Kembleite still say that after seeing Irving play Mathias in *The Bells*?). Kean's Gothic roles (the title role in Maturin's *Bertram* is the best remembered) are played at a higher emotional pitch than Kemble's. He revealed passion at intervals throughout, where Kemble concealed passion until the climax of the drama. It is in their contrasting treatment of second-rate material that the essential difference of their Shakespearean styles can be seen most clearly.

It would be an unpardonable oversimplification, though one which Kemble would have appreciated, to settle on a contrast between steadiness that wins its slow way to the audience's heart and brilliance that regularly tingles the nerves. The missing dimension in the work of both men is comedy, either as a genre in its own right or as a mode of playing that might add complexity to tragedy. Kemble, with the example of Garrick close (and that of John Henderson closer) behind him, was particularly conscious of this deficiency, but his attempts to prove his versatility *proved* nothing of the sort. Kean, like Laurence Olivier for example, had sufficient mischief in his histrionic armoury to have tackled comedy at its angry end, and could have reached the bitter humour of Edmund in *King Lear*, if a less black-and-white text of that play had been available to the theatre of the time. But Lewes' perception is acute: 'He had no gaiety; he could not laugh; he had no playfulness that was not as the playfulness of a panther showing her claws every moment.' On and off stage, Kemble was too solemn, Kean too frantic. Neither mode is suitable for comedy. But these variant deficiencies, like their differing qualities, do nothing to account for the violence of the battle between the opposing camps of their supporters. My suggestion is that there were two main bones of contention. One belongs to socio-cultural history, the other to biography. I conclude by dealing with them in turn.

13. Quoted in FitzSimons, p. 104.

Kemble was the product of an age that held fast to notions of human perfectibility. The calmness of neo-classical art and architecture, its submission to order, has behind it not complacence, but aspiration. Its goal is the sublime. Kemble was a collector of prints as well as books. His taste was for the baroque and Poussin was his idol. On the evidence of Richard Westall's painting of Kemble as Coriolanus before the pleading women of Rome, David George has persuasively argued that Kemble based his staging of the scene on Poussin's 'Coriolanus'.[14] The significance of that painting for Poussin—and this is an aspect that would certainly have attracted Kemble to it—was its portrayal of 'the victory of the will over the passions'.[15] Conservative opinion in England at the end of the eighteenth century countered fearful responses to the French Revolution with the optimistic assertion that in Britain the will was master of the passions. There can be various views about the main causes of the shift in what social historians have called the *mentalité* of the British population between 1790 and 1820, but the impact of the revolution in France was certainly one, and the revolution in industry another. Dennis Bartholomeusz offers an analysis of the effect on Kemble of the volatile *mentalité*:

> Though Kemble appreciated propriety and decorum as much as Chesterfield or Pitt, his patrician air became less representative as England became more industrial and, with the increasing accumulation of men in cities, probably less secure and gracious.[16]

It was Kemble's bearing, more than his stubbornness, that created him an enemy of the people in the Old Price Riots of 1809. The loyalty of his supporters remained unbroken. Their rapturous applause and shouts of 'No farewell' when he took his leave of the stage on 23 June 1817 were genuine. But in truth his time had passed. He was politically too unquestioning for a questioning age, and aesthetically too generalizing to capture the imagination of the new self-searchers. The aesthetic distance travelled between the England of Joshua Reynolds (Kemble's world) and the England Kean knew is nicely encapsulated in two famous dicta. 'Nothing can please many, and please long, but just representations of general nature', wrote Samuel Johnson. 'Nothing can permanently please, which does not contain in itself the reason why it is so, and not other-

14. *Theatre Notebook*, vol. 46, no. 1 (1994), pp. 2–10.
15. Anthony Blunt, *Art and Architecture in France, 1500–1700* (Harmondsworth: Penguin, 1953), p. 189.
16. Bartholomeusz, *Macbeth and the Players* (Cambridge: Cambridge University Press, 1969), p. 150.

wise', wrote Samuel Taylor Coleridge. Kemble was generic, Kean *sui generis*.

The biographical roots of the quarrel are simple in outline, however complex their internal shaping. The extraordinary career of David Garrick, and his exemplary marriage, had confirmed the social acceptability, *under certain conditions*, of actors. More than that, his nose for publicity had given actors a special access to the growing hoard of journalists. They provided good copy, and lots of it. As a younger brother of the redoubtable Sarah Siddons, Kemble had a good start and, often by the skin of his teeth, he made the most of it. It would be quite easy to mount a scurrilous case against the gentlemanly Kemble. He had a drink problem; he attempted to rape a young actress in January 1795; his marriage was a loveless sham; he was addicted to opium. The significant point, though, is that the case was never made. There was something about Kemble that won the trust of his social equals and betters at the same time as it alienated his social inferiors. The reputation of the acting profession was safe in his hands. It was quite otherwise with Kean. He was known to consort with prostitutes; his wife left him; when the going got tough he took himself off on week-long drinking 'benders'. Worst of all, he was officially found out. Maria De Camp did not take Kemble to court for his assault on her (in the fullness of time, in fact, she married his brother, a match which puts a curious spin on the idea of 'keeping it in the family'), though she might have done so. Alderman Cox did take Kean to court to answer a charge of 'criminal conversation' (adultery) with Charlotte Cox, though he really should not have done so. The hearing, which opened on 17 January 1825 in an atmosphere of horrified and horrific prurience, threatened, though it did not finally destroy, Kean's career. It destroyed Kean instead. However vehement his gestures of defiance were, on stage or off it, he was a little man, on stage or off it, when the chips were really down. Lewes, who can scarcely have seen Kean act before the Cox trial, probably never saw him at his best. Given the quality of Lewes' testimony, then, it is all the more certain that Kean was an extraordinary actor. But it needed Macready's strenuous respectability, and his recognition of the new seat of cultural power at the sophisticated centre of the middle classes, to restore the reputation of actors.

10

Frederick Robson
'A Downright Good Actor'

Something of nineteenth-century acting styles is necessarily recalled when television producers choose to serialize a novel by Charles Dickens, simply because Dickens conceived of character in theatrical terms. Almost invariably his plots are advanced by the behaviour of people who *look* what they *are*. The benevolent declare their innate benevolence in their cherubic features; the malevolent, even when they deceive the naive protagonist, betray themselves to the reader by telltale physical signs.

The semiotics, that is to say, are broadly melodramatic. They begin in the dressing room, where Dickens applies the make-up. It is not my intention to downgrade his novels. Melodrama, which can venture to the edge of the dreadful chasm and then have the temerity to draw back, is the mode that best represents the high Victorian temperament; the same fiction could both conjure up the unspeakable horror of the human condition and lull the unspeakable into comforting silence. It can reasonably be argued that dramatized Dickens is a doddle for any half-competent actor with a knowledge of make-up, and it is not surprising, given the available resources and an audience's abiding delight in thrilling plots, that Dickens comes across well on television. Recent serializations of *Martin Chuzzlewit*, *Our Mutual Friend*, *Oliver Twist* and *David Copperfield* have amply demonstrated that. There is such abundance in the novels that we forgive the slender contrivances of the 'main' plot: the riches of social truth are in the surrounding circumstances, where the humour also lies. But Dickensian comedy is often double-edged. The comic characters (and they are 'characters' in a recognizably theatrical sense) are not exempt from the evil impulses that threaten to overwhelm the narrative. When two people in dialogue use verbal tricks as elaborate as dance steps, they may make us laugh; but what if they are word-dancing on a grave? The human comedy reaches a point of emotional complexity when we laugh because we are unnerved. Shakespeare's Richard III is an evil comedian, placed disconcertingly at the centre of a play. Dickens characteristically situates his comedians at the fringes. The competent actor will accommodate the ambivalence of 'funny evil', but it takes an extraordinary actor to embody it. Albert Camus, when he wrote *Caligula*, was looking for that extraordinary actor, someone to carry a complacent audience into confrontation with the valueless 'absurd'. And Dickens, however strenuously he tried to suppress them, had intimations of the void to which a certain kind of laughter opens access.

The elusive Frederick Robson (1821–64) was, by common consent, a Dickensian actor, but that is not a description that gets us very far. Fagin is not the same kind of performer as Bill Sikes, nor does it much help to note that, during his early years at the Grecian Saloon/Theatre, Robson played Bailey Junior in an adaptation of *Martin Chuzzlewit* and later recited a monologue as Sarah Gamp. The Victorian stage had no shortage of 'comic men' who could play to brilliant effect the eccentric figures of farce or the obligatory good-hearted rustics and servants of melodrama. In general, though, such actors played according to type in parts made to their measure. Their task was to fulfil expectation, not to exceed it. Robson's special capacity—it leaps out from virtually every commentary on him—was to astonish audiences by embellishing the commonplace. Not one of the plays which he made remarkable in their time survived into the twentieth century because, with two arguable exceptions, they are time-locked. They were written for audiences that accepted and enjoyed a drama that was essentially content to recycle, rather than to invent, plots and characters. Any regular theatregoer—and each of London's theatres had its own adherents—would know the nature of the part from the name of the actor. Familiarity brings its own kind of satisfaction, but it is clear that Robson gave familiarity a jagged edge. It may, of course, be my fancy, but I felt the cut of it when watching the vivid scenes between Silas Wegg and Mr Venus in the televised adaptation of *Our Mutual Friend*. I mean no discourtesy to Kenneth Cranham when I say that it was particularly Timothy Spall's Mr Venus that gave meaning to the idea of the 'Dickensian' actor. Spall is physically unprepossessing, flabby-cheeked and puff-bodied, and Venus is manifestly a minor character, a small trader on the edge of the law, surrounded by the dust and clutter of his dubious trade. How, then, did Spall make so much of Venus? It was a studied performance, certainly. The speaking voice was slow-moving, spiced with a nasal whine, and he had the disconcerting habit of staring straight at Silas Wegg as if ignorant of normal decorum. Above all, though, it was Spall's embodiment of a bland immunity to morality that disconcerted me. Here was a man who lived mundanely on 'the other side'. It was a glimpse into perfunctory evil, the darkness of the everyday—and it was very funny. It was also, I think, intrinsically Dickensian.

Robson, like Dickens (like Tennyson, too, but Tennyson couldn't deflect it into humour), lived with a sense of darkness at the centre. He was the son of Philip Brownbill, probably a stockbroker in Margate, but it was father Brownbill's diminutive wife Margaret who reared him. The implication is that his parents' marriage was no more successful than his own would be. Subsequent memoirists (biographers would be too grand a word for all but Mollie Sands) like to believe that his mother took him to the Coburg Theatre in 1831, to see Edmund Kean in decline playing Richard III, Lear, Othello and Sir Giles Overreach. They like to believe that because Robson's acting in his maturity put old-timers in mind of Kean, but there is no reliable evidence to convert what looks like wishful thinking into reliable fact. By the middle of the 1830s, probably only with his mother who may or may not have been already a widow, young Brownbill was living in South London while working as an apprentice to an engraver in the Strand. He was, like his mother and Edmund Kean, decidedly short (about five feet or 1.5 metres) but well-proportioned. In 1840, having completed his apprenticeship, Thomas Brownbill set up his own engraving business in Brydges Street, but he was already living a second life as Frederick Robson, entertainer and would-be actor. A fascination with the double life, which features so prominently in Victorian literature from *A Tale of Two Cities* through *Dr Jekyll and Mr Hyde* to *The Picture of Dorian Gray* and beyond, exercised a particular pull on actors, generally to the detriment of their personal lives. It was his unparalleled on-stage duality that Robson's admirers would celebrate, and it was almost certainly the doomed off-stage attempt to keep pace with his reputation that destroyed him.

It would have been comparatively easy to write a maudlin Victorian novel around Robson's life, or at the very least a cautionary tale to illustrate a sermon. In early 1842 he was Thomas Brownbill, engraver. This was the man whom, on 21 September 1842, Rosetta Frances May married. By the end of 1842 he had become Frederick Robson, strolling actor. Or had he? According to the birth certificate (dated 26 July 1846) of his second child, a daughter to follow Frederick Henry (born 17 December 1843), he was Thomas Frederick Brownbill, engraver. And yet he had been a member of the acting company at the Eagle Saloon and Grecian Theatre in the City Road ('Up and down the City Road/In and out of the Eagle/That's the way the money goes . . .') since February 1844. There is no stable sense of a self here, though it would be speculative to talk already of a double life. It is not an easy thing to abandon a name. Henry Irving, when he ceased to be John Brodribb, had already set himself to a fierce refashioning of the self, but certainty came less readily to a small man with a small reputation. Brownbill, in the middle-class world to which an engraver aspired, would not have been proud of Robson's association with the Grecian, however that 'low' theatre was loved by the artisans of North London. Irving silenced Brodribb, but Robson never silenced Brownbill. Even at the height of his fame, he was tormented by doubts about his true identity. Eventually he had to drink in order to act, and the drink killed him at the age of forty-three. He was not the model for the dying clown in *The Pickwick Papers*, but he might have been; which is to say that Brownbill was so exemplary a Victorian self-tormentor that the Victorian Dickens had already invented him before he became Robson of the Grecian.

Thomas Rouse, the manager who employed him, was an exemplary Victorian of quite another kind. Having progressed from bricklayer to master builder, he used his wealth to satisfy his passion for bettering the lot of the working classes—not through charity but through culture. The Eagle Tavern and Grecian Saloon was to become, in his vision, North London's rival to the Vauxhall Gardens. By 1838 he was advertising 'Concerts in the open air, dancing and vaudeville in the Saloon, set paintings, cosmoramas, fountains, grottoes, elegant buildings, arcades, colonnades, grounds, statuary, singing, music'. The theatre or concert hall was one of the elegant buildings: a rotunda that housed nightly performances as well as providing an alternative dancing space when the weather was too inclement to encourage patrons to polka on the marked-out lawn. The young Dickens wrote a patronizingly humorous account of Samuel Wilkins' attempt to impress Miss Jemima Evans by taking her there in the 1830s.[1] It is a journalist's mockery of Rouse's aspirations, but Rouse was not easily deterred. His own love (he was the poor man's Alfred Bunn) was for opera, and he staged in the Grecian rotunda, for the edification of a largely artisan audience, works by Rossini, Auber, Boieldieu, Donizetti and others, as well as the predominantly farcical afterpieces for which Robson was engaged. The taste of North Londoners was not so easily elevated as Rouse had hoped, and losses on gate-money had to be compensated for by profits on the consumption of food and drink.

Robson made his first appearance at the Grecian (as Justice Shallow in a pillaged version of *The Merry Wives of Windsor*) in front of an audience of up to 700, many of them with glasses and plates on the shelves in front of their seats. 'Enormous piles of the thickest sandwiches, and mountains of pork pies were nightly consumed at the Grecian.'[2] Even so, it was there, in a revival of Samuel Beazley Junior's *The Lottery Ticket*

1. 'Miss Evans and the Eagle', in *Sketches by Boz* (1839).
2. Erroll Sherson, *London's Lost Theatres of the Nineteenth Century* (London: John Lane, 1925), p. 10.

(1826), that Robson gave the first indication of his idiosyncratic emotional range. The question raised by this performance—and similar questions may be asked about all of his characteristic achievements—is 'how did Robson endear himself to audiences in the part of a hunchbacked, malicious clerk whose chief activity and delight is meddling with other people's lives?'. It is one of those questions that leaps over history. They *liked* Robson's Wormwood at the Grecian in the 1840s: I *liked* Spall's Mr Venus in the 1990s. And yet Wormwood and Venus haven't an endearing trait between them. It is not simply that we like the actor in spite of the character; rather that, in defiance of our own moral judgement, we like the character because of the actor. This (temporary) upsetting of our value systems is something that fine acting can bring about. If, as actorphobes fear, this disturbance were permanent, a liked Macbeth would make us murderers. Alternatively, the quality of the performer extends the range of our moral understanding. Robson was a fine enough actor to challenge, through the felt reality of his performances in plays that bore little relation to reality, the Victorian audience's self-deluding eagerness to polarize good and evil. There was an irresistible exultation in his playing of Wormwood, but the basis of it was observation. Westland Marston would later remember that 'nothing . . . could be more microscopic than his observation of characteristics'.[3]

It is not surprising that the details of Robson's early stage career are obscure. Local notoriety was the immediate reward of his engagement at the Grecian, but no critical attention. We can be fairly sure, though, that he performed solo 'turns' for the volatile crowds, and that the most successful of these were built around songs. There was an attempt by some of Robson's friends, after his death, to suppress stories of his early successes in London's Song and Supper rooms, of which Evans's is only the most famous. These 'friends' were fearful of demeaning him by association with the music halls. Robson, late manager of the Olympic, was above such things, they boasted; he was no Sam Cowell. In the turmoil of his immature maturity, Robson may well have endorsed the suppression, but the ability to sell a song to a rowdy audience is a special skill. A little man, strangely dressed, stands on a stage to deliver a 'serio-comic ballad', with spoken commentary between the verses, convulsing the audience with laughter at one minute, and in the next silencing them with a throbbing episode of 'orrible murder, hideous cruelty, despairing suicide or a pauper's death. There is no agreement about when Robson first delivered the song with which he became lastingly associated, 'Vilikens

3. Westland Marston, *Some Recollections of Our Recent Actors* (London; Sampson Low, 1890), p. 363.

and his Dinah'.[4] I can no longer trace the anecdote which records his distress when this pathetic ballad was interrupted by laughter, and I don't believe it anyway.

He may well have sung it 'straight' to begin with, adding a semi-improvised interspersed commentary when he found himself having endlessly to repeat it on demand—just to sustain his own flagging interest—but it is a piece that cries out for laughter to alleviate it, like the song of the cockney mother whose baby was 'so tiny an' fin' that it vanished down the plug-hole when she 'turned rahnd fer the soap on the rack'. Mollie Sands refers to the version of 'Vilekens', in Number 691 of Davidson's *Musical Treasury*, in which E.L. Blanchard has recorded the spoken interludes of at least one performance. The conflicting tonalities of song and speech, still to be heard in recordings of later artists like Dan Leno and George Robey, gave scope to Robson's gift for extreme emotional contrasts. Whether or not he had sung it before, it was his incorporation of 'Vilikens and his Dinah' in a revival of Henry Mayhew's one-act farce, *The Wandering Minstrel*, that made both the song and the play popular.

By the time he played Jem Bags in *The Wandering Minstrel*, Robson had left the Grecian, perhaps aware that he had attracted the attention of one or two managers of the more obviously 'legitimate' theatres in London's West End. There is an unconfirmed claim that William Farren, then lessee of the Olympic in Wych Street, advised him to test himself in Dublin before confronting the London critics. Possibly. Farren was a major figure in the comedy of the first half of the nineteenth century, and he has a place in Robson's story. It was certainly in Dublin from 1850 to 1853 that Robson laid the foundation for his decade of glory. His place in the stock company was that of 'low comedian'. In Dublin, as in London, each actor had his or her line of business. The acting edition of Colin Hazlewood's *Waiting for the Verdict*, produced at the City of London Theatre in 1859, details the 'line' opposite the name of each character. Rearranged for easier reading, the list is as follows:

Leading man
Leading lady
Juvenile [lead]
First heavy man
Second heavy man
First old man
Second old man

4. See Appendix 3 (pp. 143–45) of Mollie Sands, *Robson of the Olympic* (London: Society for Theatre Research, 1979).

First walking gentleman
Second walking gentleman
Responsible [there were two of these in *Waiting for the Verdict*]
Utility [and three of these]
Very responsible [here is an actor who will represent the aristo-
cracy or judiciary]
First low comedy
Second low comedy
Chambermaid [or *soubrette*][5]

A nineteenth-century playwright who failed to take account of such lines
of business had little chance of success. Robson may have begun as
'second low comedy' at the Queen's Theatre, Dublin—we can be certain
he was never a bland 'utility' player, since his physique disqualified
him—but if so he was quickly promoted. On 17 June 1850 he presented
a one-man show, *Seeing Robson* (it was played again in 1852), and was
given his first Shakespearean outing, as Lancelot [*sic*] Gobbo in *The
Merchant of Venice* before the end of the season. He would later play,
without evident distinction, Autolycus in *The Winter's Tale* and Bottom
in *A Midsummer Night's Dream*. Robson was at his best in contemporary
dramas, in which his extravagant developments of observable mannerisms and witty parodies of modern dress were readily recognizable. It
was not until the Olympic years that he discovered his own style of
historical grotesquerie in J.R. Planché's antique fairyland. The crowning
event of the Dublin seasons came with the opening, on 22 February
1853, of Mayhew's *The Wandering Minstrel*, almost certainly the first
occasion, though by no means the last, on which he sang 'Vilikens and
his Dinah' during the course of a play.

Jem Bags was the first of Robson's famous roles. Mayhew had created
him out of his intimate knowledge of the London poor: a scrounging
street-vendor, purveying broadside ballads—ineffectively because his
singing voice is cracked with hunger. (Even so, 'Vilikens and his Dinah'
rarely got by without an encore.) The surviving photograph of Robson
as Jem Bags, published in Mollie Sands's biography, is graphic evidence
of his approach to the part. In a tattered tailcoat and torn and patched

5. The list is taken from Gilbert B. Cross, *Next Week—East Lynne* (London: Associated
University Presses, 1977), p. 52. Cross does not mention, and may not have realised,
that Hazlewood's play was a dramatization of Abraham Solomon's sensationally
popular picture 'Waiting for the Verdict' (1857), perhaps amalgamating or perhaps
anticipating its sequel, 'The Acquittal' (1859). The interplay of drama and painting in
the nineteenth century is brilliantly explored in Martin Meisel, *Realizations* (Princeton,
N.J.: Princeton University Press, 1983).

8. Robson as Jem Bags: a little boy lost in adult rags.

MR. F. ROBSON,

AS JEM BAGGS, IN "THE WANDERING MINSTREL."

9. Robson as Jem Bags: resentment has replaced bewilderment.

trousers (Gilbert was certainly alluding to Robson in his wandering minstrel Nanki-Poo, 'a thing of shreds and patches'), gamely challenged by a fanciful hat and a brocaded waistcoat, Robson gazes upwards as if appealing for divine compassion, a little boy lost in adult rags. It is a tableau of pathos. Just how much is invested in an actor's face is evident if the original photograph is compared to the C.P. Nicholls engraving of it. The photographer has captured Robson with his mouth slightly open and soft bags under his eyes to hollow them into exhaustion. The engraver has closed the lips and lowered the corners of the mouth to form a sullen scowl. Resentment has replaced bewilderment. Looking at the photo, I remember how uncomfortable the diminutive Charlie Drake used to make me feel, with his round face and child-like voice, and his near-masochistic accident-proneness (not to mention the beatific smile that turned his pudding-face into an emblem of all that twinkles). There was something in Drake's *persona* that threatened my heartstrings, and I had to fight to laugh. Looking at the engraving, I remember how untouched I was by Norman Wisdom who, knowingly or not, tried to revive the Robson tradition of mingled laughter and pain. Quite simply, Wisdom was too self-conscious, too attention-seeking to achieve what Robson achieved. The audience needs to be able to look away and find their man still there when they look back.

Dublin had not established Robson, but it had given him a legitimate claim on the London stage. He was lucky, though, to find his permanent base so quickly. His years in Ireland had probably delivered the final blow to what was already a rocky marriage. In a declaration dated 8 December 1879, Rosetta Brownbill states that she and her husband lived apart from 1850 to 1861. If there was any stability in Robson's life during his brief stardom, it was provided by the Olympic Theatre. It was William Farren who first employed him there, and Farren was an actor of substance. David Rinear has interestingly argued[6] that his long career—he made his debut in 1806 and retired from the stage in 1855—marks the shift in comic acting from the high artificial style towards the comparatively colloquial. By 1853, when Robson joined the Olympic company, Farren was past his best but he was still a useful model for an untried comedian. He continued to play the 'old' comedies (he was unrivalled as Sir Peter Teazle in *The School for Scandal*) in the artificial style that he felt they demanded, but he was alert enough to tone down his performance in contemporary plays. G.H. Lewes, that most discerning of Victorian critics, calls him 'eminently an intellectual actor', meaning by that description 'an actor who produces his effects not by the

6. See *Theatre Notebook* 31, 1 (1977), pp. 21–27.

grotesqueness or drollery of his physique, but by the close observation and happy reproduction of characteristics'.[7] But Lewes has another point to make about Farren, one which accentuates the contrast between the old actor and his new employee. 'He could touch a chord of pathos gently, but he was quite incapable of expressing any powerful emotion.'[8] This is a deficiency which Lewes observes also in another contemporary hero of the comic stage, Charles Mathews the Younger. It was not a deficiency of Robson's, as Farren surely recognized. The new actor might complement but would never rival him, could play hot to his cool. In the event, it was Robson's singing of the popular street-song, 'The Country Fair', in Charles Selby's *Catching an Heiress* that first endeared him to the Olympic audience. According to Mollie Sands, it elicited from Farren an exclamatory, 'That's very good; he's an actor.'[9] Robson could act a song as well as sing it.

Above all else, his first season at the Olympic established Robson as the genius of burlesque, a Victorian mode that survived fitfully into the twentieth century, not least in the plays that Ernie Wise claimed to have made to the measure of himself, Eric Morecambe and their guest celebrity to provide a lofty conclusion to one series of 'Morecambe and Wise Shows'. While Charles Kean's grandiloquent *Macbeth* was running at the Princess' Theatre, Farren took his cue to revive Francis Talfourd's *Macbeth Travestie*, and gave Robson the role of Macbeth. The result was, in its own way, revelatory. Before Robson, burlesque actors played for laughs. Robson left the laughs in the puns and played the part in earnest, not Shakespeare's Scottish tyrant, of course, but 'an equivalent character drawn from "low life"'.[10] The performance was met with an echoing chorus of critical praise, the common burden of which was the startling introduction of genuine emotion into a kind of drama that had until then been considered antagonistic to it. Henry Morley would write retrospectively of a performer who 'while other people were burlesquing reality, could put such a startling reality into burlesque'.[11] The effect was not to stifle laughter but to increase it (as someone before Robson ought, surely, to have guessed). In Samuel Butler's gloomily autobiographical novel *The Way of All Flesh*, Ernest Pontifex, newly released from prison, visits the Olympic in no condition to enjoy the *Macbeth Travestie*, but

---

7. G.H. Lewes, *On Actors and the Art of Acting* (London: Smith, Elder, & Co., 1875), p. 58.
8. Lewes, p. 56.
9. Sands, p. 45.
10. This perceptive comment is from George Taylor, *Players and Performances in the Victorian Theatre* (Manchester; Manchester University Press, 1989), p. 75.
11. Henry Morley, *The Journal of a London Playgoer, 1851–1866* (London: Routledge, 1891), p. 52.

ON ACTORS AND ACTING

'laughed till he cried' when, after the little Macbeth confessed that the sight of Duncan's boots had deterred him from committing the murder, his wife tucked him under her arm and carried him off the stage. (Butler gets the actress wrong—it was the statuesque Mrs Alfred Phillips, not the petite Mary Keeley—but no matter.)

The financially relieved Farren followed up the success with another Talfourd revival, *Shylock, or the Merchant of Venice Preserv'd*. Again the critics were unanimous. As Shylock, Robson 'adhered to the principle— exclusively his own—of grounding his eccentricities on a really tragic basis'. 'Many of his bursts are truly tragic, and might have done justice to Edmund Kean in his best days. . . . Is there after all but a step from the sublime to the ridiculous?'[12] George Taylor's insight is important: 'for Robson the passions of a local Jewish tailor were just as powerful as those of the Venetian money-lender'.[13] Played this way, burlesque has a social point to make, comparable with the political drive that impelled Brecht to write his telling 'Rehearsal Scenes from Shakespeare'. I have a sense that Robson was an impassioned observer of social injustice, and that the heavy drinking which was already beginning to take its toll was in part the displacement activity of an angry dissident. Only in part. Robson was unnerved by success, terrified that he would be unable to sustain it. As the years passed, he needed to drink before he dared to act, and the exertion involved in playing the most violent of his roles (in general, those in burlesque and the extravaganzas which I will shortly consider) cried out for the recuperative aid of alcohol. This was partic- ularly the case with the third of Robson's great burlesque performances, the title role in Robert Brough's travesty of Legouvé's *Medea*, which drew crowds to the Lyceum to see the regal Adelaide Ristori in the summer of 1856. Ristori's *Medea* opened on 6 June and Brough's bur- lesque on 14 July at the Olympic. Morley wrote of Robson's 'personating jealousy by a wild mingling of the terrible with the burlesque',[14] but his fellow actors noticed the inconsistency of his performances during the run. Uneasy in his relationship with his own children, Robson found Medea hard to keep at a distance. After little more than three years at the Olympic, he had completed most of his best work. I need to backtrack to 1853.

Farren had surrendered the management of the Olympic to another gentleman comic, Alfred Wigan, in 1853, and Planché provided Wigan with an occasional prelude to his first season. *The Camp at the Olympic* is Planché's verse review of the current state of London's theatre.

12. These two quotations are from Sands, p. 51.
13. Taylor, p. 75.
14. Morley, p. 135.

Tragedy, comedy, opera, ballet and spectacle are allowed to speak for themselves. So is burlesque, and the part of Burlesque was allotted to Robson. His Macbeth and Shylock had made it his by right, and Planché gives the character (and the genre) a fair opportunity. Robson presented the case for burlesque as the righteous opponent of tragic 'bombast and puff' and the possessor of some personal dignity:

> When in his [burlesque's] chaff there's not a grain to seize on,
> When in his rhyme there's not a grain of reason,
> His slang but slang, no point beyond the pun,
> Burlesque may walk, for he will cease to run.[15]

The identification with burlesque threatened to dictate Robson's future career, shutting off even the opportunities promised by Jem Bags—of developing a line in little men doing their best in a world too big for them. It was more probably audience demand than managerial preference that ensured him some variety. Alfred Wigan was never entirely easy about the popularity of his low comedian, and certainly not about his addiction to alcohol. Jacob Earwig, the eponymous *Boots at the Swan* in Charles Selby's play, was in the Jem Bags line. Robson had performed it at the Grecian, and revived it at the Olympic in Farren's time: his audience called for it at regular intervals, and Wigan was bound to concede. Jacob is deaf and prone, therefore, to misinterpret his orders, but he has the best possible intentions. It was a charming gift to Robson, who had the gift of charm.

Altogether more serious was the role of Samson Burr in John Oxenford's *The Porter's Knot*, the hit of the 1855–56 season at the Olympic. Samson, having scrimped and saved during his working life as a porter in order to pay for his prized son's training as a doctor, relishes his retirement with the wife he loves. But the spendthrift son has accumulated massive debts. To spare his wife the discovery of her son's depravity, Samson pretends that the debts are his and returns to his job as a porter. The mawkishness is difficult to stomach now, but the Victorians were unembarrassed by sentimentality. According to Clement Scott, '[t]he reconciliation between father and son as played by Robson was one of the most affecting things I ever saw on stage. The audience did not cry; it alternately sobbed and howled.'[16] William Charles

---

15. Of the Planché pieces referred to here, all are in the five volumes of Planché's *Extravaganzas*, published by Samuel French in 1879. *The Camp at the Olympic* and *The Discreet Princess* are in Donald Roy's edition of *Plays by James Robinson Planché* (Cambridge: Cambridge University Press, 1986).
16. Quoted in Sands, p. 102.

Macready, recently retired from the stage, had been a masterly portrayer of suffering fatherhood, a favourite Victorian theme. So, evidently, was Robson. According to one memoirist—and every contemporary critic says much the same in different words—'he stood alone on a peculiar piece of ground—half-way between tragedy and comedy'.[17] For the ductile regulars at the Olympic, Robson was a living image of the divided self. He was neither one thing nor the other, but both contradictory things at once. What he was to himself is not at all clear to me. He was again the little man bewildered as Pawkins in Oxenford's *Retained for the Defence* (1856), a comic role which provided him with Robertsonian opportunities to invent comic business while being defeated by food, but in the title role of Palgrave Simpson's *Daddy Hardacre* he had to make contact with a darker self. For many of his contemporaries, this was his finest dramatic achievement. The play is a fairly straightforward theft from its French source, *La fille d'avare*, but it reaches forward in English literature to George Eliot's *Silas Marner* (1861). Daddy Hardacre loves his daughter and his money—nothing else. And he is deaf even to his daughter's pleas that he help his brother, who has suffered financial ruin and is threatening suicide. It is, of course, his beloved Esther who steals his money to save her uncle. This is a comedy and needs a reconciliation, but the tone of Robson's playing was, at key points, disturbingly violent. Westland Marston's long description of it is startlingly vivid, a window on a vanished theatre.[18] Given scope by the dramatist, Robson could paralyse his audience. Playing 'in earnest' topped the list of Macready's rules for acting; Robson carried the principle from the tragic to the comic stage. He was, concluded Henry Morley, 'a downright good actor',[19] giving authoritative voice to a unanimous verdict.

It is the unanimity of admiration that makes Robson a necessary subject in any serious consideration of nineteenth-century acting. His performance of Daddy Hardacre revived with new vigour the critical demand that he should be given a chance in tragedy. The stage had offered nothing so fiery since the glory years of Edmund Kean; if anyone could restore passion to the frigid tragic drama, surely this was the man. But Robson, however powerfully he struck high tragic notes, never played in tragedy. Was that because he lacked confidence, or was it because he knew his limitations? Seymour Hicks recalled an evening at the Garrick Club, where Irving had invited him to dine. Among the old actors they talked of was Robson. This is Hicks' memory of what Irving said:

17. J.C. Hotten, quoted in W. Clark Russell, *Representative Actors* (London: Frederick Warne & Co., n.d.), p. 416.
18. Marston, pp. 363–67.
19. Morley, p. 51.

Yes, Robson—er—Robson—a good actor, but not great—no, not
great—yes, yes, he was great! He was great enough to know that
he could only be great for three minutes! The stuff they talk
about his being able to have played tragedy, had he wanted to,
is wrong. Three minutes of it—yes—but the whole evening—oh,
dear no![20]

The appearance of authenticity is increased by Hicks' artful reproduction of Irving's famous tricks of speech. It is a well made point, and one
Irving might well have made. But Irving is unlikely to have seen Robson
at his best. There is no evidence of his visiting the Olympic before 1856,
and from then until Robson's death he was only sporadically in London.
As Daddy Hardacre, at least, Robson was called on to sustain pathos on
the borders of tragedy for much longer than three minutes. The secret
of his appeal, though, was in his abrupt transitions from the intense to
the ludicrous. 'He is partly Liston and partly Kean', said the *Quarterly
Review* in 1854,[21] indicating Robson's reliance on the traditions of both
comic mugging and tragic gesture. There were moments, certainly, when
he seemed as ordinary and as recognizable as the man next door, but the
totality of a Robson performance was in no way 'natural'.

The old debate about natural acting has a new focus here. G.H. Lewes
had no truck with those who advocated on stage 'the familiarity of daily
intercourse'.[22] For him, the art of the actor is one of representation. 'He
has to use natural expressions, but he must sublimate them'. All performances, Lewes insists, are necessarily conditioned by *l'optique du théâtre*.
'The art of acting is not shown in giving a conversational tone and a
drawing-room quietness, but in vividly presenting character, while never
violating the proportions demanded on the one hand by the *optique du
théâtre*, and on the other by what the audience will recognise as truth.'
To present a Hamlet whose manners and reactions were those of a
servant would be 'not natural, consequently not ideal, for ideal treatment
means treatment which is true to the nature of the character represented
under the technical conditions of the representation'. Robson would have
understood Lewes' argument. When he was 'natural', it was for theatrical
purposes—for effect. An effortless normality was one of the available
styles in a system of performance based on rapid changes of mood. At
his peak, Robson was a virtuoso; people came to see him *act*, not simply
be. His true Victorian successor was not the loveable low comedian J.L.

20. Hicks, *Seymour Hicks by Himself* (London: Alston Rivers Ltd, 1910), p. 123.
21. Quoted in Clark/Russell, p. 417.
22. This and subsequent quotations are from Lewes' Chapter 10, 'On natural acting'.

10. A. Emery, Robson as the Yellow Dwarf: a malevolent grotesque.

Toole, who inherited many of his comic roles, but Henry Irving, whose virtuosity was similarly salted with mischief.

It is unlikely that Robson on stage would have elicited such compassion for victims and losers if Robson off stage had not felt it. However artfully contrived, his performances were powered by feeling. If he is remembered primarily as the maestro of burlesque, it is because it was that genre that his acting transformed. Lewes, no fan of burlesque, recognized in Robson the proof that 'burlesque acting is the grotesque personation of a character, not the outrageous defiance of all character; the personation has truth, although the character itself may be preposterously drawn'.[23] There was no comparable shift in the writers: this was a reformation led from the stage itself.

Planché was the only playwright to recognize and develop Robson's range in the distinctive world of Victorian nonsense, that curious combination of jocularity and frenzy. *The Camp at the Olympic* had signalled his return to the theatre for which, under the management of Madame Vestris in the 1830s, he had written his first extravaganzas. These flimsy pieces had flourished on their charm, exquisite staging and Planché's skill in the matching of characters to actors. It was that same skill that clinched the triumph of the Christmas extravaganza he wrote for Alfred Wigan at the end of 1854. The plot of *The Yellow Dwarf* was drawn from a fairy tale by Madame d'Aulnoy, but its true provenance is entirely theatrical. Gam-Bogie, the title role, is a malevolent grotesque, and Robson played him in full yellow, with a bald wig and great flaps of false, pointed ears. In the oil painting at the British Theatre Museum, he looks uncannily like the Mekon in 'Dan Dare', a nightmare figure of great importance to the early success of the *Eagle* comic. The play is not a burlesque, not concerned to mock a source, but freestanding for all its dependence on the rhyming couplets and frequent puns that were a staple of burlesque. If an actor of Robson's quality could be found, it would be a fine alternative to our over-familiar Christmas pantomimes, ideally played in a double bill with Planché's next Olympic extravaganza, *The Discreet Princess*. Gam-Bogie (this is a great entrance for a monster of depravity!) is discovered in the branches of an orange tree, beneath which Queen Indulgenta falls asleep. The Queen is on a pilgrimage to find a husband for her spoiled daughter, the Princess Allfair, but she has ventured into dangerous territory. As his reward for saving her from the two-headed lion, Gam-Bogie extracts a promise that she will see him married to the beautiful Princess. In triumph, he sings a song to a tune from *Der Freischutz* and dances a Lancashire clog hornpipe. Planché has appended a wonderfully disdainful note on the dance in the collected edition of his extravaganzas: 'Introduced specially for Mr. Robson who

---

23. Lewes, p. 70.

had made a popular feature of it in the provinces. Neither song nor dance are required in this situation and their omission, as in all cases of forced introduction would be an improvement'. Perhaps he is right, but the sinister glee of the yellow dwarf's dance resonates with Rumpelstiltzkin. This is not the sleazy demon-king of twentieth-century pantomime, but a hideous shape in motion; as if a tormented and tormenting figure from Bosch's imagination were winding his way across a canvas by Watteau. By the time Gam-Bogie reaches Queen Indulgenta's palace, Princess Allfair has surprised herself by falling in love with Meliodorus, King of the Gold Mines (a breeches part for the pretty singer Julia St George), but Meliodorus is deceived and imprisoned, and Gam-Bogie courts the Princess in a scene that alludes to the ferociously comic wooing of the widowed Lady Anne by Richard III:

DWARF: If thy revengeful heart cannot forgive,
            Lo, here I lend thee this sharp-pointed sword,
            And humbly beg my death. *(kneeling)*

ALLFAIR: *(taking the sword)* Upon your word?

DWARF: Aye; do not pause. I cribbed your mother's cake,
            But then I stole it only for your sake.

(Allfair gives him a poke with the sword, but it does not pierce him)
            Go it again! I floored King Meliodorus,
            But 'twas your face made me so indecorus [sic].

(she gives him another poke, without effect, and then flings the sword down)
            Why drop the sword?

ALLFAIR: The deuce is in his luck,
            I try to stick him and he won't be stuck.

DWARF: Take up the sword again, or take up me.

ALLFAIR: You are much sharper than your sword, I see.
            What is the reason through I haven't thrusted you?

DWARF: *(rising)* Because you can't—or I should not have trusted you.
            You don't think such a fool I could have been?
            I'm jolly yellow, but not jolly green.
            This sword a fairy for my father made;
            No cutler ever knew so keen a blade;
            A better tempered weapon cannot be,
            It makes a point of never hurting me.[24]

24. *Extravaganzas*, vol. 5, pp. 60–61.

11. Caricature of Robson as the Yellow Dwarf: that curious combination of jocularity and frenzy.

This is delicious fooling for an informed audience, but there is an undercurrent of sexual exploitation and the climax of the action is disconcerting. Meliodorus escapes from captivity, and returns to the palace to claim his bride, but Gam-Bogie creeps up on the loving couple, recovers his magic sword and kills Meliodorus. The Princess then snatches the sword, stabs herself and dies at Gam-Bogie's feet.

According to Planché, Robson's four lines of lament (the monster really loved the maiden), 'slightly parodied from the wail of Othello over the dead body of Desdemona, moved Thackeray, "albeit unused to the melting mood", almost to tears'. His own verdict endorses the response of that hard-headed novelist: 'So powerful was [Robson's] personation of the cunning, the malignity, the passion and despair of the monster, that he elevated Extravaganza into Tragedy'.[25] *The Yellow Dwarf* does not end on a tragic note, of course. In the finale, Allfair and Meliodorus are magically restored and Robson sings a moral-free 'moral' to the tune of 'Vilikens and his Dinah'. Planché's note is again wry: 'A song in Henry Mayhew's farce of *The Wandering Minstrels* [*sic*], which Robson had previously made exceedingly popular by the dramatic power he threw into it'.[26]

I have described *The Yellow Dwarf* in some detail, partly because it is a work of real quality, but more because the nature of Robson's achievement can be understood only by reference to the material that came his way. As Prince Richcraft in Planché's Christmas extravaganza for 1855, *The Discreet Princess*, he had to impersonate a sadistic villain. Bent on destroying the whole tribe of Ganders, he plans a nasty death for the discreet Finetta:

> Would she had forty thousand lives, that I
> Might forty thousand ways to take 'em try,
> Or that she had but nine lives, like a cat -
> But as she has but one, I will take that
> In such a way that no cat of nine tails,
> Could ever raise of woe such horrid wails.
> Get me a barrel, stick it full of spikes,
> So sharp, nobody ever felt the likes!
> In it I'll cram the baggage like a ball,
> And roll it down the Brockenneckerthal![27]

25. *Extravaganzas*, vol. 5, p. 37.
26. *Extravaganzas*, vol. 5, p. 74.
27. *Extravaganzas*, vol. 5, p. 131.

Delivered with relish, as Robson certainly delivered it, this is Marlowe's Tamburlaine in rhyming couplets, but it is on the work of a slightly later dramatist that Planché calls when Richcraft's murderous scheme is thwarted. After delivering a mad tirade, Robson is instructed in a stage direction to deliver the 'business of Sir Giles Overreach'.[28] It was by his acting of Overreach's madness in Massinger's *A New Way to Pay Old Debts* that Edmund Kean was widely rumoured to have thrown Lord Byron into a fit. The probability is that Planché's stage direction here is less an instruction to the actor than his attempt to describe, in theatrical shorthand, what Robson actually did.

Neither Gam-Bogie nor Prince Richcraft is a particularly long part, but the demands they make on the actor—the frenetic energy and acrobatic engagement that they require—are very considerable indeed. *The Yellow Dwarf* ran for 122 nights, *The Discreet Princess* for over 100. Both were entirely dependent on Robson's exertions. By the Christmas of 1856, when Planché had provided him with another (admittedly lesser) vehicle in *Young and Handsome*, the challenge was beyond him. Planché's introduction makes a slenderly veiled reference to Robson's drinking; '[he] was suddenly attacked by a serious complaint to which he was unfortunately subject, and compelled to give up the part'.[29] Four years at the Olympic had very nearly burned him out. From 1857 until his premature death he performed unpredictably; those who saw him on a good night noticed no diminution in his powers, those who saw him on a bad night put it down to 'the old complaint'. Crabb Robinson, a constant admirer, thought him still at his best in July 1859, but the last of his diary references, dated 13 February 1863, is a sad one: 'The charm of Robson's acting is gone.'[30] G.H. Lewes makes a telling point about Victorian acting: 'Vehemence without emotion is rant; vehemence with real emotion, but without art, is turbulence.'[31] Robson's career on the stage began turbulently and ended in turbulence. It is a career that contradicts any claim that an actor's life is an easy one. I cannot vouch for the truth of Barton Baker's story that 'his terror of facing the audience became so great that while waiting for his cue he would gnaw his arms until they bled', but it may be true. What is certain is that the normally controlled Baker leaps into purple prose when he tries to describe Robson's effect on an audience.[32]

28. *Extravaganzas*, vol. 5, p. 134.
29. *Extravaganzas*, vol. 5, p. 150.
30. Eluned Brown (ed.), *The London Theatre: selections from the diary of Henry Crabb Robinson* (London: Society for Theatre Research, 1966), p. 210.
31. Lewes, p.95.
32. See H. Barton Baker, *The London Stage* (London: W.H. Allen & Co., 1889), vol. 2, pp. 30–31.

11

Irving and the Lyceum
Volcano and Cathedral

Irving was not at all like those actors who are normally recognised as 'great' in their own time, and whose reputation for greatness lingers into future generations. Burbage was strong and athletic, Alleyn monumentally self-assured, Hart and Mohun handsome and gentlemanly after the taste of the time, Betterton refined, Quin stately, Garrick compellingly graceful in action, Kemble dignified, Kean explosive, Macready earnest, but Irving was peculiar. He was neither strong nor athletic; his self-assurance was a mask (as those inside the Lyceum on his painful first nights were likely to notice); he was neither handsome nor gentlemanly; he was certainly not graceful or dignified; his attempts to 'explode' betrayed the weakness of his voice; and his earnestness about the art of the theatre was contradicted by the mischief of his own performances. You would be closer to a twentieth-century equivalent if you thought of David Warner rather than Gielgud or Olivier: 'We called him ungainly Irving and the irreverent name of "the telescope" was applied to him, for we never could gauge his length. When ever it was thought that this had been demonstrated, he would suddenly shoot out half a foot longer in the verve of his acting.'[1]

In the Lyceum company, it was William Terriss who had the attributes of the 'great' actor, not Irving. Sarah Bernhardt listed them in her posthumously published *L'Art du théâtre:* a retentive memory; excellent bodily proportions; and a fine voice. Irving had only the first of these, and might have been expected, according to the distinctive 'lines' of nineteenth-century actors, to be confined to secondary roles. During his years in provincial theatres, he was generally placed as a light comedian, though already with a recognized gift for the sinister. The *Liverpool Courier* reported in 1867 that he had 'fully proved his right to be placed

---

1. Quoted from the *Era* of 27 December 1890 in *First Knight*, vol. 1, no. 2 (1997), p. 60. It should be said that the 'old playgoer' was recording his time with Irving in Manchester in the 1860s. In maturity, Irving eradicated some of his quirkiness.

in the first position on the stage as a light character eccentric comedian',[2] and it was still the opinion of a man as discerning as Charles Reade, at a time when Irving's reputation was at its height, that he should be seen as 'an eccentric serious actor' in distinction from 'an eccentric comic actor' like the American Joseph Jefferson.[3] Irving was alert to the paradox of his own greatness. 'For an actor who can't walk, can't talk and has no face to speak of, I've done pretty well', he said to Ellen Terry.[4] In fact, Irving's face was a craggy asset, but his voice was notoriously unreliable and his legs an invitation to satirists. 'If we Irvingites ever raise a statue to our idol, the anti-Irvingites should pay for the lower half; for without Mr Irving's legs, they would have had little enough to go upon.'[5] He had 'a walk somewhat resembling that of a fretful man trying to get very quickly over a ploughed field', wrote his admiring friend Edward Russell,[6] and William Archer was tempted into an even more graphic analogy: 'It seemed as though locomotion with Mr Irving was not a result of volition, but an involuntary spasm, complicated by extraordinary sidelong and backward skirmishing, reminding one of the movement of a napkin-ring shot out from under the forefinger.'[7]

Since it was clearly not to his physical attributes that Irving owed his supremacy, we have to wonder what it was about him that convinced his contemporaries. Sarah Bernhardt's verdict that he was 'a mediocre actor, but a great artist' is glossed by the explanation that, though his articulation and pronunciation were defective, 'his expression was profoundly thoughtful'.[8] What makes Bernhardt's comments pertinent is her own similarity to Irving. Once her years of youthful beauty were past, she played more and more on her idiosyncrasies and on the evidently strenuous display of her emotional resources: 'I have myself unconsciously created a personal technique, in order to heighten the sonorous music of verse, the melody of words, and the music and the melody of thought.'[9] Bernhardt was not rewarded as readily as Irving with the reputation of being an intellectual actor that neither of them merited; for both of them, though, it was the expenditure of nervous energy in calculated self-display that was interpreted as evidence of an

2. Quoted in Laurence Irving, *Henry Irving* (London: Faber and Faber, 1951), p. 142.
3. See Percy Fitzgerald, *Sir Henry Irving* (London: T. Fisher Unwin, 1906), p. 31.
4. Quoted in George Taylor, *Players and Performances in the Victorian Theatre* (Manchester: Manchester University Press, 1989), p. 157.
5. 'An Irvingite', *Henry Irving* (London: Routledge, 1883), p. 36.
6. Quoted in 'An Irvingite', p. 52.
7. Quoted in Taylor, p. 156.
8. Bernhardt, *The Art of the Theatre*, trans. H.J. Stenning (London: Geoffrey Bles, 1924), p. 65.
9. Bernhardt, p. 124.

active intellect. Their intelligence was an intelligence of feeling that valued 'the music and the melody of thought' above its content. Bernhardt, though, would have been perceived as great in any theatrical era; Irving could have been perceived as great only in the later nineteenth century. This chapter will endeavour to explain that statement.

That the Victorian age experienced a crisis of confidence in the nature of the self is not much in dispute. The effect on the theatre, though, has not been seriously explored. Because Irving manufactured a personality to cope with success, and because that manufactured personality replaced almost entirely—in the public eye, at least—the troubled person it concealed, he offers himself to scrutiny as a peculiarly transparent example of the theatre's response to cultural urgencies. Consider first the manufactured self: his 'huge silk hat, monkish face, iron-grey hair, loose Chesterfield were as subtly distinguished as they were carefully unobtrusive'.[10] Irving's demeanour and the street-costume, described here by the industrious journalist H.G. Hibbert, declared the soberly religious Victorian at the same time as it advertised the star of the Lyceum. It was not at all unobtrusive, but it pretended to be so. The painter Mortimer Menpes, whose sketches of Irving capture the face of a benevolent grandfather with a sternness all for the world, not for the grandchild, knew only the public Irving: 'He radiated some subtle force before which all men became modest and even reverential. What was this mysterious influence? If we could answer that question truly we should solve the problem of what made Irving great.'[11] Menpes ignores the human tendency to pay homage to success, and his conclusion that Irving 'never spoke without thinking' echoes those admiring critics of Irving's acting who assumed that there was profound thought behind every detail of his acting. The achieved image is of an intellectual giant, and if Irving carries some of the responsibility for this absurd projection, it is only because he chose to permit it. In his public life it would seem, as in his acting, even when out of his depth he contrived to be 'interesting'. It is a gift, if not a profound one. Actors need to know their assets and their limitations. If Irving's legs were weak, his wrists and hands were marvellously expressive. Seymour Hicks recognized the art of a fellow professional: 'His hands with their long tapering fingers were eloquent, and he used them with masterly and unerring effect on the stage; the sleeves of his costumes were always cut to show them to full advantage.'[12] Irving had a highly developed sense of himself as the focal point of a stage

10. H.G. Hibbert, *Fifty Years of a Londoner's Life* (London: Grant Richards, 1916), p. 27.
11. Menpes, *Henry Irving* (London: Adam and Charles Black, 1906), p. 41.
12. In H.A. Saintsbury and Cecil Parker, (eds), *We Saw Him Act* (London: Hurst and Blackett, 1939), p. 115.

12. Mortimer Menpes, portrait sketch of Irving: 'line by line, he modelled the beautiful, sensitive face'.

picture. He explained to the Edinburgh Philosophical Institution his view of the drama as 'the art of human nature in picturesque or characteristic action'.[13] Graham Robertson's is a fascinating verdict:

> His artistic life was one long struggle towards perfection; fault after fault he conquered, one by one he laid by his mannerisms,

13. Irving, *The Drama Addresses* (London: Heinemann, 1893), p. 20. The speech is dated 8 November 1881.

line by line he modelled the beautiful, sensitive face that he had evolved from his original immobile and rather ordinary features. To the hour of his death he worked incessantly, his whole career was a progression and those who witnessed his last performance probably saw him at his best.

But Robertson also gives a disturbing account of the price of this 'surrender of self to Art'. Robertson was a painter, and the biographical canvas may be overcoloured, but the odder thing is that it may not:

> His art was his life—his soul. He had vowed himself to it by a pact as awful as that between Faust and Mephistopheles; like Peter Schlemihl, he had sold his reflection; the mirror of memory gives back a score of counterfeit images, but of the true Irving, the dweller in the innermost, hardly a trace.[14]

The ferocity of Irving's commitment to the art of the theatre is a common theme in the reminiscences of those who knew him. Ellen Terry dates it from his failure in the 1867 *Taming of the Shrew*: 'I think this was the peculiar quality in his acting afterwards—a kind of fine temper, like the purest steel, produced by the perpetual fight against difficulties'.[15] But there is an element of disingenuousness in much that Ellen Terry wrote and said about Irving. She willingly gave scope to his self-fashioning, even when she saw through it. Not that the ferocity is in doubt, but the religious solemnity with which Irving presented it masked the pagan puckishness which humanized it. This was something that his old adversary George Bernard Shaw acknowledged long after Irving's death:

> He was utterly unlike anyone else: he could give importance and a noble melancholy, bound up with an impish humour, which forced the spectator to single him out as a leading figure with an inevitability that I never saw again in any other actor until it rose from Irving's grave in the person of a nameless cinema actor who afterwards became famous as Charlie Chaplin.[16]

Dan Leno, who loved to imitate Irving in his major roles, may have anticipated this startling Shavian vision of a jester in the make-up of a king, but Shaw doesn't finish there. On 13 May 1897 he had suggested to Ellen

14. Robertson, *Time Was* (London: Hamish Hamilton, 1931), pp. 162–63.
15. Terry, *The Story of My Life* (London: Hutchinson, 1908), p. 74.
16. Christopher St John, (ed.), *Ellen Terry and Bernard Shaw: a Correspondence* (London: Reinhardt and Evans, 1949), p. xxv.

Terry that Irving became an actor 'to escape from himself'. In the Preface to the *Correspondence*, written in 1929, he tries to place Irving's acting more precisely in historical perspective:

> He achieved the celebrated feat of performing Hamlet with the part of Hamlet omitted and all the other parts as well, substituting for it and for them the fascinating figure of Henry Irving, which for many years did not pall on his audience, and never palled on himself. If those present could have remembered Barry Sullivan's Hamlet in the eighteen-sixties or foreseen Forbes-Robertson's Hamlet of the eighteen-nineties some of them might have said that Irving's Hamlet was neither skilled classic acting nor Shakespear's [*sic*] Hamlet, and that compared to Sullivan he was a limp duffer and compared to Robertson a freak; but most of them would have paid their money none the less to enjoy the performance as an avatar of Henry Irving.[17]

It is a fair comment on the Irving cult, because it acknowledges the extent to which Irving's imperfections enhanced it. The presentation of a new angle on himself was what his public came to see. Irving was the naked actor par excellence. He had manufactured a personality because only that way could he present himself. And the self he presented was as confused and tormented as anyone in the audience. The Lyceum was a confessional theatre in an age of moral concealment. Shaw was half right in 1897: through his acting Irving hid himself from himself, but not from anyone else.

There is nothing far-fetched about that suggestion. Irving was brought up in the context of a humourless Cornish Methodism, and the best educated part of him was his conscience. The defect of a conscience is that it doesn't obstruct sin, it simply ensures that you suffer for it. In order to enter a theatre, the young Brodribb had to embrace guilt: in order to become an actor, he had to cease to be Brodribb. He had had the sermons of the evangelical Edward Irving read to him in his childhood, and he had read Washington Irving's *Sketch Book* for himself. The choice of a name carries its own indications. 'Rip Van Winkle' had an uneasy effect on me in the Methodist manse that was my home: it spoke of change, dissociation and fragile intimacy in ways I could only dimly apprehend, but whose very dimness heightened the effect. When Brodribb elected to become Irving, dissociation must have been in his mind. Because he had been modestly educated, he had no confidence in

17. St John, p. xxviii.

his intellectual powers, but his bottled-up feelings gave him access to forbidden worlds. He would spend his whole theatrical life on the threshold of the forbidden. Unnerved by the ideas to which he was constantly exposed in his professional life, he was peculiarly susceptible to the anxieties of his age. His marriage was a futile attempt at a further self-fashioning, as well, probably, as a bid to subdue the demons of sexual temptation. After its decisive failure, which coincided with his own theatrical success in *The Bells* (1871), he lived in bachelor isolation, but continued to reserve a first-night box for his wife and sons throughout the period of his Lyceum management. His grandson claims that he never spoke to her after their separation.

To younger actors, like John Martin-Harvey and Seymour Hicks, Irving seemed set in unpeopled gloom: 'no man that I ever met was so truly lonely as he', wrote Martin-Harvey, and Hicks found him 'a man of solitary habit and a deep sadness'.[18] Even so, he received and enjoyed the attention of women. Ellen Terry may never have been his lover—though we would do well to wonder whether it would be less strange if she had been—but she refers jestingly to his various 'flames'. If he suppressed his sex drive, it must have been at considerable cost. If he did not, it was a considerable achievement to suppress gossip. After Irving's death in Bradford in 1905, a photograph of himself pasted back-to-back with one of a young woman was found in his pocketbook. Since the publication of Laurence Irving's biography in 1951, it has generally been accepted that the young woman was Nelly Moore, who died in 1869: a touching story of love surviving death, and one which sustains the image of a sentimental Victorian who is master of his urges. But the photographed face, it now appears, was that of a little-known singer called Zare Thalberg, who was about ten years younger than Irving and still alive when he died.[19] None of this *matters*, of course, since we cannot recover the negative and positive effects of sexual loneliness or physical love on Irving's acting, but it is naive to suppose that it made no difference one way or the other. A period so fixated on the moral and medical consequences of masturbation invited neurosis in its population.

The diagnosis and treatment of neurosis was among the most sensational of nineteenth-century developments. Irving played Hamlet as a neurotic; a fundamentally sane man, driven into solitude by bereavement and betrayal, and pitched finally into hysteria by the demands of revenge. Edward Russell's response to the Lyceum performance is indicative:

18. Saintsbury and Parker, pp. 126 and 114.
19. See Alex Bisset, 'The Thalberg mystery', in *First Knight*, vol. 1, no. 1, pp. 7–10.

Hamlet is evidently one of those who . . . find in solitude a licence and a cue to excitement, and who, when alone and under the influence of strong feelings, will abandon themselves to their fancies. Such men . . . will pace rooms like wild animals, will gaze into looking-glasses until they are frightened at the expression of their own eyes, will talk aloud . . . will do almost anything to find vent for emotions which their imagination is powerful enough to kindle, but not fertile or methodical enough to satisfy.[20]

What Russell records is Irving's way of acting out a recognizable nineteenth-century condition: there were men like this in Broadmoor. The Victorians did not yet know enough to deal with the too much they knew. Irving was one of them, and there were many more in his audience. Even friendly critics observed a hysterical quality in his acting, control maintained by the exercise of art against nature. Neurosis caused by a guilty conscience and straining to express itself in hysteria struggles against the will to conceal in many of Irving's best known roles: Mathias, Eugene Aram, Sir Edward Mortimer in *The Iron Chest*. These men, as Irving portrayed them anyway, suffer paroxysms of guilt because of the atrocious crimes they have committed. Their attempts to escape detection are doomed by their own self-knowledge. 'You cannot escape your own conscience' was simultaneously Irving's reminder to himself and his message to the audience. Guilty creatures at the play must have contributed significantly to the ethos of a Lyceum production. Moral health was a middle-class obsession, and neurasthenics were skeletons in family cupboards. There were bedsides at which doctors and churchmen were interchangeable. Irving was inevitably affected by reports of advances in the treatment of neurosis, but his theatrical interest was more in the manifestations of extreme mental states. On visits to Paris, his grandson tells us, he would visit the morgue to study the faces of those who had come to identify the dead. The urge to study grief at first hand may have been uppermost in his mind, but the whiff of the morbid is unmissable.

Death as a theme in Victorian drama, as well as in Victorian society, deserves a study in its own right. Few actors have died more often than Irving. On occasions he could do it mischievously, after the style of Frédérick Lemaître, as he did in the English version of Lemaître's *Robert Macaire* (1883), when, shot through the chest at an upstage window, he walked nonchalantly downstage to lean on a table, smiled and crashed

---

20. Quoted in Alan Hughes, *Henry Irving, Shakespearean* (Cambridge: Cambridge University Press, 1981), p. 51.

13. Irving on holiday in Cornwall, typically with his dog: 'a man of solitary habit'.

down dead. Usually, though, he settled for variations on the established tradition of protracted stage deaths. He did not underrate the importance of observation, but he was unlikely to let probability stand in the way of a strong effect. His guilt-created fatal stroke in *The Bells* owed nothing to medical science. There is a point of some interest here. I do not know whether Irving knew anything of Cesare Lombroso's studies of criminal degeneracy, but the French actor Constant Coquelin certainly did. Lombroso was newsworthy throughout the second half of the nineteenth century, and actors in the intellectual stream would certainly have heard of him. When Coquelin took on Mathias, he played him unsympathetically—as a murderer bearing the physical signs of criminality that Lombroso had identified. Irving's Mathias was an upright bourgeois whose life was blighted by a single crime, committed impulsively on behalf of his impoverished family. When it came to it, and despite his talent for the macabre, Irving was not at ease with sheer evil. Although his dramatic preferences were essentially melodramatic, he could not stomach playing the conscience-free villain. His Iachimo in *Cymbeline*, for all its Mediterranean flourishes, ended up as blood brother to his Eugene Aram.

There is no quicker way of coming to an appreciation of Irving's mastery of a Victorian audience than to read W.G. Wills' mawkish text of *Eugene Aram*. Thomas Hood's then-familiar poem, which provided Irving with his most famous party piece, is travesty enough. The historical Eugene Aram did not carry a burden of guilt into his new life as a schoolmaster, and was not at all relieved to be arrested for the murder he had committed fourteen years earlier. Wills worked according to Irving's instructions in making *Eugene Aram* a follow up to the success of *The Bells*. Aram is shown on the eve of his marriage to the parson's daughter, who has seen in him a 'haunting melancholy' (Irving was undoubtedly good at haunting melancholy) that seems to her discordant with 'A life as gentle, blameless, and as pure/As blows the wind o'er beds of lavender'. Wills, it will be clear, uses blank verse to gloss over the slackness of his similes. The idyll is troubled only by Aram's anguish when people praise him for his virtue, until the arrival of Houseman, shameless accomplice in the crime that led to the murder. In two short acts, the whole action is over. It has been prefigured in the play's third speech, when Jowell the gardener warns his eight-year-old son that '[a] bad conscience, Joey, is like baby at home; it sleeps all day, and then wakes up with a squall!'. The final act, set in the churchyard, is occupied with Aram's confession to Ruth and his remorseful death. The murder, it turns out, was committed in outrage at the heartless wronging of a woman he loved. Ruth is all compassion and Aram dies, having seen his 'first, faint glimpse of Heaven' in her eyes. Clement Scott's notice was largely devoted to the slenderly written Act Three:

> The confession was listened to with the deepest attention, and the oncoming death, now at the tomb, now writhing against the tree, and now prostrate upon the turf, brings into play an

157

amount of study which is little less than astonishing, and an amount of power for which credit would have been given to Mr Irving by few who have seen his finest performances. We feel we have but incompletely given an idea of the high thought and judgement given in the play . . .[21]

There is no hint of high thought and judgement in Wills' text, any more than there was any 'astonishing' study behind Irving's portrayal of 'oncoming death'. The triumph of the production was a triumph of sheer theatricality over semipoetic drivel. Irving's dance of death in *Eugene Aram* shows how fully he shared the age's sentimental addiction to the numinous. If there are intimations in the play of a growing contemporary interest in psychopathology—something which might, after all, explain Clement Scott's evaluation of it (Scott was inclined to take a tabloid interest in the new science)—I cannot detect them. It would seem that the mere portrayal of a criminal's remorse was, in 1873, sufficient incentive for Wills and Irving. What continues to puzzle me is the question of the reception of such a play by a dumbstruck audience. What did *they* think it was about? And what were they sensing while Irving's neurasthenic hero paced the stage? The freight carried by the story of Eugene Aram is far heavier than Wills' play admits. Eighteen years earlier, Tennyson had published his battering monodrama *Maud*, which chronicles the descent into madness of a man who kills for love. Tennyson described his poem as 'a little *Hamlet*, the history of a morbid, poetic soul, under the blighting influence of a recklessly speculative age'. Its virtuosity has contributed to its being often underrated in post-Victorian England, and that is a pity. Tennyson writes from inside the skin of the tortured self he has projected into the poem. He *is* the narrator more wholly than Irving *was* Eugene Aram, but not necessarily more wholly than was suggested by Irving's performance of the 'morbid, poetic soul'. *Maud* is an eccentric masterpiece, a visceral journey into the nineteenth-century nightmare of neurosis. For a man of Irving's temperament, it was natural to invest Eugene Aram with the fevered imagination of Tennyson's narrator, of Tennyson himself. It was not until late in both their lives that Irving and Tennyson joined forces in the Lyceum. It was as Tennyson's Becket, a twelfth-century archbishop traumatized by Victorian doubt, that Irving ended his theatrical life, and that is oddly appropriate. The two men were accepted as representative 'great' Victorians: the first poet to be made a Lord, the first actor to be knighted. But there is more to it than that. Tennyson and Irving shared

21. Saintsbury and Parker, p. 68.

a capacity on the one hand to pulverise the public by their virtuosity, and on the other to resemble the public in their struggle with demons. In their confessional imperative, too, they are representative Victorians.

In private life Irving occasionally revealed a rakish sense of humour, but he was squeamish in the theatre. Ibsen's themes disgusted him more even than Shaw's. It is legitimate here to wonder what is masked by a strenuous adherence to propriety. The argument that sexual and emotional repression were among the dynamics of empire building is a familiar one (the narrator of *Maud* escapes from madness through patriotic participation in the Crimean War). Irving's empire was the Lyceum, and his magnetism was such that he convinced the London public that it was the proper home of Shakespeare and the classic drama when, in fact, his Shakespeare was a pictorial artist and the 'classic' drama was melodrama. There was, however, no conscious hypocrisy in his credo: 'All Art is worthy, and can be seriously considered, so long as the intention be good and the efforts to achieve success be conducted with seemliness.'[22] He would like to have kept the Lyceum clear of the raging debates about the sources of human behaviour; so, at least, his head told him. Instead, his performances embodied many of those debates. They would not have seized the public imagination otherwise. Here, three of them are considered.

It was rarely his intellect that guided Irving into his probings of the psyche. His engagement in debate was sometimes involuntary, sometimes intuitive. The softening of villainy in his creation of Mathias, Eugene Aram, Shylock and Richard III, for example, drew down on him accusations of effeminacy at a time when issues of gender were coming under scientific scrutiny. Richard von Krafft-Ebing's *Psychopathia Sexualis* was published in 1882, and its vocabulary of 'inversion', 'perversion', 'sadism' and 'masochism' spread much more widely than the book itself. In England it intervened in the debate about manliness that had been popularized by Charles Kingsley and the 'muscular Christians'. The shackles of manliness tightened in the second half of the nineteenth century and the male came to be presented in two contradictory ways. He was the beast whose appetite threatened the female 'angel': he was the strength that stabilized the wavering woman. (Truth is 'manly', Lombroso argued: witness the derivation of 'testament' and 'testimony' from the Latin *testis*.[23]) It was Kingsley's remarkable project to reconcile

22. *The Drama Addresses*, p. 143. The speech to the Edinburgh Philosophical Institution is dated 9 November 1891.
23. See G.F. Drinka, *The Birth of Neurosis* (New York: Simon and Schuster, 1984), p. 164.

the conflicting versions of masculinity. Yes, the male was bestial, but that bestiality could be harnessed to strength if it was acknowledged rather than suppressed. The whole male self is inspired by 'some deep, dark, central force' which can be made to work for good.[24] A manly man, that is to say, should acknowledge the source of his manhood: a primal force with the explosive power of a volcano. For Claude Mellot, in Kingsley's novel *Yeast* (1850), his beard is 'a testimony and a sign that a man has no right to be ashamed of the mark of manhood'. Irving was self-consciously aware that beardless actors stood out in the society of his time, and for a while tried to tone down the feminine grace of his hand movements on stage. But the most effective counter to those few critics who saw in the Lyceum a temple of the epicene was Ellen Terry. Hers was the essential female presence in the hothouse atmosphere of Irving's theatre, and he had the wisdom to recognize it. He was not equipped, as William Terriss was (or Wilson Barrett), to play out the manly man. At his subtlest, though, he could call on a sensitivity that was 'feminine'.

Irving was unwilling to be drawn into debates about gender and sexuality, but that did not prevent him from being a subject in some of them. The controversy in which he engaged most openly was that over hypnosis. The word had been coined in mid-century by the Manchester surgeon James Braid, and it is probably evidence of the superficiality of Irving's interest that it is the more old-fashioned figure of the mesmerist who features in *The Bells*. The scientific study of hypnotism reached its peak in the 1880s, when its centres were in Nancy, Vienna and Paris rather than London. Even so, probably more so because responsible knowledge was hard to come by, England was hospitable to wild speculations throughout Irving's life. In late adolescence he had allowed himself to be hypnotized by a friend,[25] and the mystery intrigued him. It intrigued many other people as well. The 'good' hypnotist might have the power to alleviate suffering or even to cure illness, it was claimed, but what about the 'bad' hypnotist? Hippolyte Bernheim, working in Nancy, explored the possible connection of hypnotism and crime. In a particularly gruesome experiment, he tried to hypnotize subjects into committing a fantasy murder, and he made legal history by arguing in court that two felons had been hypnotized into committing their crimes by people of overpowering evil.[26] It is the coincidence of murderer and

24. The quoted phrase and much of the argument and the subtitle of this chapter are derived from an essay by David Rosen in Donald Hall (ed.), *Muscular Christianity* (Cambridge: Cambridge University Press, 1994), pp. 17–44.
25. See Laurence Irving, p. 51.
26. See Drinka, pp. 153–54.

mesmerist that *The Bells* is overtly concerned to sensationalize: the criminal can be hypnotized into confession. But if the criminal, why not the non-criminal sinner? What of the exposure of the bestial primal force within the manly man of muscular Christianity? The unconfinability of hypnotism, its potential invasion of the unspeakable aspirations or past misdemeanours of the secret self, exercised a powerful grip on the Victorian psyche, and *The Bells* remained in Irving's repertoire throughout the last thirty-four years of his life. The troublesome issue is, of course, the location of the true self. Do we make our selves or are we made by them? If I am not what I seem, who is? And brooding over all these questions in the Lyceum is the slippery self of the chameleon actor. It is small wonder that *The Bells*, however shallow its scientific base, unnerved Victorian audiences.

With Herbert Beerbohm Tree as Svengali in *Trilby*, the subject of hypnotism received slightly more adult treatment, and it was probably in a spirit of emulation (Svengali should have been *his* part) that Irving commissioned Robert Hichens and H.D. Traill to write *The Medicine Man* (1898). This was the only play staged under his management in which Irving appeared in contemporary dress, and its failure may have owed something to that. The pictorial splendour and loose folds of period costume went some way towards disguising his awkward angularity. The older he grew, the more awkward he felt on stage in modern dress. The plot of *The Medicine Man* required from him the exhibition of will power as a rational version of hypnotism. Dr Tregenna does not hypnotize his victims, he overwhelms them into submission. As so often, critics wrote of the magnetic power of Irving ('animal magnetism' was the name Franz Mesmer gave to the fluid in the human body that his treatments aimed to regulate), and of his mesmerizing eyes. It is not uncommon to find references to the hypnotic force of great acting, and it may be delusion to believe that the force was ascribed to Irving more often than to any other actor. He certainly employed all the artificial aids available to him—costume, lighting, scenery, the arrangement of actors on the managed stage—in order to enforce focus on himself; and this carries some equivalence to the swinging pendulum or to the fixed point of focus of the hypnotist. Louis Parker's jocular description of the aura of the Lyceum contains the truth it almost succeeds in deriding:

> The house became a temple. Even the pit was holy ground. We were inclined to take our shoes off on entering; the people in the more expensive seats were obviously the cream of London, and the plays—ah, but this was a very mischievous effect of the

161

spell!—the plays were all heaven-sent masterpieces, and were all equally great. We lost all sense of proportion. *The Corsican Brothers* seemed as notable as *Hamlet*; *The Lyons Mail* was as great as *Macbeth*, *Eugene Aram* as great as *Othello*.[27]

Parker's point that the Irving spell warped the judgement of his 'subjects' is a perfectly serious one. The artful mixing of sincerity with chicanery was a hallmark of the Lyceum, and the figure of the hypnotist is not inappropriate to it.

The third area of debate is the one which engaged Irving most comprehendingly. He was as enthralled by images of the double life as any reader of *Dr Jekyll and Mr Hyde*. This is not a point that needs labouring. Any consideration of Irving's repertoire of roles enforces the recognition that he specialized in expositions of duality. The archetypal moment occurs towards the end of Act Three of *The Lyons Mail* when the virtuous Lesurques is about to be condemned for a crime committed by his vicious double, Dubosc. 'This man', says the magistrate Daubenton, 'is a monster, or a martyr'; but the option is a false one. The actor is both monster (Dubosc) and martyr (Lesurques), and the audience is complicit in his duality. It is an inviting illusion of Stevenson's fiction that the evil in a man can be totally separated out from the good, incarnated in bodies that no longer resemble each other. The Victorian leitmotif of the double life rarely relies on such transparency to ensure resolution. Concealment of evil remained a possibility in life: Dorian Gray is still beautiful. Many of the stalwart Victorians in the Lyceum audience would have been familiar with duplicity: it was the price exacted by rectitude in an unforgiving society. Irving paid it as often as anyone. The well-attested alliance between actor-manager and faithful audience at the Lyceum was delicately balanced. It involved an agreement that Irving would create characters in whom opposite qualities were seen in unlikely combination. There was not much subtlety in Lyceum dramaturgy: it was only the acting that entertained complexity.

Irving was not a classical actor. He conceived his characters in terms of moral contradiction and developed them through detail. It is in his by-play that we can read his true strangeness. Henry Arthur Jones recalls him as Dubosc, patting a horse as he murdered a postboy: 'There was a relation in it. He could not have patted the horse like that if he hadn't just murdered his postboy.'[28] What Jones has perceived is that Irving could be more terrifying in his gaiety than in his terror. This pairing of

---

27. Saintsbury and Parker, p. 101–2.
28. Jones, *The Shadow of Henry Irving* (London: Richards, 1931), pp. 44–45.

sublimity and buffoonery is unusual, but not unique. Théophile Gautier claimed it for Garrick and for Lemaître: 'He is awe-inspiring and ludicrous; he terrifies you and amuses you; he is afraid of nothing, not even triviality, for he knows that in a moment he can be sublime if he wishes.'[29] Irving's route to sublimity took him through triviality. He built his cathedral complete with gargoyles, holy and unholy in eerie proximity. But the Lyceum was, for a time at least, a Gothic cathedral dedicated to the art of the theatre. That is how contemporaries *felt* it. Irving's official language was as spiritually soaked as Stanislavsky's, but he had an unofficial language as well. Its vocabulary, I believe, was one which welled up from what was then conceived as the volcanic centre of his manhood. It was through performance that he strove to resolve the inner conflicts that oppressed him. What the Lyceum audiences witnessed, and what the most suggestible of them experienced, was a sort of *psychomachia*: a struggle within the psyche. They were onlookers, they were voyeurs, and those under the 'fluence' were also invited to acts of introspection.

---

29. Quoted in Robert Baldick, *The Life and Times of Frédérick Lemaître* (London: Hamish Hamilton, 1959), p. 245.

Part Three

SHAKESPEARE IN THE TWENTIETH CENTURY

A Note to Part Three

There is a need for some explanation of the form in which Part Three is presented. It is a return, from a more determinedly twentieth-century perspective, to issues explicitly treated in Part One and implicitly in much of Part Two. Whether or not we like the fact, the British theatre remains improbably reliant on Shakespeare. Directors and actors make reputations for themselves through interpreting his plays, regional playhouses schedule them for peak-time playing, and many children owe their first experience of 'live' theatre to a national syllabus that dares not exclude him. Because my experience of the New Globe has given me grounds for optimism about that playhouse in particular, and a breath of hope for the beleaguered British theatre at large, it seems apt to conclude the book with a chapter about it. The open stage and the insistently *present* audience have, after all, renewed the 'old' invitation to actors to assert themselves (and the new-fangled director to take a back seat). That is not to say that the New Globe is uncontroversially a triumph of historical reconstruction, but any playhouse that is good for actors is a cause for celebration.

The Shakespeare Memorial Theatre at Stratford has seen some fine performances, but it is not a generous acting space. Much of the innovative work there during the last half of the twentieth century has involved architectural and scenic efforts to transform it into a different playing place, but the auditorium remains stubbornly itself. I know: I have slept there. The Swan is unique and vibrant, The Other Place is hospitable, but Stratford's main house is a problem. My first experiences of it belong to the 1950s, when the D'Oyly Carte company was still making annual Gilbert and Sullivan visits. I have vague memories of Emlyn Williams as a tattered Shylock, Alan Badel as Hamlet, Anthony Quayle as Othello. It was during Quayle's period as artistic director (he was too modest to become an actor-manager in the Benson-Tree-Wolfit tradition), from 1948 to 1957, that Stratford began to steal its star performers from London, and the theatre was already on the global tourism circuit by the time Peter Hall was appointed artistic director in 1960. Hall, whatever one's views of his quality as a director, was a manager in the league of Garrick and Irving. The Royal Shakespeare Company was his creation, but a change of name could not transform the Royal Shakespeare Theatre. To remain solvent, the Company had (and has) still to fill it. During the 1960s, though, the old monumental playhouses were coming under pressure from theatre-workers whose ambition was to go *out* to find new audiences rather than to stay *in* and wait for visitors. Without much personal involvement, Hall incorporated Theatregoround as a satellite, and The Other Place became a sort of garden shed appendage to the main house. I have a hazy memory of hearing the young Mike Leigh talk about his vision for its development, and the iconoclastic performance-artist Roland Conrad Miller was, I think, part of an unlikely team. The RSC opened its London base at the Aldwych in 1960, received its first Arts Council subsidy in 1963, and had built up a healthy deficit by the time Hall handed over to Trevor Nunn in 1968.

It was in 1970 that Kenneth Muir, then editor of *Shakespeare Survey*, asked me to write the journal's annual report on the Stratford season. With the exception of 1971 (Muir had forgotten to tell me that the invitation was for three years), I continued to write these reviews until 1975. Since then, I have been quite often asked for permission to republish extracts, and it is partly for that reason that I have thought it proper to make available here some of the material that has been long out of print. But there is a more important reason. My work for *Shakespeare Survey* forced me to question the function of a drama critic. I had recently delivered a series of undergraduate lectures on acting from Betterton to Irving for which my best sources had been Colley Cibber, Lichtenberg, Charles Lamb, Hazlitt, Leigh Hunt, G.H. Lewes, Dutton Cook, Westland Marston, Barton Baker, Joseph Knight and Clement Scott. More immediately in my experience was the weekly alternative of Harold Hobson or Kenneth Tynan. The task of a drama critic, it seemed to me, was to reproduce in words what it was like to be *there*, but without ducking away from a responsibility to enter into contemporary debate. *Shakespeare Survey* gave me a lot more space than that allotted to newspaper reviewers and, since my reports were not published until well on into the following year, I was not going to affect attendance at the theatre. But my efforts simultaneously to emulate Hazlitt and Tynan increased my respect for both men.

The first half of the 1970s was a period of simmering excitement in the British theatre as a whole. With the recent abolition of dramatic censorship, a new and more strident generation of playwrights was making its voice heard. The RSC had strengthened its hold on the Arts Council, on the global audience at home and abroad, and even, to some extent, on schools and universities, but it wasn't easy for Stratford to escape the tang of irrelevance when so much was happening on the fringe. Looking back now, I realize how much harder it was for Margaret Thatcher to inflict damage on Shakespeare than on the alternative theatre—the one that claimed its right to intervene in the political life of the nation. My personal allegiance was to that alternative theatre, and my annual forays to Stratford were those of an observer. An impulse to shake Shakespeareans by the throat may have affected what I wrote, but then, so may a contradictory impulse to *become* a Shakespearean. My experience as a reviewer of performances made me aware of the insidious tendency to look over one's shoulder at the cleverer person next door.

The first of my Stratford years included Brook's *A Midsummer Night's Dream*, and the last included Buzz Goodbody's *Hamlet*. They were the most exciting performances I saw. In their very different ways, they both encouraged the critical tendency to place the RSC as a director's theatre in opposition to the actors' theatre that Olivier had established at the National. But it was the *acting* that excited me in both these remarkable productions. My reviews of both are included in the extracts that follow, along with those of two versions of *Measure for Measure* (1970 and 1974) and one of *Twelfth Night* (1974). Readers will also find examples of my engagement in debates that seemed important at the time. It has been pointed out to me by friendly advisers that this chapter sits oddly in such a book as this. Much of it makes uncomfortable reading for me, too (Tennyson's reference to 'stepping-stones of our dead selves' has always a ring of truth); but the 1970s were my present tense when these reviews were written, and that is the tense in which I still try to write. The theatre we have in 2000 is not the one I expected in 1970 or 1975.

12

Shakespeare at Stratford
1970–1975

The Season of 1970

Trevor Nunn in 1970 must have been uncomfortably aware of the inevitable comparison with Peter Hall in 1960. What are the prospects now? There is a company unique in the British theatre, an audience unique anywhere, and an international reputation which can as well diminish as increase. Above all, after the daring of the previous decade, the conditions are right, for the first time since the Restoration, for the establishment of an English ensemble theatre with a style of its own and an aim in view.

The 1970 season has left all the roads open. Trevor Nunn's decision has been not to decide. Each of the first seven plays had a different director; there was no evident linking of the repertoire; there were as many designers as directors; no clear message for the seventies emerged. The confirmed existence of a Royal Shakespeare *Company* has, for several years, tempted speculation about a 'company style'. Over the season I observed none that could be usefully separated from the actors' individual expression of their variable sameness. There is no master method of voice production that can link Sebastian Shaw's habit of hesitating among words with Ian Richardson's masterful summoning and dismissal of them. There is no single rigorous leadership seeking to expose to these two actors their tendency to discover in each character they play a psychological reason for speaking as they most naturally and confidently speak. There is no new uniformity in the verse-speaking, though the 'pushing and chopping technique' which Gareth Lloyd Evans described in *Shakespeare Survey* 22 is still prominent. There is no doubt, nor *need* there be any regret, that the Royal Shakespeare Company in 1970 continues to accommodate more ideas than it defines.

Measure for Measure (1970)

Nothing unthought happens in a play directed by John Barton. The Duke's desk, in the opening scene of [this production], is piled high with dusty books, probably the overspill of this endearing eccentric's untidy library. Angelo uses the same desk in II.ii., but there are no books on it. He loves neither dust nor scholarship. The desk has become a judgement table. Angelo is busy at it when Isabella is first admitted. 'You're welcome' he announces tonelessly, then looks up, *sees* her, and continues, 'what's your will?'. The pause is not a long one, but a lot of work is done in it. The process begun there is confirmed in II.iv when Angelo, admitting his lust, moves from behind the judgement table impulsively towards Isabella, and she, in escaping, replaces him. Isabella, at that moment, judges Angelo. (It was, I think, at II.iv.125.) There is some danger that, in the pursuit of significant detail, Barton will shy away from Shakespeare's larger gestures. There is nothing certainly wrong in having Claudio (in a blonde wig suggestively similar to Angelo's) eat a prison meal whilst the Duke exhorts him to 'Be absolute for death', but, in offering an alternative object of attention, such an action is, I think, false to the text. Such falseness is less obvious where the pursuit of truth is less meticulous; and it should be stressed that this *Measure for Measure* is serious, intelligent, and sometimes dull. The dullness gathers around Sebastian Shaw's Duke. To the Shakespeare Conference, John Barton described the Duke as a 'complex, inconsistent man', adding that 'the *point* of the part is its inconsistencies'. Shaw spoke it like a man conscious of his own complexity and willing to keep slow pace with it. He found prose rhythms even in the octosyllabics of III.ii, but only by blurring stress and unstress and placing the words round pauses. If the pipe-smoking eccentric of I.i. seemed wise, it was partly because his sniggering councillors behaved foolishly; and if the good humour remained with him, even embracing a quizzical fondness for Lucio, it wasn't always distinguishable from simple-mindedness. Certainly the gravity with which this Duke followed his own thought processes exposed more triteness than sagacity in his pronouncements. At the end of the play Isabella was left alone on stage, puzzled still for an answer to the Duke's proposal. Such an ending is, of course, a rejection of comedy convention in the pursuit of psychological consistency—unnecessary but not uninteresting. Estelle Kohler's Isabella was always imperfectly aware of her real feelings. I am uncertain whether Miss Kohler was acting the character's uncertainty or making drama out of her own uncertainty about the character. Something was missing, although a lot was there. Neither the Duke nor Isabella held me as Mariana and Angelo did. Watching Sara Kestelman this season, as Jane Shore, Mariana and

171

Hippolita/Titania, I have felt in touch with future greatness. Mariana is given unusual prominence in this production. She is, writes Anne Barton in a programme note, the one character who 'exists as an uncriticized absolute', and, by placing the interval immediately before the play's move to the moated grange, John Barton has reinforced his view that *Measure for Measure* undergoes a radical shift of emphasis with the introduction of Mariana. Hers is the dominant presence in Act V (should it be?), a pale, auburn-haired, pre-Raphaelite beauty whose dejection has produced in her no hesitancy. Angelo was given a less helpful introduction. The Duke's [Act I] announcement of his deputy was met with concerted chuckles by the assembled officers. (Even stranger was the giggle with which Friar Thomas greeted the Duke's, 'hence shall we see, / If power change purpose, what our seemers be'.) I was disturbed by this. Right government was *not* a serious issue in I.i., so that Claudio's subsequent condemnation lacked political definition. It seemed as peripheral as the trial of Froth and Pompey, a scene that was neither funny nor controlled in this production. It was left to Ian Richardson to establish his own authority as Angelo. Richardson's indi-viduality is strongly marked in this Company. Dangerously so, perhaps. Buckingham, Proteus and now Angelo stood out as cold-blooded, precise figures whose disdain for baser men was signalled in the carriage of the head, the subtle modulation of the voice, and the sparse, carefully expres-sive gestures. All accurately acted, they were all improbably similar. But the theatrical delight of such accomplished playing is irresistible—the greeting of Isabella in II.iv when, seated on his desk, he pulls a chair towards him with his foot and indicates with a flick of the right hand that she should sit; the distaste with which he handles the Duke's dusty books in I.i.; the fastidious wiping of his fingers, which becomes an image of his misanthropy, later to be parodied in the Abhorson/Pompey scene; the desperate phrasing of,

> Would yet he had liv'd!
> Alack! When once our grace we have forgot,
> Nothing goes right: we would and we would not.   (IV.iv.35–37)

There must be some questioning of so physically 'beautiful' an Angelo, and of Barton's decision to have him seize Isabella's hair in II.iv. to pull her down on to the judgement table and stroke her body from breast to groin, but there is no doubt of the continuing control of Richardson's performances. John Barton suggested to the Shakespeare Conference that *Measure for Measure* is 'Isabella's play'. Timothy O'Brien's set pushed it further towards Angelo. The wall-blocks of panelled wood indicated, but did not complete, a box-set. Continued into semi-parquet flooring and slung, wooden ceiling, they had a clinical (puritanical?) cleanliness and a forbidding solidity. But the perspective was sharply exaggerated, a distortion of the geometrical form it adumbrated, and a realisation almost of Angelo's mentality. It must have been a beautiful model. Full-size, it tended to crush the play.

A Midsummer Night's Dream (1970)

[I watched the second night of this famous production.]

When Peter Brook directed *Measure for Measure* at Stratford, he illustrated Pompey's account (IV.iii.1–21) of the inmates of the prison by bringing them on in a hideous parade of corruption and disease. John Barton followed the idea in 1970, but his gathering of felons became a jolly thieves' kitchen with a *Beggar's Opera* tunefulness. Peter Brook and John Barton could scarcely be more different. Barton looks for ways of revealing theatrically what he has discovered in reading a text. Brook prefers to make his crucial discoveries in rehearsal, believing that theatrical revelation must not be anticipated but 'risked'. The opposition of an 'intellectual' and a 'spiritual' theatre might be argued from their differing approaches. Peter Brook's production of *A Midsummer Night's Dream* is the sensation of the 1970 season. Those who did not respond to it will feel compelled to argue against it. Those for whom it was a uniquely joyful experience will regret the cribbed confinement of the cavillers, who lost the light for a handful of prejudices. I am decidedly of the second party, and can only with hesitation undertake to analyse an experience that came to me whole. I think I understand now what Brook means when he describes himself as a man 'searching within a decaying and evolving theatre.'[1] It is not enough that the Royal Shakespeare Company should serve Shakespeare. It must be prepared, from its position of privilege, to serve the British theatre, which finds itself, in 1970, threatened materially by, for example, a new minimum wage for actors, and spiritually by a loss of faith in the holiness of its art. One member of the *Dream*'s cast told me that working with Peter Brook was 'fantastic. It changes your life'.[2] England has a bad record in its treatment of wayward theatrical genius. Some of the attacks on Peter Brook ring like repeating history, but no one to whom I talked at Stratford was ready with outright condemnation of *A Midsummer Night's Dream*. One Shakespearean scholar confessed that he shut his eyes during the performance, loving the way it was spoken, hating the way it was

1. Brook, *The Empty Space* (London: McGibbon & Kee, 1970), p. 100.
2. For the record, this was Ben Kingsley, who played Demetrius.

presented.[3] And yes, it was superbly spoken, despite the fact that Brook gave no textual notes throughout the rehearsal period.[4] I choose to believe that the actors spoke well because the director had renewed in them a generous anxiety to communicate with the audience. It was no accident that the programme notes featured Meyerhold's insistence that 'There is a fourth *creator* in addition to the author, the director and the actor—namely, the spectator. . . . From the friction between the actor's creativity and the spectator's imagination, a clear flame is kindled'. At the end of the performance Puck's 'Give me your hands, if we be friends', was taken as the cue for the actors to leave the stage and walk through the auditorium shaking hands with the audience. It was the culmination of a feast of friendship. I was moved.

The design by Sally Jacobs set the play among white walls rising to about eighteen feet and topped by a practical gallery from which actors not on stage were constantly surveying those who were, and contributing where necessary to the mechanics of the staging. Two upstage doors, much narrower than their Elizabethan counterparts but similarly placed, provided the only access at stage level, but there were ladders at the downstage end of both the side walls, and trapezes slung from the flies could lower and raise Oberon, Puck, Titania and the four fairies. The costumes were vivid, of no single period, aiming at beauty and the actors' comfort. Puck was in a glossy yellow clown-suit and blue skull-cap. Demetrius and Lysander wore smocks of the currently popular smudged pastel design over pressed white flannels, Helena and Hermia long, side-slit dresses with the same smudged pastel decoration. Oberon wore deep purple, Titania bright green, the Mechanicals the working clothes of British labourers in the age of austerity. The Fairies, unobtrusive amid the colour, wore practical suits of grey silk. Against white walls, costume stands out. So do properties. The trees were coiled wire mobiles, hung out from the gallery, which produced metallic music as they twisted and settled. Hermia, walking alone at the end of II.ii., was threatened and snared by them in a nightmare realisation of 'the fierce vexation of a dream'. At the amazing end of III.i. (immediately followed by the interval), the stage was a bedlam of flying plates and flashing tinsel darts, the wild confetti for the 'marriage' of Titania and Bottom. The play's magic was replaced by circus tricks. Brook has described the reasoning:

> . . . Today we have no symbols that can conjure up fairyland and magic for a modern audience. On the other hand there are

3. I can reveal, after all this time, that the scholar was Harold Jenkins.
4. According to a conversation with John Kane, who played Puck.

a number of actions that a performer can execute that are quite breathtaking. So we went to the art of the circus and the acrobat because they both make purely theatrical statements. We've worked through a language of acrobatics to find a new approach to a magic that we know cannot be reached by 19th-century conventions.[5]

I am not convinced of the necessity of the substitution, but its effectiveness in the theatre can be assessed only in the theatre; and even there not argued, only perceived or denied. At II.i.246, Puck swings down on a trapeze, spinning a plate on a rod. Oberon, on a lower trapeze, looks up to ask, 'Hast thou the flower there? Welcome, wanderer', and Puck leans over to tip the still-spinning plate on to Oberon's rod—'Ay, there it is'. The plate does not *become* the flower. Instead, the act of passing it becomes the *magic* of the flower. In order to harry Lysander and Demetrius in III.ii., Puck climbs on six-foot stilts and darts around the stage in a new-established convention of invisibility that makes stage poetry out of a scene normally surrendered to a dead convention. I feel no inclination to defend any of Brook's decisions. I doubt whether the play could have been so well spoken if it had been seriously falsified. It should, however, be recorded that there was doubling of Theseus and Oberon, Hippolita and Titania (the change at IV.i.102 was simply managed, though with remarkable poignancy, by having Oberon and Titania walk up to the stage doors, don cloaks and turn to walk downstage as Theseus and Hippolita), Philostrate and Puck, Theseus's courtiers and the fairies, so that the lovers carried with them into their dream all the familiar faces of the Athenian court. And it should also be admitted that a man more musically accomplished than I would annotate the variety of Richard Peaslee's score where I can only applaud it. More than anything I have ever seen, this production declared its confidence and delight in the art of performance. In doing so, it went, for me, beyond the meaning of the play to a joyous celebration of the fact that it was written. And it did all its work in full view of the audience. I am reminded of another of Peter Brook's stated beliefs: 'This is how I understand a necessary theatre; one in which there is only a practical difference between actor and audience, not a fundamental one'.[6]

[I am astonished to discover that my review makes no mention of the Mechanicals. In fact, it was their utter seriousness, the fact that they

---

5. Quoted in an excellent discussion of the production by John Barber in the *Daily Telegraph* of 14 September 1970.
6. *The Empty Space*, p. 134.

were doing their very best to turn in a decent performance for the Duke, that most excited me at the time. It was a celebration of the honest endeavour that goes into any acting that is worth watching.]

The Season of 1972

The 1972 season, despite Trevor Nunn's understandable public hedging, was intended to be a very special one for the Royal Shakespeare Company. It saw Shakespeare's four Roman plays 'performed in a group for the first time anywhere', Rank Strand Electric's new computer system for stage lighting 'used for the first time', what the programme called 'radical alterations' to the auditorium designed to bring it closer to 'the "one-room" relationship between actor and audience' that will be a feature of the company's Barbican theatre, and the installation of complex hydraulically-operated staging to permit sudden transformations of the whole stage picture.

Of at least equal theatrical significance (though, by contrast, quite unsung) was the confirmation of a change in casting policy. The three-year contracts that were a feature of Peter Hall's organisation have been replaced by single-season contracts. If this does not represent a total surrender, it is certainly a retreat; and its artistic implications are unmistakable. The British actor, we are to assume, comes ready-trained to this as to any other repertory theatre, there to be *deployed* by the British director. There is no time for serious discovery in such a system, no possibility of evolving a style of acting that will distinguish this company from every other. (Against Yeats's search in London for a professional actress to play Deirdre, Synge 'would rather go on trying out people for ten years than bring in this ready-made style of acting that is so likely to destroy the sort of distinction everyone recognises in our company'.) So what is to be distinct about the Royal Shakespeare Company? On the evidence of 1972 not the acting—unless through the locally superb performance; and such individual excellence you might see also at the Bolton Octagon, the Chester Gateway, or the Swansea Grand—but the staging. A false emphasis, surely. It's harder, of course, to train actors than to costume them, and the rewards are often less immediately apparent. But the life of the theatre is in the actor, not the edifice, nor the lighting, nor the costumes and stage properties. The announced total cost of the alterations during the winter of 1971–72 is 'approximately £90,000', and right enough by me that the Royal Shakespeare Company should have that kind of money. What, I wonder, is the actor's share? There were too many subsidiary actors, in 1972, who

176

seemed quite simply inadequate, ill-at-ease with Shakespeare's language and evidently unable to sustain a conviction of their own importance. Did they feel less crucial to the season than the new stage? That way lies artistic bankruptcy and the first hydraulically-operated Bingo Hall in England. It is in its acting that the Royal Shakespeare Company should aim to excel. The current emphasis on conspicuous expenditure exposes those weaknesses of the acting company that it may at worst be intended to disguise. It is an obstruction that could be overcome by a single artistic decision. There is enough money in Stratford not only to employ but also genuinely to care for a uniquely-talented group of actors. Meanwhile the revival of *The Comedy of Errors* ten years after its first production provoked unfavourable comparisons with the original performance. What the actors achieved was not precision itself but the shadow of precision. They lacked exuberance because they lacked the skill that earns it. Synge's metaphor will serve to define my response to the performance as a whole. Here was a ready-made cast in a production once made splendidly to measure. I do not intend to make any special comment on the 1972 *Comedy of Errors*. 'The present newly-cast revival', said the programme, 'is the production's fourth at Stratford'. The reasons for pumping it back into the repertoire after seven years were, I suspect, more cogent off-stage than on it, and I find it hard to see how the actors stood to benefit. Not many prizes are given for dancing in dead men's shoes. As it was, the production highlighted the inflexibility of the company's middle actors. Hazlitt would have regretted their lack of the *gusto* essential to comedy, and in the Roman plays a general lack of urgency. It is a long time since the fifty-lines-and-under speaking parts were played so badly at Stratford, and that, however you look at it, is serious.

[1972 was the year in which Ian McKellen and others founded The Actors' Company. In an interview with Gordon Gow, McKellen explained that, at the National and the RSC, 'the actors are one of the last things to happen in the process of putting on a production'.[7]

The Season of 1973

[The best of this season's productions were John Barton's *Richard II* and Buzz Goodbody's *As You Like It*, but my comments on the acting are disappointingly slight. I was embroiled in two debates, one about the proper scope of the Shakespearean director, and one about the academic

7. See *Plays and Players*, 19, no. 12 (September London: Michael Joseph, 1972), pp. 36–7.

response to theatre. We have moved on since then, I think, but the debate has enough historical interest to justify an excerpt.]

The experience of three years as the reviewer of the Stratford season for *Shakespeare Survey* has increased my awareness of the breach between universities and the theatre, a breach that has been made wider by the development of English studies. After attending a performance at Stratford, students and teachers of English will often talk as if Shakespeare were peculiarly their property. He is not. He belonged and should be restored to an excitable and unpretentious audience, from which most of us are, by inclination and training, debarred. We rarely contribute generously to the atmosphere in the audience of a Shakespeare play, since we are there for private, acquisitive reasons, self-centred rather than communal. Our tendency is either to reject or to hoard, to relish the experience more for the judgements it allows us to *make* than for anything we simply *receive*. We lack the ability to suspend judgement for a time that is a natural skill of the unsophisticated audience. I'm reminded of a point Northrop Frye makes about Shakespeare's comic plots: 'it seems clear that no audience of Shakespeare, whether Elizabethan or modern, is allowed to think at all. They have the power to like or dislike the play, but no right to raise questions, as long as the action is going on, about the plausibility of the incidents or their correspondence with their habitual view of life.'[8] Nor should the theatre audience test what is done on stage against their habitual view of what *should* be done. Far too often, students, scholars, and scholarly critics ignore what is there in order to draw attention to what has been missed, or concentrate more on the distortion (which is, after all, not necessarily anything other than an alternative to a particular preconception) than on the experience. A performance should serve a text, certainly, but cannot answer to it at every point. There is still much cogency in the sort of distinction George Hauger draws between what lies on the page as a *script* and what becomes, in performance, a *play*.[9] In these terms, a play is defined by a performance that it can never precede, and no play, not even one by Shakespeare, is a book. I do not wish to re-open an old debate, since I have nothing to add to it, but it does seem to me important that academics should be sympathetic to a theatrical question ('how can we make this script into a play?') they are unlikely ever to have to ask. Whatever the prevailing pieties, Shakespeare's work does not play itself, and much of what I hear castigated as directorial perversity is a faithful reproduction of authorial complexity.

8. Frye, *A Natural Perspective* (New York: Columbia University Press, 1965), p. 13.
9. Hauger, *Theatre—General and Particular* (1966), pp. 24–25.

I'm not trying to defend against all comers the professional theatre in general and the Royal Shakespeare Company in particular. The power of the modern director has established patterns of behaviour, but not standards of performance. In the mind of a Meyerhold or a Brook, an image may translate itself almost instantaneously into its *mise en scène*, something to capture and contain his imaginative energy until it is released through rehearsal; but inspiration has become compulsory for all directors, and those who don't have it must be severely tempted to cultivate the appearance of having it. It has become the rule to adopt a leading idea about a play, and use every available theatrical method to force it across to the audience. Over-simplification is almost inevitable if the dramatist is Shakespeare, and this can have a dangerous charm in the theatre, as it did in John Barton's substitution of Bolingbroke in disguise for Richard II's friendly groom. Over-emphasis, on the other hand, is theatrically offensive too. I doubt whether this year's *Richard II* will have more friends among the purists than *Romeo and Juliet*, yet it displayed a far greater theatrical intelligence than Terry Hands's vulgarly ingenious production, in which the over-emphases were sometimes hysterical. The 'director's theatre' post-dates Shakespeare by 400 years, and cannot lightly be assumed to be suitable for the production of his plays. Its English advocates have tended to look to Stanislavsky for authority. The vexed issue in this context is that of the 'super-objective': 'what we need is a super-objective which is in harmony with the intentions of the playwright and at the same time arouses a response in the soul of the actors. That means that we must search for it not only in the play but in the actors themselves'.[10] Stanislavsky stresses the collaboration of the whole company, but in a director's theatre (and whatever he *says*, Stanislavsky cannot escape all the responsibility) it is the director who decides on the production's super-objective. Design will reinforce that super-objective, and so will the director's more obviously 'original' ideas. There are times—as in this year's *Romeo and Juliet* and, sometimes, in *As You Like It*—when the resources seem to have been used to give a specious consistency to an unhappy idea, but Stanislavsky can furnish an alternative text:

> The usual impression is that a director uses all of his material means, such as the set, the lighting, sound effects and other accessories, for the primary purpose of impressing the public. On the contrary. We use these means for their effect on the actors. We

10. Stanislavsky, *An Actor Prepares*, trans. E.R. Hapgood (Harmondsworth: Penguin, 1967), pp. 274–75.

try in every way to facilitate the concentration of their attention
on the stage.[11]

Where the director's theatre addresses its serious attention to the art of
the actor, it is, I suggest, the highest development of western theatrical
method *so far*.

[It would have been more honest of me to admit that Stanislavsky was
talking about actors in *both* the quotations I used: but the pursuit of a
super-objective had been passed over to the director some years before
1973, and actor-training licensed a myopic concentration on the
individual character that directors found it convenient to encourage.]

The Season of 1974

Twelfth Night (1974)
It was largely through individual performances that this production
recommended itself. [Peter Gill was the director.] Nicol Williamson's
Malvolio was a studied grotesque—a pinched, Scottish elder of the kirk
with the distorted sexual aspirations of the 'unco' guid'. He held his
voice in the back of his throat, and only his bottom lip was mobile. The
walk was a heron's prance, and, at times of supreme self-satisfaction, his
head leant towards his shoulder and his eyes glinted like an alert bird's.
The run was an absurd lope, which carried his legs as far sideways as
forwards and left the top half of his body almost static. His black
costume was striped with white lines of various thickness and density
and topped with a ruff. It had a *trompe l'oeil* effect, seeming to hold a
tiny head an impossible distance from the bottom of the long, mean legs.
He was happiest in this costume. Comically night-shirted in II.iii, and
villainously cross-gartered in III.iv, he was willing to let the absurdity of
the dress usurp his comic force. But in the gulling scene he was brilliant.
He explained 'play with my—some rich jewel' (II.iv.67–68) by a gesture
sharper than a footnote, lifting his chain of office then slapping it down
with self-annoyance. His attempts to twist his mouth into a meaningful
pronunciation of M, O, A, I, were as hilarious as his sudden, irrational
conclusion that they said 'Malvolio'. Remembering his dignity, he just
resisted the invitation to 'revolve' contained in the letter, but 'smile' he
would, and did. First he had to remember how to do it, and then, almost
imperceptibly, force his lips wider and slowly wider into a look of such
joyless jollity as might have been worn by Miss Hotchkiss at the ITMA

11. Stanislavsky, p. 171.

office party. His subsequent entrance to Olivia, pushing Maria aside and 'smiling' as he smeared his body along a property tree, was perfect, but the scene declined into ungainly knockabout and was only saved by the soliloquy. Twice, then, he stood to acknowledge with reverent hypocrisy Jove's hand in his well-merited glory, but for the rest of the time he sprawled beside a table in gangling self-love.

The tone of Frank Thornton's Aguecheek was set by the long face and longer silence that preceded his lifeless question, 'Shall we set about some revels?' (I.iii.146–47). He was thin and melancholy, devoid of energy, dyspeptic and consumptive. There was a consciousness of real loneliness beneath the surface of the comic scenes, that affected not only Aguecheek but also Feste and Sir Toby. David Waller was, on his first entrance with Maria, dignified and relaxed, but drink depressed and depraved him. He made his reading of the character clear to his *Guardian* interviewer (18 September 1974):

> Toby's first line is: 'What a plague means my niece to take the death of her brother thus? I am sure care's an enemy to life'. That suggests to me a man who is, as it were, protesting too much. He is protecting himself, a wounded man—hence the drinking. . . . Nearly his last words are 'I hate a drunken rogue'. And it seems quite clear to me that he's referring quite consciously to himself.

That, expressed with admirable clarity, was the key to Waller's playing of Sir Toby. Patricia Hayes's perky Maria was a decade older and too happy below stairs to give credibility to her standing in Olivia's household. And Feste? How fascinating that it can be played so variously. Ron Pember spoke like a Londoner, dressed like a faded Harlequin now reduced to busking, and hinted always at a radical's social distaste for the antics of privilege. He despised the effeteness of Orsino's court, and his angry assumption that Viola considered him a beggar (III.i.9.) had all the spikiness of class-pride. But there was more than this. One member of the audience interestingly compared him with Bosola,[12] another joker who declines to laugh at his own jokes. He was discomforting, an outsider, almost malevolently saturnine, defying the sentimental response to Malvolio's plight by pressing home his final accusations with heartless accuracy in Act Five. (Yet he, with Fabian, guided Sir Andrew off the stage after Sir Toby's cruel last rebuff.) The majority of George Fenton's music for the production had a 'Victorian

12. The malcontent figure in Webster's *The Duchess of Malfi*.

Elizabethan' tone. Against that, Pember sang his songs with the gritty voice of the modern, unaccompanied folk-singer. He was a working man among the leisured classes, deeply critical of their behaviour and bitterly dissatisfied with his own. The rough-and-ready air of the curtain-call was, perhaps, his triumph over the formality of Illyria. The four lovers had whirled and weaved their way around, involving Antonio in their dance, but leaving him bemused and lonely when they went out and the stage wall slid shut behind them. And there Antonio stood, upstage alone, while Ron Pember sang his song of mutability to us. I shall never forget this Feste.

[The fact is that, until I reread this review, I had forgotten Pember's Feste—but I remember it now, and that's something . . . .]

Measure for Measure (1974)
The idea in itself was witty. We were, as the desultory openings of the production made clear, watching a *performance* of the events of *Measure for Measure*. And the performers were recognisably members of a discontented stock company, making do with available scenery (Mariana could not be afforded the splendour of a moated grange—she sat, instead, at the top of a high step-ladder) and timeworn costumes. The musicians were untidily concealed at stage right, the overstage lighting was open to the audience, the technical work (black-outs, sound-cues, costume changes) was intentionally sluggish, and the play began with its actors strolling onto the stage out of character to await the cue. The Duke was among them, in a splendid robe-of-office (the company's other precious property[13]), with his back to us. The lethargic opening music went on too long, and the actors fidgeted until the Duke turned to address to us the opening word. But what a Duke! Barrie Ingham was made up black-haired and sleek as the heavy villain of melodrama, and his voice and air-sawing gesture were in keeping. In such a company, Michael Pennington's Angelo was the juvenile lead, Escalus the first old man, and Lucio the comic man. But there was an extra twist to all this. The actors hated their overweening actor-manager. The suggestion of the costuming is, on the one hand, that everyone in Vienna is poor, and on the other, that the Vincent Crummles who plays the Duke underpays his actors, earning for himself an unpopularity that is more theatrical than social. That, I take it, was the idea; and it was a potential asset of

13. The first precious property was a statue of Christ the King, slightly battered, but too good to be missed, even if its relevance to the present play was unclear. It was an emblem of the aesthetic, as well as the moral, confusion of this particular stock company.

this production that its director [Keith Hack, on loan from the Glasgow Citizens' Theatre] brought to it more passion than had been evident in the rest of the season. There was a desperate need for something to excite the audience's imagination even where it offended. It was a severe blow to the Royal Shakespeare Company that the critical reaction was unanimously hostile. The reaction was not surprising, though it might have been ungracious. Whereas the theatrical imagination that had conceived the production was impressive, it operated at a distance from the text (take as evidence the cutting of the Duke's lines to allow villainous intention to replace sincere bewilderment), and it had not adequately communicated itself to the actors. A director who imposes on his actors an idea of whose validity he fails to convince them is the modern theatre's equivalent of the egocentric actor-manager, so that, despite the energy of his interpretation, Keith Hack must stand condemned by his own theatrical image . . .

Against the figure of so villainous a Duke, Angelo seemed strangely innocent, and Pennington played him without the ice-in-the-blood strength of, for example, Ian Richardson's 1970 performance. Subversion in a society governed so evilly might have been admirable, but the low-life characters, with the exception of Lucio, were charmless. Even Claudio, sporting unexpectedly a single ear-ring, was too ugly and wretched to wring a tear. But the outrageous hypocrisy of the Duke overwhelmed the lesser hypocrisy of Angelo and of an Isabella who not only wore black lace in the convent, but also touched Angelo before he touched her. The audience sniggered at his reference to 'the love I have in doing good' (III.i.202), and laughed aloud at his comically inappropriate 'Benedicite' to Juliet (II.iii.39). In disguise, the Duke wore a single black glove, and, in criticism of the Elizabethan convention, took the further precaution of hiding his face from all who might recognise it. Eventually (in IV.ii) he would reveal himself to the Provost in unnecessary anticipation of the fine unmasking in Act Five. His change of heart was mocked by having him descend from the flies off-cue on a crudely constructed bar, and transformed now into a golden-haired god [*ex machina*]. The over-acting of the Duke in Act Five was intended to undermine our belief in the happy ending he contrives. All the world's a tatty stage, and no one in authority is to be trusted.

Nothing in this production interested me more than Barry Stanton's Lucio. Here, certainly, was a *picaro*, his fashionable finery reduced to scabby tatters. Stanton is big, even fat (though without flabbiness), but astonishingly light-footed. His strut was as dainty as a bird's, and his fastidiousness was feline.

[I relished this production more than I managed to convey in this review. I suspect that I was nervous of taking on the editorial board of the *Shakespeare Survey*. Keith Hack had asked Edward Bond to write a programme note, and the two men were clearly in agreement about the play. Bond wrote: 'It is ironic that the academic theatre and the critics take the Duke at his face value, and remain caught up in the whole pretence of "seeming" that Shakespeare attacked. In fact, our politics are still run by Angelos, made publicly respectable by Ducal figure-heads and theories, supported by hysteria (Isabella), and mindlessly obeyed by dehumanised forces (the Provost and Abhorson).' Hack's iconoclasm was not accidental. He saw Stratford as part of the Ducal establishment.]

The Season of 1975

Hamlet (1975)
I would be doing the late Buzz Goodbody a disservice if I called the production of *Hamlet* at Stratford in 1975 hers. Against the tide of our 'director's theatre', over which the Royal Shakespeare Company has long exercised a moon-like influence, she found the courage and the skill to release the play to the actors. The actors, for their part, responded with a performance whose alertness to the text was not only exemplary but constantly invigorating. For the second time this decade Stratford has provided us with a major theatrical exploration of a familiar text; and this *Hamlet*, unlike Brook's 1970 production of *A Midsummer Night's Dream*, is imitable.

I was once in a production of [John Arden's] *Ironhand* which over-whelmed audiences in Manchester's small University Theatre. Trans-ferred to the Teatro Regio in Parma it dwindled. *Hamlet* was not performed in the main house, but in the bare and comfortless small studio/shack named, or unnamed, The Other Place. To call the produc-tion imitable is not to claim that it is transferable. It belonged to the physical context in which it had been rehearsed, and which it exploited. There was no sign whatsoever of the conspicuous expenditure which is still a trademark of the Royal Shakespeare Company. A student society's budget could have serviced it. The tickets are one price (70p), and you sit where you can on backless benches. For *Hamlet* an end-stage had been built opposite the auditorium's single access door. The 'scenery' was a line of screens, simply constructed of paper stretched over a wood frame. 'You can be sure somebody will come bursting through that', I whispered to a colleague before the play began. I was wrong. The line of screens left an acting area about ten feet in depth, with the actors clearly sharing a room with the audience. On this narrow platform stood

184

Francisco at the play's opening. Torches provided the only light, and their beams, thrown across the audience, picked out the Ghost at the back of the room. It was simple and effective, and it set the tone of a production which *never* strained for its effects. There was no deception, no trickery. It was appropriate that the door through which the Ghost vanished, on which Laertes would later batter, and through which Fortinbras would make his final portentous entrance, belonged in each interval to the audience. We were sharing with the actors a neutral space whose primitive amenities became startlingly appropriate whenever they were used. There was remarkably little sense of a performance taking place. Rather, we were silent participators in a series of events whose intense logic required that they take place here and nowhere else. We were being shown neither a case-history, nor an outlandish fable. That evening (it was 1 October when I saw it) in that place *Hamlet* was a likely story. It was likely, in large part, because the actors made it so, but also because our presence and participation guaranteed its likelihood. I wonder, too, how much was owed to the costuming. This was a modern dress *Hamlet*, but without ostentation or self-conscious ingenuity. The clothes were, in effect, gestic, expressing the gist of the characters, their gesture and their social context. Claudius, in a finely tailored blue suit with broad white stripes, was as strong and clean-cut as an industrial trouble-shooter in George Baker's authoritative performance, a formidable man whose wardrobe carries the Establishment's seal of approval. There is nothing more disheartening to one who knows the need for change than a group of reasonable men in pin-striped suits. This is not a frivolous point. Most of us must, at some time, carry our reforming fervour into the board-room, where even the preliminary task, that of persuading colleagues of the existence of those flaws which they embody, is a formidable one. What we saw clearly in this production was Hamlet's attempt to ruffle composure by flouting good form, its initial success and feckless, fumbling climax. The readier way of changing governments is vigorously presented by the brash final entrance of a cynically opportunistic Fortinbras: 'I have some rights of memory in this kingdom,/Which now to claim my vantage doth invite me'. His costume, that of a paratrooper, and his demeanour leave no doubt of his intentions towards Denmark. Like Fielding's Fireblood,[14] he 'would have ravished her, if she had not, by a timely Compliance, prevented him'.

The benefits of careful costuming were further illustrated by a Polonius [André van Gyseghem] who could follow the fashion of his monarch without a hint of competition, an Osric in impeccable jodphurs, and a

14. In *Jonathan Wild*.

Reynaldo whose city pin-stripes wittily contributed to the portrait of an ambitious civil servant who would flatter his superiors only to replace them. Laertes had a student's hair and beard, but his father's taste in clothes. Ophelia, more tendentiously . . . wore a loose, off-white dress in pre-Raphaelite style. It might have implied her independence of courtly fashion, but the performance proved nothing conclusively. Sid Livingstone, one of those rare, composed actors who makes any line appropriate and could probably convince us that Macbeth was a Lancastrian, presented a north-country Horatio in frayed brown corduroys, loose overcoat, and long scarf; a scholarship boy. The court cold-shouldered him, and he chose not to press the point, but the friendship with Hamlet was real and attractive. The players came from the same rough world, working actors who respected the craft they practised. 'The Mousetrap' was performed in the centre of the shallow stage, with Hamlet and Ophelia stage right and the rest of the court extreme stage left. There was no attempt to make of the play-within-a-play more than an adequate pretext for the disturbance it causes. Bob Peck, who doubled as First Player and Gravedigger, is greatly talented but also wisely disciplined.

On an undecorated stage, costume is doubly telling. The actors of *Hamlet*, I surmise, had been invited to select and wear with comfort the modern clothes that best expressed their characters. Hamlet himself was smart in his original black jacket and pin-striped trousers, but the smartness was nicely mothballed and Sunday-best. The neat brown suit that replaced his mourning was both in contrast and in keeping with the grimly proper court. Ben Kingsley is a conscientious actor, devoid of flamboyance. His study of Slender for *The Merry Wives of Windsor* was built on the rational development of a single gesture—something like the awkward thrusting out of a hand to take a glass that is being offered to someone else and its convulsive withdrawal just as the glass is about to be placed in it after all. It requires strict concentration to perform every up-beat action on the down-beat. It might have become routine for Kingsley by the time I saw *The Merry Wives*, but his Hamlet certainly had not. There were 'original' readings, the relaxed jocularity with Yorick's skull for example, but the impressive thing was the constant testing of the sound of the words against their meaning. Kingsley, sallow of complexion and primly cut, is too austere to satisfy romantic tastes, but there was great charm in the honest speaking of the lines, the charm of an actor modestly encountering a poet.

That, in all frankness is the point. The achievement of this production is to be measured, quite simply, by the fact that the actors meant what they said. Buzz Goodbody had coaxed the play into their hands, and they respected it. It is not easy to *mean* someone else's words, not even consistently to *sound* as if you mean your own. One tendency of those modern actors who strive most earnestly for meaning has been to draw too much of the character's life into themselves, away from the audience, draining in consequence the oral strength of the pentameter. The Other Place is small enough to be lenient to such shortcomings, and it would be a mistake to suppose that what has been discovered and accomplished there can be readily transposed to the Aldwych or the Royal Shakespeare Theatre. Even so, the achievements of The Other Place over the last two years offer a vital criticism of the attitudes that still govern performances in the main house. They also provide some indication of the way that may have to be followed by an impoverished professional theatre in inflationary times. That is no council of despair. To judge by the responses I heard, poverty could not have come at a better time. *Hamlet* is not the only one of The Other Place's productions to have excited its audiences. *Perkin Warbeck* was warmly received, for *Man Is Man* there is a black market in seats, and *Richard III*, which has just opened as I write, with Ian Richardson playing the title role, promises again to upstage the costlier productions at the Theatre. Remembering how Stanislavsky closed the Moscow Art Theatre's Studio when Meyerhold's alternative style was beginning to establish itself, I fear for the future of The Other Place. Its present scope and style seem better suited to the time than anyone (even Buzz Goodbody?) had predicted, but it is utterly dependent on its parent company. It is too small, and too inconvenient, to sustain on its own even a mediocre ensemble, yet under the cloak of the Royal Shakespeare Company it has presented in successive Octobers Nicol Williamson as Uncle Vanya and Ian Richardson as Richard III. And this *Hamlet*.

[Buzz Goodbody had killed herself in April, three days after the first preview of this *Hamlet*. She was young and very gifted. We laughed a lot when we met for the first time, but she was dead within a week.]

13

The New Globe
Monument or Portent?

It is almost certainly too early to try to determine the appropriate future direction of performances at the New Globe. Pauline Kiernan, in the first book-length study,[1] makes no attempt to do so. She stands towards the professional aspect of a theatrical project as academics are often inclined to—discreetly, respectfully, quietly. If she has spotted mistakes in policy, or observed what is better in one production and worse in another, she has not evidently felt it her place to say so. Her position, perhaps, was an invidious one. As a research fellow, with the specific brief to study Shakespeare in performance at the New Globe, she had to earn the confidence of the players, and in retrospect she is nervous of betraying that confidence. I can see why. For a variety of reasons, the whole Globe project is an open invitation to academic assertiveness. There are those who believe the building should never have been erected at all, those who disagree with the outcome of the 'best-guess' approach that guided the architectural decision-making, and those who deplore the standard of performance of the professional company.

The first objection is both unanswerable and now irrelevant. The New Globe is a fake addition to the heritage trail and has its hold on cultural tourism. So much was admitted in the paper prepared by Philip Brockbank for ratification by the International Conference at North-western University in June 1984:

> While the Globe Centre will concentrate on its Shakespearean aims, it is to be expected that considerable tourist interest will be excited. The new theatre will contribute much towards making the riverside from Waterloo to Southwark attractive enough to draw Londoners and tourists to the area. It will be an important magnet for both the purposeful and casual visitors, and will help

---

1. Kiernan, *Shakespeare at the New Globe* (London: Macmillan, 1999).

the area to recover some of the importance as a centre of popular civilization that it had in Shakespeare's time.[2]

Will the tourists drop in to the converted power station that is now the Tate Gallery of Modern Art on their way from Waterloo to the Globe? John Drakakis' argument that the interests of the people of Southwark had nothing whatever to do with the plans for the New Globe applies equally to that pile. It will not be long before homes are converted to restaurants to cater for the influx of visitors. Local pubs with theatrical connections (Doggett's Coat and Badge on one side of the Globe, the Anchor on the other) may allow themselves to be incorporated into an 'olde worlde' theme park in order to compete with the brash new pub on the waterfront. Scoffing at such developments is its own kind of snobbery. It is, after all, one thing to try to obstruct the erection of a building, and quite another to refuse to use it once it's there. The New Globe nestles amid concrete like a spilled heirloom. By the time this book is published the Inigo Jones Theatre will have been added to the Shakespearean one. Their architectural status may be on a level with a drawing by Walter Hodges or an isometric plan by Richard Leacroft, but you can walk into them, test their sightlines with your own eyes, even perform in them, and that makes them different.

This palpable difference does nothing to invalidate the second kind of opposition to the Globe project: that the planners have got their historical reconstruction wrong, and that the outcome therefore threatens to impede the very pursuit of authenticity that it sets out to assist. What is undeniable is that the Globe is not, on the available historical evidence, the easiest of Elizabethan playhouses to reconstruct. The foundations of the Rose are *there*, and where they proffer different conclusions from those represented in the New Globe, they function as a critique of the reconstruction. The plans for the Fortune might, if a team of scholars got to work on them, yield corrective guidance. The reconstructed Fortune in the grounds of the University of Western Australia was built with unobtrusive modesty, according to an interpretation of the Elizabethan plans. Its building materials are not 'authentic', and it has none of the *bijou* charm of the New Globe, but it is a place in which students, actors and scholars can test ideas against a recognizable source. The drawing of the Swan, reproduced by a man who *wasn't* there after a sketch by a

---

2. Quoted in John Drakakis' angrily eloquent essay in G. Holderness (ed.), *The Shakespeare Myth* (Manchester: Manchester University Press, 1988), pp. 24–41, which brilliantly argues the case against building the New Globe. Drakakis pitches the visionary Sam Wanamaker against the roadsweeper, Charlie Cox, who was quoted as saying 'If Shakespeare moves in 'ere, I'm moving out'.

man who *was*, has inspired the construction of several models (I was involved in the making of one of them in the 1970s). But the Globe was 'Shakespeare's theatre' in a way that the Rose (even if it housed his early plays) was not, and national culture meets with national myths in that magic name. '[E]ven if they discovered after all that Shakespeare was Christopher Marlowe or a wandering Kentish tinker', Terry Eagleton acutely says, 'it would be a brave man or woman who would try at this late date to close down Stratford.'[3] The Globe it is, then; no longer a toy theatre of the historical imagination, but a full-size permanent feature of Bankside reality. And it is that very notion of permanence that diminishes the building's veracity. Despite their cost and original splendour, London's Elizabethan playhouses achieved no permanence. They were subject to regular alteration, and the entrepreneurs who made money out of them seem to have accepted their obsolescence with something like equanimity. The New Globe, spared fire and earthquakes, will last as long as it is financially viable, and then a little bit longer.

But at what point in historical time is it to be frozen? The Rose underwent a major facelift in 1592, only five years into its brief life. It is probably a good sign that, in preparation for the 1999 season, the stage-balcony at the New Globe was enlarged and extended out from the facade of the tiring-house (or *frons scenae*), perhaps under the influence of the film *Shakespeare in Love* or perhaps simply to accommodate Cleopatra's monument. This is, after all, a working theatre whatever its alter ego as a museum. And perhaps the most important thing to say about it is that it is an immensely exciting performance space. When it is in operation, it need not matter that it is the fake outcome of a committee of Van Meegerens whose whole endeavour was to reproduce the appearance of authentic antiquity. We do not have to forget that we are in an enclosed space that bears a relationship to the original Globe, not far from where it was, and quite like it may have been, but we don't need to dwell on it while the performance is in progress.

The third complaint—that performance standards have been unacceptably low in the New Globe—is probably more the product of high hopes than of reasonable expectation. Scholars have been claiming for so long that the full richness of Shakespeare can be revealed only in the original circumstances of production that disappointment was likely to express itself in abuse. It is not easy to assemble a company of actors all of whom are capable of projecting Elizabethan English in an open-air playhouse to an audience whose most vocal members are not necessarily reverential. Some of the New Globe players will have had experience of interacting

---

3. Holderness, p. 205.

with an audience, but not in Shakespeare's plays. The relationship has to be negotiated and the terms are oddly contradictory. Until the audience begins to assemble, the space is closed to trespassers. You pay for admission in the modern foyer off New Globe Walk, and gain access only under the tutelage of a guide. But the conditions of a performance are radically different. The buzz in the auditorium before the play begins is more like that in the big top at a circus than in the dimly lit, all-seats theatres with which sophisticated playgoers are familiar. Globe actors sometimes talk of a football stadium. Bill Stewart goes further: 'When we first came out it was like footballers coming out of a tunnel. You know, you come out, and the crowd are going "Yeah!"'[4] This, though, is both to overstate and to understate the case. If people knew more about the behaviour of cricket crowds (frequent appreciation, regularly mumbled outrage and the occasional streaker) they would find an apter analogy there; but sporting crowds, like spectators at a circus, acknowledge that the significant space belongs to the players. In the New Globe, particularly when the groundlings are lively, there is a potential dispute over ownership. On the occasions when the contest is prolonged, watching and listening to the play can be an uncomfortable effort. Even when, as almost invariably happens, the audience concedes to the actors, it retains a formidable presence. The overriding concern of the first performers at the New Globe has been with the audience. 'What did we learn last year?', asked Mark Rylance in his programme-note for *The Merchant of Venice* (1998):

> Whether seated on a bench or standing, Shakespeare kept his audience physically aware of themselves. There is nowhere on the stage that an actor can be seen by everyone in the theatre, Shakespeare must have wanted you to look at each other sometimes while you listened, Shakespeare and his fellows placed their thoughtful observations in an emotional story, let yourself get involved. If you feel like playing as well, we would love to pass the ball to you, join in.

We should be wary of claims that audience-contact, whether with actors or with each other, is unique to the New Globe. People write too often as if the only alternative is the proscenium-arched stage of a neighbourhood repertory company. What *is* particular to the New Globe is the collision of a holy space and its unholy visitors. If that is a cause of academic unease, it is for academics to make the adjustment.

4. Kiernan, p. 149.

ON ACTORS AND ACTING

The New Globe remains, then, vulnerable to scholarly attack, and my first concern is with its capacity to teach us about Elizabethan performance. It should be recognized, in this context, that there is almost as much to be learned from a sense of what is 'wrong' as there is from a sense of what is 'right'. In the first place, then, the New Globe is too big. John Orrell, the principal historical adviser to the project, is a Hollar addict, and his calculations, based on a conviction that Hollar was precise in determining scale, have led to the construction of a building with twenty timbered bays and a diameter of 100ft (30.5m). The Rose had a diameter of 72ft (22m) and fourteen bays, the Fortune was evidently an 80ft (24m) square. Some sonic testing of the supposed foundations of the original Globe (or of the second Globe—who knows?) in, I think, 1999 have tended to confirm the computerized calculation, made during the Museum of London's dig on the site, that it, too, had a diameter of about 80ft (24m). Orrell did not agree; 'The Museum of London, under whose auspices the dig was carried out, made the mystifying claim that a computer showed the diameter to be 80ft (24m), though what instructions the computer had been fed was never made clear. Simon Blatherwick and Andrew Gurr mercifully also made a guess, based on a rather intuitive reading of the evidence, that the figure was more like the 100ft (30.5m) . . .'.[5] I find that passage unnerving. What is meant by 'a rather intuitive reading', and how is it less mystifying than a computer-reading? What kind of instructions had Orrell already fed into Gurr and Blatherwick? It is obviously to the advantage of the Globe Trust that the capacity of the playhouse should be as large as possible under modern safety regulations. Does intuition here encompass the box office and/or the recognition that the average human size has increased since the reign of Elizabeth I? Having some slight experience on the stage of the New Globe as well as in the audience, *my* intuition remains that it is too big. The Elizabethan theatre I would love to perform in is a reconstructed Rose.

I have no such quarrel with the height of the stage. Perched up at 5ft (1.5m), with the groundlings at the level of his ankles, the Elizabethan actor was both exposed and powerful. 'You're very noticeable when you're on this stage', said Matthew Scurfield after a season's experience.[6] What surprised me, though, was that I looked straight out at the spectators in the second gallery. Eye-contact was easy, natural and immediate. Whatever my feelings about the overall size of the theatre,

5. J.R. Mulryne and M. Shewring (eds), *Shakespeare's Globe Rebuilt* (Cambridge: Cambridge University Press, 1997), pp. 58–59.
6. Kiernan, p. 146.

these people were very close, at 40–50ft (12–15m) quite a lot closer, for example, than I am to the bowler when batting in cricket. It was not an oppressive proximity, but a reassuring one. Their attention was more secure than that of the groundlings. I found myself looking again at De Witt's labelling of the Swan galleries. These attentive spectators occupy the *sedilia*. Familiar with the privileged seating of the Roman theatres, De Witt has nominated the lowest gallery the *orchestra*. Perhaps that makes sense. Not too much of a struggle to get to your place, and once there clearly distinct from the penny-paying groundlings whose eyes are on a level with your finer apparel. The *orchestra* is a good position for the silent display of superior social and financial status, but from the actor's eye-view it is the obscurest section of the theatre. He must look down to locate the people there, and looking down not only depreciates his status but also engages him more immediately with the groundlings who stand between him and the *orchestra*. De Witt calls the third gallery a *porticus*, and the readiest reference is to an enclosed colonnade where, perhaps, young men and prostitutes may stroll on the way to engineering sexual assignations. The Southwark brothels were very near, and business deals with the playhouses can be assumed. But those in the *sedilia* sound like settled theatregoers. They must be taken account of by the actors. Richard Olivier, who has directed plays at the New Globe, is conscious that 'the relationship between the actors and the groundlings can make those in the galleries feel excluded',[7] and the actors are aware of it, too. 'You must play to the galleries', says David Lear. 'The yard can easily be held':[8] and John McEnerey, somatically aware of the storytelling priorities of the Elizabethan actor, admits that '[t]he ground-lings could be alarmingly distracting, unless you gave a very firm purpose to everything you were doing'.[9] The purposefulness of Elizabethan performance is a quality I have stressed in the first two chapters of this book, and it is interesting that playing the New Globe has jostled it into an experienced actor's vocabulary. My point here, though, is that the conformation of the theatre space suggests that the middle gallery was the preferred spot for the most serious playgoers. If he paid too much attention to the groundlings, the actor risked offending his best customers. (If he paid too little, he could have had his ankles bitten.) Elizabethan dramaturgy, so hospitable to the juxtaposition of 'low' and 'high' scenes, took practical account of the pull of the groundlings and the complementary pull of the patrons in the *sedilia*.

7. Kiernan, p. 140.
8. Kiernan, p. 137.
9. Kiernan, p. 139.

The platform, which looks almost unnaturally large when empty, does not *feel* so large when you are on it. It easily accommodates a natural walking pace, and it invites travel. That is to say that the on-stage area is in harmony with the off-stage rhythms of communal interaction. It is the kind of *gestic* space that Brecht would have relished. Actors in dialogue quickly recognize that they are better advised to maintain a distance. The close proximity of television conversation is utterly inappropriate. When there is wide open space all around, it implies conspiracy rather than intimacy. Diagonals have quickly become the favoured configuration of actors grouped on stage, but their three-dimensional effect is best appreciated from the sides, which the actors still have difficulty in persuading themselves to address. Meanwhile the area forward of the pillars has been identified as a 'hot' spot for direct communication with the audience, and an 'authority position' fixed 'under the "fiery cloud" on the Heavens trap, in the middle of the stage-width, forward of the *frons*, and back from the pillars.'[10] One of the discoveries that has most surprised actors who are playing Shakespeare in the New Globe for the first time is the encouragement the platform offers to speak their lines on the move. David Fielder found that 'it had a very different feeling about the relationship between the spoken word and movement—you move and speak at the same time. In modern theatres we're not encouraged to move on the line'.[11] Norbert Kentrup, the monumental Shylock of the 1998 season, spoke 'Hath not a Jew eyes?' on the move, an implicit challenge to the assumption that the great rhetorical set pieces were delivered by static actors using the aid of conventional gesture. There is no chance of clinching historical 'rightness' here. Modern solutions cannot wholly resolve ancient teasers. What is certain, though, is that, on a platform stage with solid pillars, a static actor will always be invisible to some of the spectators in a full house, and that this is an incentive to mobility. Except in formal scenes, where the protocols of precedence must be observed, there is onus on the actors to keep the stage busy. There is a general recognition among them of the need to sustain high energy levels. If a playing space properly belongs to those who are good for it, the New Globe stage is for travellers, not for squatters.

There remains some uncertainty about the effectiveness of action in the proximity of the *frons scenae*. The initial impetus of actors who enter the space through a stage door for the first time urges them forward: for Vincent Brimble in his first season at the New Globe, the pillars 'tend to

10. Kiernan, p. 63.
11. Kiernan, p. 135.

pull you down to the front. It makes it feel like a proscenium stage. The light gets very dingy at the back of the stage in the afternoon.'[12] It is obviously undesirable that a segment of the stage should be closed off, but Brimble's final point is an important one. In the debates about the orientation of the New Globe stage, Orrell's voice was again the decisive one. On a north-south axis, the Rose stage lies north-north-west, and would therefore have been in sunlight for much of the afternoon. But Hollar pitches the roof of the Second Globe in the south-west, and that is where Orrell thought it should be in the New Globe, too. For the benefit of the architect Theo Crosby, he arranged an experiment, 'placing the model of the first Globe on an improvised heliodon and noting the play of direct sunlight and shadow through its structure as we tilted and turned it in the powerful beam of a theatrical profile spot'. They discovered that, on Hollar's orientation, the stage was always in the shade, and 'whatever sunlight penetrated the building shone into the galleries rather than on the players. . . . Precisely the opposite of what most modern people expect'. According to Orrell, '[t]he effect was so radical and complete that Crosby was convinced, and went to a great deal of trouble to redesign the project to accommodate a Globe facing in the direction Hollar so fortunately recorded'.[13] From this account, it is not at all clear to me what Crosby was convinced *of*. The experiment is simply an experiment. Unlike the orientation of the Rose stage, it sheds no light on theatrical preference. In an earlier article, however, Orrell speculates on the reasoning behind what looks an unlikely decision on the part of the Lord Chamberlain's Men:

> [I]t seems that a more even, indirect or 'north' light was pre-ferred to the intenser contrasts of direct sunlight on the stage. Just such a renunciation of *chiaroscuro* effects is characteristic of Elizabethan portrait painting, and it may be that an aesthetic preference for the flat, linear style of appearance influenced the placing of the stage against the light. Elizabethan and Jacobean art commonly shows rich contrasts of colour, and these too would be visible in costumes lit indirectly from the diffused daylight reflected inwards from the yard.

The concluding sentence reads more like a rebuttal than a confirmation of the preceding argument. The rich contrasts of colour, of which (I agree) Elizabethan actors were fond, would have been more vivid in

12. Kiernan, p. 152.
13. Orrell in Mulryne and Shewring, p. 55.

direct sunlight than in diffused daylight absorbed as well as reflected by the groundlings. And Orrell is honest enough to admit that 'Hilliard, a leading practitioner of the linear style, declares in his *Art of Limning* that his models were best displayed in open sunlight, and appears to equate subdued light not only with "shadowe" or *chiaroscuro* moulding of forms but also with questionable morality'.[14] For a reason that puzzles me, Orrell even cites the reference to the stage cover at the Fortune as a 'shadowe' to support his argument, despite the fact that it seems more likely to confute it. Why use a shade unless you are in the sun? I am confused and unconvinced. 'Solving the problem of determining the theatre's orientation on the site required turning the building round', blandly records Kiernan, 'with the surprising discovery that the stage always remained in the shade, with the sun shining into the galleries.'[15] I can't see why the discovery should have surprised anyone, since it was precisely what had been planned, nor do I see it as a 'solution'. Indeed, having observed the darkness at the *frons scenae* (why have such rich icons if they blur into vague patterns?) and galleryites shielding their eyes with their programmes, I don't find it easy to distinguish the problem from the solution.

Three further issues of consequence to an understanding of Elizabethan performance continue to nag at me: the pillars; the central opening or discovery space; and the manner of opening and closing performances. I will conclude the 'historical' section of this chapter by dealing with them in turn.

I expected to enjoy the presence of the pillars more than I do. They are certainly a pleasing architectural feature when the stage is empty, and they so obviously wouldn't be there if such a theatre were to be built now that they add an impressive sense of period authenticity to an audience's sense of occasion. A feeling of being 'in the service of the building' is something Richard Olivier alludes to.[16] But the pillars are big and very stubborn, and their segmentation of the stage is an ungainly one. That is not to say that they cannot be effectively exploited. Mark Rylance as Bassanio signalled his contempt for Shylock by leaning on one of them; a playful Jessica hid from Lorenzo by darting behind one in Act Five of *The Merchant of Venice*; and Kentrup's circling of a pillar as he demanded that Antonio 'look to his bond' was mysteriously sinister. It is easy to find uses for them in any Elizabethan play. They support conventions of concealment or invisibility, provide vantage

14. 'Sunlight at the Globe', in *Theatre Notebook*, vol. 38, no. 2 (1984), p. 73.
15. Kiernan, p. 5.
16. Kiernan, p. 143.

points for eavesdroppers or spies, may become entrances to houses or serve as outdoor features as soon as an actor shows us they are so. My instinct tells me I ought to love them. Perhaps I will when the actors stop worrying about them.

The central opening at the New Globe, whatever it may appear from the auditorium, does not lead to an enclosure. Strictly speaking, then, it is not a discovery space; it is the visible part of a room behind the facade, between the permanent features of the stage doors. The room is, in fact, about half as large as the platform itself, big enough to contain a decent rehearsal or to house a warm-up. Although the Swan drawing does not indicate any central point of access to the stage, it is a reasonable inference from stage directions that the Globe had one. The danger is that actors, and in particular directors, will be tempted to use it inappropriately. As a site of dramatic action, a recessed space is irreconcilable with a thrust stage. Whatever may happen in it will be invisible to a significant segment of the spectators and inaudible to more. It may be useful for massed entries and for formal or celebratory exits and it allows the thrusting out of large pieces of furniture (Desdemona's bed is a prime example), but it must not be used as the setting for Prospero and Miranda at chess, for Hermione's statue in *The Winter's Tale* (it nearly was in 1997), or for the display of Portia's caskets in *The Merchant of Venice* (it was in 1998).

There is one compellingly modern reason for this veto. It has been difficult to persuade standing audiences to take up a position at the sides of the stage. If the scenic incorporation of a central opening becomes habitual, people will naturally congregate in such a way as to face it. There is much loose talk already about the New Globe as a theatre 'in the round'. Enough anyway to deserve a mocking grin from habitués of the Victoria Theatre in Stoke. If companies agree to employ the central opening as access to an inner stage, they will soon find themselves acting on an end-stage with curious hollows at either side. There is a further danger, exemplified by Pauline Kiernan. 'It may be', she hazards, 'that audiences will need to be given more practice in listening skills before the central opening can be used effectively as it must have been at the original Globe'.[17] What she is actually suggesting is that Shakespeare's contemporaries didn't care whether or not they could see the statue of Hermione provided that they could hear the dialogue it activated. Both Kiernan and the actors she quotes frequently claim that the New Globe has revitalized our experience of listening to Shakespeare. It rings too piously for me, and I confess that my hackles rise when I read that

17. Kiernan, p. 77.

'[e]xperimenting with the central opening as a discovery space has begun to offer experiential evidence for our understanding from the texts that listening can be more critical than looking'.[18] No theatre should make, on its audience's behalf, hierarchical distinctions between ear and eye: and the New Globe is a long way from earning the right to privilege listening over seeing. I have been happy to look around when speaking characters are hidden by a pillar: it has given me a chance to *see* the on-stage auditors while hearing the invisible actor. I would be tempted, if I were to produce *Hamlet* there, to stage the duel in the yard so that the spectators could, if they wished, concentrate on watching Claudius and Gertrude watching it. But claims that the New Globe is going to revive in the British public (not to mention the Germans and the Japanese) a delight in the art of antithesis and the pliability of the iambic pentameter seem to me sentimental; and to link those claims to the use of the central opening as a sanctuary for verse speaking is perverse.

There is no doubt that a final exit through a large gap in the middle of the *frons scenae* provides a gratifying closure to almost all Elizabethan plays. If, as seems likely, the Montagues have been using one stage door and the Capulets the other throughout *Romeo and Juliet*, an exit together through the central opening is a powerful sign of reconciliation. And comedies that end on the promise of marriage invite a mass exit *together*. Elizabethan dramaturgy deals very well with closure—except for the clowns. I have asked in chapter three of this book for a revival of the jig at the New Globe, and am pleased to learn from Kiernan's book that this has been actively considered. In 1997, work on 'an "authentic" jig in present-day language to come after each performance of *Henry V*' was abandoned because 'the preparation involved was in danger of using up valuable time and energy'.[19] The modern theatre finds it difficult to leave things to the actors, and that is a pity. In the Elizabethan theatre the clowns would have been allowed to get on with it, and the jig would have been produced without any rehearsal vetting. The New Globe has found itself, perhaps unintentionally to begin with, challenging notions of purity in the production of Shakespeare's plays, and it scarcely needs saying that our 'pure' theatre is losing audiences at the same time as it is failing to gain them. The New Globe has been an exception to the rule of dwindling attendance, in large part because playgoers feel energized and empowered there. A jig would reward the regulars, surprise first-timers and provide a pay-off for the company comics. I like the idea of a jostling in the house at the end of the mainpiece: those jostling to get out

18. Kiernan, p. 7.
19. Kiernan, p. 98.

of the way of this sacrilege meeting others jostling to get in because the jig is the only thing they want to see.

But closure, I admit, is not a problem. Signalling the start of the play has, by contrast, been a concern. How did performances begin in the original Globe? I am tempted by the idea that the clowns did turns for the assembling audience. Marcello Magni as Harlequin paraded the auditorium before *The Merchant of Venice* in 1998, and the rapport (and in some cases anxiety) he established in his improvised encounters carried over into his performance as Launcelot Gobbo. If you have skilled soloists in the company, why not use their talents? The sound produced by the musicians was too thin to overcome the audience buzz, but Magni created a circle of attention wherever he paused in his perambulation. A clown who knows the actors are ready can stand on the platform to do his final turn. His exit may then signal, more effectively than any knocking of the stage or musical introduction by the city waits, that *The White Devil* is about to begin. I select that play because it has the toughest-to-bring-off opening that I know. Lodovico has to stride onto the platform and quell the audience with no more help than the single word, 'Banished!'. Inductions and prologues seem to me, in part at least, desperate measures designed to bring an unruly audience to gradual stillness. A better alternative, certainly an alternative, would have been the improvising clown. The fact that there is no textual evidence for such a practice proves nothing, because this entertainment would have been unscripted, and the possibility that afternoons at the Globe were topped and tailed by clowning retains its plausibility.

There are intimations, in almost every performance at the New Globe, of a popular theatre; the question is, what do we do about it? In the long run, certainly, the company will nurture new writing. That process has already begun. It may also carry into the academies a recognition of the rough-and-tumble of Elizabethan theatrical practice, though there is an understandable reluctance in literature departments to accept that the reception of the great poetic plays of early modern England could have been conditioned by volatile audiences, distorted by vagaries of the weather (the actors have found that they speed up when it rains) and dependent on the memory and moods of actors. So far as we can tell, Elizabethan performers were unburdened by the sense that they were the mediators of great literature; their eyes were on the people they were speaking to. This is a focus that the New Globe necessarily entails, something that ought to be as hospitable to revivals of the 'indoor' plays of Racine and Ibsen as to the 'outdoor' plays of the renaissance. After all, if you cannot stage *A Doll's House* with two doors, it is all the more surprising that Ingmar Bergman's triumphant Stockholm production in

1989 managed with no doors at all. It is a cheering feature of the New Globe that it challenges the hegemony of the concept-hungry director. On an empty, unlit stage, it is only the story that stands between the actors and a mass exodus of onlookers. The function of the director is to manage the stage. When more is tried, as in the 1997 production of *The Winter's Tale*, the outcome is unconvincing. Northern Broadsides' single performance of *A Midsummer Night's Dream* in 1996 offers an opposite model. The company had been touring for some time, most recently in Brazil, and was accustomed (as Elizabethan companies were) to adapting their staging to the venue. Two hours of rehearsal in the New Globe was what they had, perhaps more than they needed. It is a company with a strong sense of physical presence and a hearty attitude to its audience. The occasion was spectacularly celebratory, surely an incentive to the establishment of an annual festival of touring productions. '[I]t is an actor's space. It's very, very much an actor's space', said William Russell, fresh from *Henry V* and *A Chaste Maid in Cheapside*.[20] But then, shouldn't that be true of all theatres?

20. Kiernan, p. 133

Index

201